D. B. Birney

MAJ. GEN. DAVID B. BIRNEY

LIFE

OF

DAVID BELL BIRNEY,

MAJOR-GENERAL

UNITED STATES VOLUNTEERS.

PHILADELPHIA:
KING & BAIRD, 607 SANSOM STREET.

NEW YORK:
SHELDON & CO., 400 BROADWAY
1867.

CONTENTS.

APPENDIX.

INDEX.

PARENTAGE.

DAVID BELL BIRNEY was born in Huntsville, Alabama, on the 29th day of May, 1825. His father, James G. Birney, was one of the most remarkable men of his generation, and his son inherited some of those qualities which have made his father's name a household word wherever the love of truth and freedom prevails. After graduating with honor at Yale College, James G. Birney studied law in Philadelphia, in the office of Alexander J. Dallas. When admitted to the bar, he went to Kentucky, his native State, and remained there for several years.

After his marriage, he removed to Huntsville, Alabama, where all the children of his first marriage were born. He associated himself with Arthur G. Hopkins, (who subsequently became Governor of the State,) and was soon one of the leaders of the Bar of Alabama.

In 1834, the Legislature of the State appointed James G. Birney a Commissioner to go North and select the members of the Faculty for the State University, then about to be established at Tuscaloosa. His learning, fine social qualities, and keen judgment of human nature, eminently fitted him for this duty, which he successfully performed.

Among other gentlemen selected by him, was F. A. P. Barnard, lately elected President of Columbia College, New York, whose attainments and reputation as a scholar and man of science, have fully justified the discrimination which more than thirty years ago called him to a seat among the faculty of the Alabama University. The writer passed the early part of his collegiate life at this institution, and can bear witness to the fact, that few institutions of learning in our country have been directed by more able or more competent instructors.

During his visit North, James G. Birney, actuated by a liberality of spirit which at that time was seldom found among men living south of Mason and Dixon's line, attended Anti-slavery meetings in Philadelphia, New York, and Boston. By the arguments he heard advanced, he became convinced that it was the duty of every slaveholder to give his slaves every opportunity of going to Africa, and he returned home a strong Colonizationist. In the right of his wife, and by purchase, he was the owner of a number of slaves, and to all who desired to go to Africa, he offered every facility. Many went, but he still remained the owner of enough to make any man poor during the years of the rebellion. In a few years his professional business again called him North, and the result of the second visit was that he became an Emancipationist. On his return home, he emancipated all his slaves, and though partially impoverished by this course, became desirous of converting others to his (at that time) peculiar theory. This, however, did not suit the latitude of Huntsville, and his residence there was uncomfortable. This induced him to take his little family northward, and in 1838, he returned to Kentucky, with the intention of establishing an Anti-Slavery paper in that State. From this, however, he was dissuaded by his friends, and they convinced him that such a course would do more harm than good to the cause of which he had become so zealous an advocate. He then removed to Cincinnati, and established the "*Philanthropist*," the first press of the country devoted exclusively to the cause of freedom. Even in that city public opinion was unprepared for such an institution as an Anti-Slavery paper, and three times the office was mobbed and the types thrown into "pi" in the streets. But the editor was in earnest, and never failed to get out his edition as per contract.

During his residence in Cincinnati, James G. Birney made many warm friends among the progressive men of that city and vicinity. Among others, Salmon P. Chase, now the Chief Justice of the United States, was drawn to him and aided his enterprize both by his personal and professional character. Judge Chase was then a hard-working lawyer in Ohio, but he was a big-hearted and liberal-minded man. He aided by all the means in his power the Pioneer in the Anti-Slavery movement, and in later years he did all he could to secure the success of David B., the son of his former friend, James G. Birney, because; as he once told the writer, "his heart was in the cause by hereditary right." All honor to a man who has never in public life deserted the principles of his early manhood, and may he long live to adorn the highest judicial office of the Western Continent.

In 1844, James G. Birney was nominated as a candidate for the Presidency by those men of the Anti-Slavery party who at that early day thought it their duty to their country to organize, believing that the time would come when, from their small beginning, the entire North would be converted to their way of thinking. Their candidate never entertained the hope of securing an electoral vote, but this did not deter him from accepting the nomination. He believed that the organization of a regiment would be the nucleus of an army which would carry its standard from the Atlantic to the Pacific, from the St. Lawrence to the Gulf of Mexico. As old John Brown, in 1860, marched into Virginia with a mere squad of men, on an expedition which he knew was Quixotic, and would result in the sacrifice of his life, so James G. Birney, in 1844, headed an expedition which resulted in his political death. The vote stood in the aggregate as follows: for James K. Polk, 1,335,834; for Henry Clay, 1,297,033; for James G. Birney, 64,653. The result of the election to Mr. Birney was his bitter denunciation by the friends of Henry Clay. Every press in the country of Whig principles, and every politician disappointed in his aspirations for office, aided to build Birney's political tomb. In social circles the same feeling prevailed, and the name of Birney was, throughout the Union, put on the same page of history with that of Nero, Jefferies, Arnold, &c. But "tempora mutantur." In 1861, the first shot fired on Fort Sumter drove away the fog, and when it was lifted from the ground, the men who stood by James G. Birney in 1844, came forth to vindicate the principles they had so long advocated, and they were reinforced by an army which is "marching on" to freedom and the vindication of the rights of man.

James G. Birney, however, was not influenced by any considerations which could swerve him from what he considered the path of duty. His principles were not altered by the opinions or conduct of those around him. He died in 1858, believing that he had done his duty, as a patriot and a man, to his country and his generation, without any regret that he had not held office, and blaming no one because his life had been an unappreciated struggle for an idea in advance of the age in which he lived.

EDUCATION AND EARLY LIFE.

EDUCATED by such a father, and under such auspices, it is not at all strange that the subject of our sketch should have been a few years ahead of the age in which he lived. Until the commencement of the rebellion he never had an opportunity of giving a practical effect to his early notions of the duty of a man in the nineteenth century in America. He never essayed to go beyond his own social circle, but in this his political opinions were well known and ridiculed, until the country learned to understand them.

He was educated at Andover, Massachusetts, and though after leaving college his pursuits were of an active character, his retentive memory never lost that training he had received at college. At all times, in conversation or in writing, his quotations from the classic or English authors were correct and appropriate. There are few men whose avocations after graduation were like those of General Birney's, who retained so much of the mechanical part of education.

After leaving the University he embarked in business in Cincinnati with a house that had been established for some years. Disaster soon overtook them, and the junior partner—the future major-general—before he was of age, found himself overwhelmed by debt. This, however, did not dampen his energy. He accepted a position as agent of P. Choteau & Co., and went to live at Upper Saginaw, Michigan, then a trading station with the Indians. Here, for several years, he devoted himself incessantly to the interests of his employers, and his services were duly appreciated. The climate, however, did not suit his health, and in spite of favorable offers to remain, he cut himself loose from the advantages of several years' connection, and with his wife and one child sought his fortunes anew.

During his residence in Michigan he had studied law, and was admitted to the bar. The profession, however, did not afford him a livelihood, and he was compelled, by necessity, to seek other means of subsistence. Coming to Philadelphia in 1848, he accepted the first situation that was offered him, a position as transcribing clerk in a mercantile agency, at a salary of six dollars a week. This, however, was only the entering wedge, and in less than three months he was the selected travelling agent of the establishment, and spent six months in travelling throughout the country and establishing those relations for the institution (then an experiment) which laid the foundation of its subsequent usefulness and success. Within less than a year from his first connection with the agency he was its chief manager and director. In this position he remained until July, 1856, during which time he formed the acquaintance of the principal business men and firms of Philadelphia. They all entrusted him with their confidence, and many of them were indebted to him for their prominence and success. It was his faculty to make friends of all with whom he came in contact, and many houses availed themselves of his judgment and sagacity in the prosecution of their business.

On the 17th of June, 1856, a circumstance transpired which made him determine to give up the management of the agency. He had for some time been contemplating a business arrangement with a friend, and during the day on which he resolved to give up his position in the agency, he sent for the writer, and requested an interview at his house that evening. This took place, and in less than an hour, new business arrangements were effected. By the next morning at ten o'clock, General Birney and his new partner had taken an office on Third street, Philadelphia, by buying out a lease and going into possession at once. This business was purely of a legal character, and suited his tastes and education better than any in which he had ever been engaged. He prosecuted it with eminent success until the 16th day of April, 1861, when he left office and practice to engage in the war which had been commenced to test the right and capacity of man for self-government. His duties in the partnership were the office practice and the correspondence, which under his care became very large. His clients were among all classes of the community, and in all branches of business. For all he had an attentive ear and timely suggestions. Few men have ever been able to attach their clients to them personally more closely than Birney. A business acquaintance with him nearly always resulted in a lasting friendship, and when he gave up the office for the tent his absence was a loss to many of his old friends during the commercial troubles of 1861.

This faculty of making friends extended to his numerous

correspondents. Few men could write a letter with more ease and grace than Birney; using very few words, but those well chosen and expressive of his meaning. He exchanged friendly letters with many men whom he had never met, and the frankness with which his correspondents in all parts of the country, many of whom were leading men in their respective localities, expressed to him their views, was unusual in letters whose chief purpose was business. With the South his correspondence was very extensive, and during the summer and fall of 1860, he thus had an opportunity of knowing the sentiments of men in all parts of the South and Southwest.

MILITARY TRAINING.

FTER the election of Mr. Lincoln, Birney formed and expressed the opinion that many of the Southern States were really in earnest in their threats of secession, and that they would make the effort in a body. This idea was then several months in advance of the times, and he found few who agreed with him. Having always been an independent thinker, the failure to make converts to his views did not disconcert him in the least; nor could any argument convince him that he was in error. He resolved that he would engage in the coming conflict, and at once put himself under instruction in the mechanical duties of a soldier, and studied closely the best authorities on tactics, engineering, &c. Thus he had the advantage of nearly six months longer preparation than others who went into the army from civil life, and this preparation told effectually upon his military career. So well known were his views and efforts to qualify himself for the vocation he intended to adopt, that after the inauguration of a new Governor of Pennsylvania, in January, 1861, some of the leading men of the State urged upon Governor Curtin the appointment of Birney as Adjutant-General of Pennsylvania. The place had been a sinecure for years, its principal labor being the receipt of a small salary, and the incumbent always left the office a "General" for life. In January, 1861, the time was approaching when Pennsylvania would be compelled to burnish up the rusty old sabres in her arsenals, and make an effort to fire powder and ball from the old muskets which had only been of service to frighten little boys at a militia training. The men who urged Birney's name had began to believe that the crisis was really approaching, and knowing his energy of character and unusual business qualifications, wanted such a man in the office. Birney, however, took little interest in the movement, saying he would prefer active service to "fancy duty," and was not appointed, because he could not control his precinct or carry his ward. Having never been proprietor of a corner grocery store, his political influence was somewhat limited, and his fitness for a civil office was not easily demonstrated.

Among other preparatory measures which Birney adopted, was to secure his election in December, 1860, as Lieutenant-colonel of a regiment of Philadelphia militia. This organization was like others of the same kind in Pennsylvania, a mere skeleton, and had never been together even in its dilapidated condition, except at an election for officers or a dinner. The whole militia system of the State was a by-word and disgrace to any community. Better have had none than the feeble imitation of other States which existed, and which only entailed upon the Commonwealth expense without advantage. Yet, in times of peace, there may have been some excuse for such neglect, but what criticism can be made when it is known that now (April,

1865) our system is still upon the peace basis! Four years of war and three invasions of Pennsylvania could not convince our law-givers that there has been necessity for organization and for efforts which a regard for our common welfare should call forth. When our homes have been invaded, the defence which came from State authority has been purely spasmodic, and our militia have become a jest and by-word from Maine to Colorado. Yet this is not from any want of courage or willingness on the part of our *people* to do their whole duty.

In 1862, when General Lee and his veterans, preceded by Stuart and his cavalry, were marching up the Cumberland Valley, the people of Pennsylvania responded nobly to the call of their governor. More than seventy thousand men volunteered to take the field in less than ten days. When they came forward by companies and regiments they could get no arms, equipments, or tents. The promises made them were broken; they were subjected to every inconvenience which human nature could endure, and it was not until late in 1863 that they were paid the small pittance which the State promised them. When, in 1863, General Lee again came into the Keystone State, is it any wonder that the same men who had been badly treated the year before hesitated to respond to the calls from Harrisburg until they knew what was in store for them? It is sometimes impossible to believe that the rulers of Pennsylvania ever discovered that a civil war was raging in the land. Their neglect of plain duty and disregard of all sense of manly honor can be explained on no other hypothesis.

It is true, that in May, 1864, after more than three years

of war, a law was passed to organize a militia system, and by its provisions all the volunteer organizations throughout the State were swept away, though they were then, and have been for years, the only nucleus of organization. This blunder was rectified in August, 1864, by a supplement, passed at the extra session; but it was then almost too late. The damage had been done. Up to April, 1865, the efforts to put in operation the provisions of the law have been feeble and unsuccessful. Had David B. Birney been Adjutant-general of Pennsylvania in 1861, there would have been a different order of things. It is possible he might have increased the State debt, but he never would have exercised the power and influence which such an office would have given him without providing some system by which a population of more than two millions of people would have been able to make, in the time of danger, an effort to defend themselves.

This, however, is a digression. The object of this sketch is to narrate what has been done, and not to theorize or to find fault with things as they are, unless it can be shown how they may be improved.

When Birney was, in pursuance of the election held in December, 1860, commissioned as "Lieutenant-colonel of the First regiment of Artillery of the uniformed militia of the Commonwealth of Pennsylvania, in the Third Brigade of the First Division, composed of the uniformed militia of the city and county of Philadelphia," by Governor Curtin, on the 22d of February, 1861, his qualifications for the office, though beyond the average standard then existing, consisted in the knowledge he had acquired by three months of study, and by his experience as a member of the First Troop of Philadelphia City Cavalry.

This organization dates its existence as far back as November 17, 1774; and during the Revolution performed services for which they were commended by General Washington in official orders, which they acknowledged, on September 15, 1787, by giving to the general "a splendid entertainment at the City Tavern, Philadelphia." In 1794, during the Whiskey Rebellion, they were in the saddle for three months, going to the western part of Pennsylvania. On March 20, 1799, after two hours' notice, they took part in the Northampton expedition. On May 29, 1812, they volunteered their services in the anticipated war with Great Britain, and were in service during the war. In December, 1838, they took part in the "Buckshot War" at Harrisburg. After this, with the exception of aiding occasionally to quell a riot in the city of Philadelphia, they rested upon their laurels until May, 1861, when, after considerable delay in procuring horses and equipments, they served the United States for three months. In June, 1863, after less than thirty hours of preparation, they were again in the saddle for ninety days. Though not in the war for three years as a body, more than eighty of their members have been in the service, filling commissions of all grades, from second lieutenant to that of major-general.

During Birney's connection with the Troop the duties of the members consisted principally in eating an annual dinner, in acting as the Body Guard of the President of the United States whenever he came to Philadelphia, and in attending the funerals of their deceased members. All these duties

Birney performed for years with the most punctilious exactness, and though he was one of the best horsemen in the troop, and was always well mounted, he could never attain any position higher than that of a private. This, however, gave him opportunity for exercise, which his sedentary life made so necessary for him, and made him familiar with the volunteer organizations of the city, so that when his commission of February, 1861, as lieutenant-colonel arrived, he was fully competent to fulfil all the requirements of the position.

OPENING OF THE REBELLION.

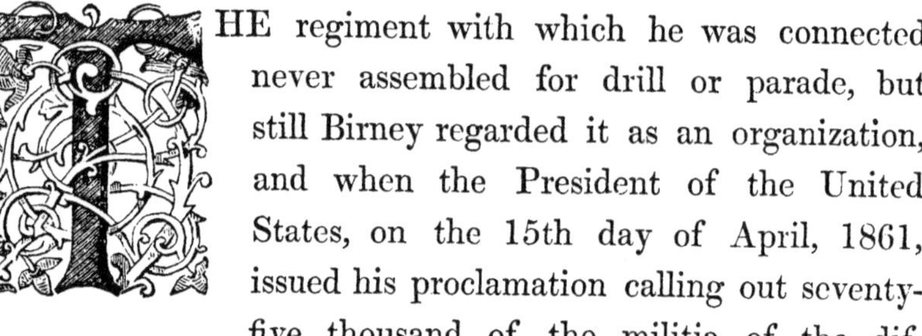

THE regiment with which he was connected never assembled for drill or parade, but still Birney regarded it as an organization, and when the President of the United States, on the 15th day of April, 1861, issued his proclamation calling out seventy-five thousand of the militia of the different States, Birney determined to act. The proclamation was posted on the bulletin boards of the city about twelve o'clock of the day of its issue. Without consulting any other officer, Birney at once telegraphed to Harrisburg that his regiment would respond to the call of the President. The same night, about midnight, he was answered that his regiment would be accepted, and he was requested to report the number of men ready to take the field. A response to this message demanded some inquiry, and the next morning Colonel Birney set about making it. By eleven o'clock (Tuesday) he ascertained that his course was approved by very few officers except the colonel. They thought he had been precipitate and wanted some time to reflect.

This demand for time did not suit either Colonel Charles P. Dare or Lieutenant-colonel Birney. They were anxious to be off, and wanted no "straggling." They came to Birney's office, and after a consultation determined to raise a regiment, and went to work without delay. A selection of officers was made from among their acquaintances, and with the aid of these gentlemen recruiting offices were opened in different parts of the city before two o'clock of that day. On Thursday (April 18th) the regiment was full. One thousand determined and resolute men had been gathered together, who were willing to leave home for three months to aid in crushing secession and bringing back the rebellious States to an allegiance to the Union. The greatest enthusiasm existed, and the first regiment ready to start was able to get the most men. Out of one fire-company in Philadelphia, consisting of seventy-five members, sixty enlisted in a body, and those men were the flower of the regiment.

After the men were assembled and ready to go, the great question was, what to do with them. Neither the General Government nor the State could furnish them with arms, clothing or equipments, nor was there any officer at hand to muster them into the service of the United States. To send them home with orders to report when wanted, would have dampened the ardor of the men. What to do with them was a problem which Lieutenant-colonel Birney solved by procuring from Major-general Patterson, then in command of the Philadelphia Division of the Pennsylvania militia, the use of the State Arsenal in the city, where the men were quartered and fed at private expense, of which Lieutenant-colonel Birney bore a considerable share, until they could be sent away.

FIRST CAMPAIGN.

ON Sunday afternoon, the officers were able to get arms, and during the night, uniforms, and on Monday, (April 22d,) four companies, under command of Lieutenant-colonel Birney, left Philadelphia as a portion of the Twenty-third regiment of Pennsylvania volunteers, and went to Perryville on the Philadelphia, Wilmington and Baltimore Railroad, on the north bank of the Susquehanna, to guard the railroad. In a few days the remainder of the regiment, under Colonel Dare, went down on the same mission, and the duty of guarding the road and protecting the workmen in the repairs of the damage which had been done by Trimble and his associates, was performed by the officers and men with alacrity. The Twenty-third Pennsylvania was thus "the first from Philadelphia in the field." [*Philadelphia Inquirer, April* 26, 1861.]

For some time the regiment was divided: Colonel Dare, with half the companies, was north of the Susquehanna river, and Lieutenant-colonel Birney, with the remainder, was south. During this period of inaction Colonel Birney made efforts to apprehend Trimble, the famous bridge burner. At one time he thought he was successful, and so informed his friends in Philadelphia, but his efforts were unavailing. Trimble escaped the rope and bough, which certainly would have been his fate had he fallen into Birney's hands.

During the early part of this railroad protection Birney's men were poorly clad. The uniforms furnished them were of the poorest description, and their under-clothing was only such as they had on their persons when they laid aside their citizens' clothes for those of soldiers. Before they had been away from home a month they were well provided by the voluntary contributions of citizens, and especially by the efforts of the Rev. Dr. Boardman's congregation of Philadelphia. In the meantime Birney required his men to observe the greatest particularity in their habits of personal cleanliness. Every day a portion of the men were required to wash their underclothing in the river. Not having a change at hand, their personal appearance, while the daily ablution was being performed, shocked the propriety of some of the citizens of Havre de Grace. These gentlemen waited upon Lieutenant-colonel Birney, and remonstrated with him because of the exhibitions which his men made daily. He answered by regretting the necessity for shocking the nerves of the people of the town, but insisted that the health and comfort of his men was an object of paramount importance. He offered, however, to compromise the matter, by sparing the feelings of the citizens if they would furnish the companies with a change of linen, and in that event promised that the men should keep on a shirt while they washed the soiled one in the river. This proposition was not accepted, and until the citizens of Philadelphia provided for the comfort of the Twenty-third regiment, the citizens of Havre de Grace were under the necessity of enduring the grievance.

SECOND CAMPAIGN.

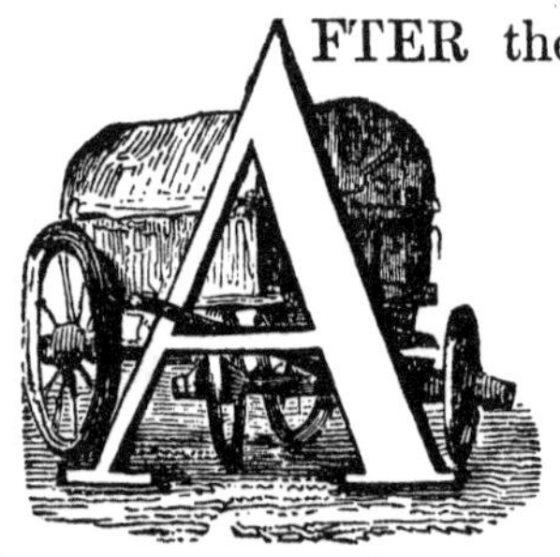

AFTER the road from Philadelphia to Baltimore was fully repaired, and communication with the North and Washington restored, the Twenty-third regiment became uneasy in their position. The officers and men wanted to see more active service. The field officers applied to Hon. Simon Cameron, then Secretary of War, for a different position. The application met with a favorable response, and on the 22d day of May, 1861, the regiment was ordered to join General Patterson, who was then in the Cumberland Valley. The order was cheerfully obeyed, and the men embarked from Havre de Grace for Baltimore. Frank Birney, a lad of fourteen years, had been for several weeks with his father, Lieutenant-colonel Birney, and had become a favorite with the men. To him was accorded the privilege of carrying one of the regimental colors through the Monumental City, which at that time was something of a triumph for the boy and the old flag, which was not then beloved by many of the people of Baltimore.

The regiment went direct to Chambersburg, where it was placed in the brigade of General Thomas—the same officer who, in December, 1864, gladdened the hearts of all his loyal countrymen by the signal victory over the army of the rebel General Hood near Nashville, Tennessee. On June 14th the brigade, consisting of four companies of regular cavalry, the First Troop of Philadelphia City cavalry, two companies of regular infantry, under Captain (since Major-general) Doubleday, the Sixth Pennsylvania, Colonel Naglee, the Twenty-first, Colonel Ballier, and the Twenty-third, Colonel Dare, moved from Chambersburg towards Williamsport, Maryland,—the Twenty-third having the right of the line.

During this campaign, which lasted until the term for which the men had enlisted expired, little transpired to vary the monotony of camp life. Owing to Colonel Dare's infirm health, the command of the regiment the greater part of the time devolved upon Lieutenant-colonel Birney. On the 2d day of July, 1861, General Patterson crossed the Potomac and sent forward a detachment, consisting of the Twenty-third Pennsylvania volunteers, under Lieutenant-colonel Birney, the Eleventh Pennsylvania, the First Wisconsin and the Philadelphia City Troop, to engage a portion of General Johnston's command, near Hainesville, under General Stonewall Jackson. The engagement (for such it was called at the time) took place near Falling Waters. The rebels fell back, our loss being three killed and ten wounded. In this action Lieutenant-colonel Birney displayed, for the first time, that coolness and intrepidity which always endears an officer to his men. Though the encounter, in comparison with subsequent actions, did not deserve the name of a skirmish, it was the first occasion in which the men engaged in it had ever been under fire, and they at once chose as their leaders the officers who displayed those qualities which to the private soldier are so captivating.

The correspondent of the New York Tribune, writing from Falling Waters under date of July 2d, (published July 8th,) says: "The Wisconsin regiment was supporting the battery on the left of the road and the Eleventh Pennsylvania on the right. These immediately came up into position and poured in one volley before the enemy had time to form. Just in the middle of the fight the Twenty-third Pennsylvania came up as cool as cucumbers and pitched into the chase, flanking out a considerable distance to the left and routing the rebels from all their places of concealment. Every man was cool and deliberate and their shots told with fearful effect." The regiment was the first to enter Winchester on the next day, and the men celebrated their 4th of July, 1861, in the town which has since been the centre of so many important movements.

After the occupation of Winchester, by order of Lieutenant-general Scott, some of General Patterson's best troops were taken from him, and his column subsequently retired to the Potomac. As is well known, he did not attack the forces of General Johnston, who subsequently joined Beauregard two days before the battle of Bull Run. Thus General Patterson and his men, much to their regret, were prevented from engaging in any active operations during their campaign in the Shenandoah valley. For this the general and his officers have been abused and censured in private and public circles, by civilians and by military men, by the press in America and Europe, by writers of pamphlets and of history, and even by Lieutenant-general Scott himself in his autobiography, lately published. Not only have the General and his officers been pronounced incompetent, but have been accused of a want of good faith for that government they had sworn to support. They bore all this in silence so long as they considered that the interests of the cause required that they should not disclose the orders under which they acted. These have lately been made public in a pamphlet which General Patterson has written. To any candid mind it is the most complete and unanswerable justification which could be made, and will furnish to the future historian of the great American rebellion facts from which he can photograph the scenes of the "three months' campaign," and do justice to all who participated in its management.

A NEW REGIMENT.

HE term of service of the regiment expired July 23, 1861, but before that time it was evident to the most casual observer that the rebellion was not a holiday excursion. The Government had called for men to enlist for three years, and the question of re-enlistment was discussed over the camp-fires. Colonel Dare could make no engagements for the future. He was then in a decline, and, soon after his return home, consumption did its work and buried him in an early grave. Lieutenant-colonel Birney had every inducement to return home after the termination of his first campaign. His private interests were suffering from neglect, his business needed his attention, and his family urged him to return to the comforts of home. But none of these temptations could deter him from remaining in the service. Many of the men of his regiment offered to re-enlist if he would take command. This he soon promised to do, and made an effort to get the Secretary of War to permit their re-enlistment in Maryland, thus saving the Government the expense of their transportation both ways. This, however, was not allowed. As soon as it was known that the regiment must return home, he wrote to his partner in Philadelphia, stating his intention of remaining in the service, and requesting him at once to make arrangements for recruiting a new regiment. This was done without delay. The Girard House, which for years had been the leading hotel in Philadelphia, but which was at that time closed, was taken for the purposes of recruiting, and it is doubtful whether a larger or more expensive recruiting office was ever opened in the country. The citizens of Philadelphia laughed when they saw their largest hotel used for such a purpose, but the result soon justified the means.

The new regiment met with great success, and in a week four companies were mustered in and sent to camp. The old Twenty-third returned to Philadelphia, August 17, 1861, and were escorted to the Arsenal, their old quarters, by their new comrades. The next day the men were mustered out. Colonel Birney went at once to work to organize the new regiment, and obtained permission from Governor Curtin to retain the old designation. In two more days about three hundred men of the old regiment re-enlisted for three years and were formed into three companies. These, with the four new companies, were encamped at the junction of Nicetown Lane and Lamb Tavern Road, in Philadelphia, and Colonel Birney went to work to lay out his camp for at least a month's residence, having received authority to raise a regiment of fifteen companies. On August 20th, an order was issued by the Secretary of War for all the companies mustered in, to report immediately at Washington. Birney went down the next day with his seven hundred men, and was in Washington the evening of the 21st.

4

The following notice of their march through Baltimore is from the *Baltimore American* of August 22, 1861:

"The Twenty-third regiment of Pennsylvania volunteers, under the command of Colonel David B. Birney, numbering about seven hundred men, passed through Baltimore *en route* for Washington. A large proportion of the men were under Colonel Dare, in the same regiment, which has already served three months under General Patterson. They are uniformed similar to regulars. Several of the companies are well drilled in the Zouave exercise, and also uniformed."

After the departure of the seven companies, recruiting was continued in Philadelphia with such success that before the 10th of September, 1861, there were fifteen hundred men in camp near Washington, completely organized. It composed part of General (Pike) Graham's brigade, which was in the division commanded by General Buell, as the army was organized in October, 1861, before it was divided into corps.

During the time the regiment was under instruction, and while General McClellan was organizing the army of the Potomac, the officers were greatly commended for their efficiency, and their camp was a favorite place of resort for visitors and general officers. The drills were without cessation, and every attention was paid to those duties which alone can make good soldiers out of volunteers.

PROMOTION.

DURING the winter, Colonel Birney formed the acquaintance of General Cameron, then Secretary of War, whose attention had been attracted by the fine appearance and superior condition of the regiment. Many of Birney's friends, at first without his knowledge, urged upon the Secretary his claims for promotion. The effort was successful, and the letter of appointment was issued February 17, 1862. His name was sent to the Senate the same week, and the appointment confirmed without hesitation.

On the day he received his appointment General Stone had been relieved from the command of the forces near Ball's Bluff, and General John Sedgwick ordered to take his place. The new general applied for the command of General Sedgwick, and it was given him. The brigade, consisting of the Third Maine, (Col. H. G. Berry, afterwards Major-general, and killed at Chancellorsville,) the Fourth Maine, (Col. Staples,) the Thirty-eighth New York, (Col. J. H. Ward, since Brigadier-general,) and the Fortieth New York (Mozart, Col. Riley) regiments, was encamped near Alexandria, and General Birney went to his new command the same day without returning to his regiment.

A CABAL.

FOR some time there had been jealousies existing in the Twenty-third, and a cabal was formed in opposition to the Colonel among some of the officers, resulting from some discipline to which they had been subjected. Birney scarcely knew of its existence. After his promotion, Captain Thomas H. Neill, of the regular army, (now General Neill,) was made colonel. This gave rise to some additional dissatisfaction, because the officers thought the Colonel should have been chosen from their own number. As Colonel Neill had been a friend of Birney for several years, it was alleged by the grumblers that the selection was at the instance of Birney. Shortly after Colonel Neill assumed command an order was issued, by which five of the companies were detached from the regiment and put into another. This was not a peculiar instance, for all the large regiments then existing were divided in a similar manner, but this fact was also used by the malcontents to prejudice the men against Birney, by the allegation that the division had been made in pursuance of a bargain by which Colonel Birney had been made a Brigadier. In addition to these charges, he was accused of caring little for the men, and as proof of the fact, it was said that Birney had not taken leave of his regiment with due formality. These arguments had for a time weight with the men, and on one occasion, when General Birney returned to visit his regiment, he was rudely treated.

It is not proposed to discuss these charges further than to deny them all. To any one acquainted with the mode of doing business with the War Department, they are simply ridiculous. It is true, perhaps, that he did not observe the usual formalities in taking leave of his regiment, but he was anxious to assume the active duties of his new command, and besides this, it was one of his characteristics to avoid scenes of any kind. He never did any thing for effect. His previous and subsequent career shows that he was not wanting in affection for his men. No officer in the army had warmer or more sincere friends among his subordinates.

This little incident has been referred to because it is the only instance in which General Birney was ever charged with want of heart, or sacrificing the interests or feelings of others to promote his own. It was magnified into some importance, but soon dwindled away, for very soon the men discovered the motives which prompted it, and the only result which followed was contempt for those officers who had manufactured the charges.

A BRIGADIER.

GENERAL BIRNEY, when he assumed his new command, was an entire stranger to every officer and man in it; but he soon won their confidence and esteem. He retained the command until September 1, 1862, when he took command of the division of which his brigade was a part, and this command he retained until July, 1864, when he was assigned by Lieutenant-general Grant to the command of the Tenth Army Corps; so that the regiments turned over to him by General Sedgwick were under his command while they continued in the service, under their three years' enlistment, and men and officers could not have more love for a general than these had for Birney.

When he took command of the brigade it was part of a division commanded by Brigadier-general (now Major-general) Heintzelman. On March 18, 1862, Brigadier-general C. S. Hamilton assumed command, General Heintzelman having been assigned to the command of the Third Corps of the Army of the Potomac, of which the division was a part. General Hamilton retained command until May 3, 1862, when Brigadier-general Philip Kearny, at Camp Winfield Scott, near Yorktown, assumed command, by virtue of orders received from headquarters of the Army of the Potomac, which command he retained until his death, September 1, 1862.

This division was then the third of the Third Corps, which continued under the command of General Heintzelman during the campaign on the Peninsula, and was composed of three brigades, commanded by Brigadier-generals Jameson, Birney and Berry, who are all dead.

The division continued to retain its number in the corps until August 5, 1862, when it was changed to the first. This designation it retained until April, 1864, when the old Third Corps, with its glorious record and warm associations, was broken up and its divisions put into other corps. The old first division having had the reduced numbers of the second division of the Third Corps (formerly commanded by General Joe Hooker) joined to it in May, 1864, then became the third of the Second Corps, which designation it still retains, (May, 1865.)

A correspondent of the *New York Herald*, writing from Richmond under date of May 6, 1865, (published May 10, 1865,) describing the march of the army through Richmond, refers to this division in the following language:—

"As the columns passed by, no one element was more noticeable than that of decimation. For instance, the old and honored Third Army Corps (now merged) appeared reduced to a single and small division, wearing its own 'square patch' as an *insignium* rather than the trefoil of its later affections. These goodly men, who, under their old and original organization, had been gallantly and nobly led by Heintzelman, sainted Dick Richardson, universally accepted Joe Hooker, generous and impetuous Sickles, lamented and able Birney, and the ever-reliant French, still bore earnest traces of their veterancy, and received plaudits to the echo whenever and wherever recognized. Though now forming part of the Second Corps, yet, not in the least derogating from the lustrous and never-fading glories of that organization, they still justly remember what has been accorded them for heroism at Gettysburg, and their saving grace at Chancellorsville, where they earned the honors of the day because they indisputably preserved it to our arms."

KEARNY.

BIRNEY was thus under the immediate command of the gallant Kearny during the Peninsular and Pope's campaigns, and may be said to have received his military education from this accomplished officer. These two men, though unlike in many points of character, soon became warm friends, and no event in his military life so affected Birney as the receipt of Kearny's mangled remains, from within the enemy's lines after the battle of Chantilly, on September 1, 1862. Through all the successes and trials of the Peninsular campaign, these men were side by side and did their entire duty to their men and their country. No unkind criticism of Kearny ever passed Birney's lips. He believed his old commander to be the embodiment of all that was gallant as an officer, brave as a soldier, and courteous as a gentleman; and in sharing his fortunes, identified himself, perhaps too much, with the unfortunate jealousies which, in 1862, existed in the Army of the Potomac between regular and volunteer officers. The latter believed that their education at the point of the bayonet qualified them for service quite as much as if they had been educated at West Point. These feelings, however, were soon worn down by time, and at the time of his death, no corps commander in the army was more beloved and respected than Birney, by both regular and volunteer officers. No man could be spoken more kindly of than the writer has often heard Birney mentioned by officers, from the commander of the Army of the Potomac to the second lieutenant, and by soldiers who wear the "red patch," (the red diamond, the badge of Birney's division,) or the bastion fort, (the badge of the Tenth Army Corps.) It is true, that this feeling of jealousy between officers fighting in the same cause, in the same army, and under the same flag, was eradicated by the wholesome findings of several courts-martial and the severe but just orders of the War Department, but it was necessary for the good of our cause that the knife should be used. After its skillful application dissension ceased. Willing and earnest obedience to commands was observed by zealous and true-hearted officers, and the commanders of our armies have thus been enabled to penetrate every part of Rebeldom.

Those who write the history of the rebellion will always differ about the conduct of many of the general officers who had commands in the Army of the Potomac when it was first organized, but the verdict which, in 1862, the public of the United States rendered, will never be altered. It is possible that some future Congress may remove the disability under which some officers have been placed by the sentences of the courts-martial, but the present generation will never censure the finding by which they have been returned to private life.

REVIEWS AND DRILLS.

DURING the fall of 1861, the Army of the Potomac, which since that time, through summer's heat and winter's snow, has written for itself so glorious a record, was assembled around the city of Washington. Its organization was said to have been complete early in the fall, and during the golden days of October and November, the country looked anxiously for a forward movement. The rebel rag floated from the top of Manassas hill, within sight of the dome of the Capitol, and the mounted guns on the enemy's fortifications were a daily challenge to the Union army. But the challenge was not accepted. Our leader was determined "not to move until he was ready." To prevent the army from rusting it was occasionally exercised in a "grand review," which was beheld with admiration by newspaper correspondents and little boys, and after one grand review was over and the country was astonished by the description, in scientific words, of the wonderful performances, the army was indulged—in another "grand review."

Then autumn passed away and our troops and their friends at home were nauseated with grand words and grand display. The brave and earnest men who had assembled at the call of the President were disappointed because they were not led forward to meet the enemy. They believed, and so did the country at large, that they were quite as well prepared as the rebels, and the inactivity imposed upon them by their commander was galling and humiliating.

Such was the state of public opinion and the feeling in the army, when Congress assembled on the first Monday in December, 1861, and the opinion of the people was soon made known through their representatives. It was soon made evident that this opinion was shared by our noble President and his cabinet. But then it was too late: the quantity and quality of Virginia mud prevented any movement during the winter months. The time came, however, when campaigning was possible; but it is yet a question in the minds of many people, whether the army would have been "ready" to move until this day, (1865,) had not the President, by General War Order, No. 1, ordered "that the 22d day of February, 1862, be the day for a general movement of the land and naval forces of the United States against the insurgent forces," &c., &c.

Even this order was no spur to habitual tardiness. The order produced only a long letter to the Secretary of War from the then Commander of the Army of the Potomac, and it was not until the night of the 9th of March, that an advance was ordered upon Centreville and Manassas. This advance demonstrated that our army for several months had been kept at bay by "quaker guns," *i. e.* stove-pipes and logs (not even painted) so arranged as to impress upon the timid mind the belief that they were real "dogs of war." Of course upon this advance the enemy retired, leaving "burning heaps of military stores and much valuable property."

PENINSULAR CAMPAIGN.

UNTIL the 17th of March, the commander of the Army of the Potomac was content with the victory at Centreville and Manassas. On the 13th a council of war "adopted Fort Monroe as the base of operations for the movement of the Army of the Potomac upon Richmond." It was then thought that "the line" on which, in 1864, General Grant "*proposed* to fight all summer," was not the proper route for a movement on the rebel Capital. That route, however, has proved to be the true one, and the evacuation of Richmond on April 1, 1865, has proved that, whatever military critics may say to the contrary, the direct line from Washington to Richmond—the route which lightning follows from object to object—was the true one. This, however, was not the opinion of the "four corps commanders" mentioned in General McClellan's Report, in part first of the second period. They thought it best to take to water, and on the 17th General Hamilton embarked from Alexandria with his division of the Third Corps. Of this division General Birney's brigade was a part, and he and his men were thus part of the advance of the Army of the Potomac to the Peninsula. This circumstance was of course accidental. When, however, his talent for command was appreciated, he continued in the advance, and with the men of his command occupied this much sought for position until

October, 1864, when he left his command and came home to die.

The army was moved from Fort Monroe on the 4th and 5th of April, and on the 10th "the siege of Yorktown was begun." On the day previous the commander-in-chief had received a letter from the President, in which these words occur: "I think it is the precise time to strike a blow. By delay the enemy will relatively gain upon you. * * * * Once more let me tell you it is indispensable to *you* that you strike a blow. *I* am powerless to help this. You will do me the justice to remember I always insisted that going down the bay in search of the field, instead of fighting at or near Manassas, was only shifting and not surmounting a difficulty; that we would find the same enemy and the same or equal entrenchments at either place. The country will not fail to note—is now noting—that the present hesitation to move upon an entrenched enemy, is the story of Manassas repeated. * * * * * * You must act."

Even this spur did not hasten the siege, and more than three weeks were expended in preparation. "Our batteries would have been ready to open on the morning of May 6th at latest, but on the morning of the 4th it was discovered that the enemy had already been compelled to evacuate his position during the night, leaving behind him all his heavy guns uninjured and a large amount of ammunition and supplies." In these operations Birney's brigade took little part except to do their share of digging. They, in common with the rest of the army, eagerly expected an action, and it was not until the 5th of May, at the battle of Williamsburg, that they were really under fire.

WILLIAMSBURG.

N this action "the division of General Kearny arrived at nine, A. M., to reinforce Hooker, who had succeeded by the greatest exertion in passing Casey's troops and pushing on to the front through the deep mud. General Kearny at once gallantly attacked and thereby prevented the loss of another battery, and drove the enemy back at every point, enabling General Hooker to extricate himself from his position and withdraw his wearied troops." (McClellan's Report.)

Of this division General Birney's brigade was a part, General Kearny having, on the 3d of May, been placed in command. In his report of the battle he says: "Approaching near the field word was brought by an aide-de-camp, that Hooker's cartridges were expended, and with increased rapidity we entered under fire. Having quickly consulted with General Hooker, I at once deployed Berry's brigade to the left of the Williamsburg road and Birney's on the right of it. * * * * * * The heavy strewn timber defied all direct approach. I therefore ordered Colonel J. Hobart Ward of the Thirty-eighth New York volunteers, (one of Birney's regiments,) to charge down the road and take the rifle pits on the centre of the abattis by their flank. This duty Colonel Ward performed with gallantry, his martial demeanor imparting all confidence in the attack. Still the move, though nearly successful, did not quite prevail; but with bravery every point thus gained was perfectly sustained. The left wing of Colonel Riley's regiment, the Fortieth (Mozart) New York volunteers, (also a part of Birney's brigade,) was next sent for, and came up brilliantly, conducted by Captain Mindil, chief of General Birney's staff. These charged up to the open space and silenced some light artillery, and gaining the enemy's rear, caused him to relinquish his cover. The victory was ours."

* * * * * * *

"I have to mark out for the high commendation of the General-in-chief, Generals Jameson, Birney and Berry, whose soldierly judgment was alone equalled by their distinguished courage."

General Kearny, not content with the opportunity to speak of Birney in his official report, as above quoted, wrote the following letter to the Governor of Pennsylvania:—

HEADQUARTERS THIRD DIVISION, HEINTZELMAN'S CORPS, CAMP BERRY, *May* 10, 1862.

TO HIS EXCELLENCY GOV. A. G. CURTIN,
Of Pennsylvania.

SIR:—As the commanding officer of this division, of which three regiments, the Fifty-seventh, Sixty-third, and the One-hundred-and-fifth Pennsylvania volunteers form a portion, I cannot refrain from calling to your notice the important part performed by them in the battle of Williamsburg on the fifth instant, and if not themselves the sufferers in loss, they contributed by steady and imposing attitude to the success of those more immediately engaged, and would have formed a means of subduing all opposition should the enemy have resisted on the following day. A picket of one hundred and twelve men of the One-hundred-and-fifth, under Lieutenant Gilbert, were the first to enter the enemy's works, followed by the Fourth Maine, of General Birney's brigade. Colonel A. A. McKnight, One-hundred-and-fifth Pennsylvania; Colonel Alex'r Hays, Sixty-third, and C. T. Campbell, Fifty-seventh, are in my first brigade, commanded by General Jameson.

In conclusion, your Excellency, it is not only by her noble regiments Pennsylvania was distinguished in the last great battles: I have to bring to your notice and to that of the people of the State, that the second brigade of my division was commanded by a Pennsylvanian, General Birney. This officer displayed coolness and courage, and brought into the field the talents which distinguished him among his fellow-citizens. He has proved himself a good colonel—his brigade is the model of good discipline. His genius of command was especially conspicuous on this day.

I have the honor to be, sir,

Your obedient servant,

P. KEARNY,

Brigadier-general Third Division Third Corps.

General Birney's official report of the battle of Williamsburg will be found in the Appendix. His conduct in this, really his first engagement, justified the high expectations of his friends, and gave promise of the success which afterwards attended his career. His coolness and soldierly bearing were the subject of comment in the descriptions of the battle, which were published in the papers of the day.

BIRNEY UNDER ARREST.

FTER Williamsburg, the army continued "on to Richmond," and on June 1st, the country was electrified by the following dispatch from General McClellan:—

FROM THE FIELD OF BATTLE,
June 1st, twelve o'clock, noon.

TO THE HON. E. M. STANTON,
Secretary of War:

We have had a desperate battle, in which the corps of Generals Sumner, Heintzelman, and Keyes have been engaged, against greatly superior numbers. Yesterday, at one o'clock, the enemy, taking advantage of a terrible storm, which had flooded the valley of the Chickahominy, attacked our troops on the right flank.

Casey's division, which was in the first line, gave way unaccountably, and this caused a temporary confusion, during which the guns and baggage were lost, but Generals Heintzelman and Kearny most gallantly brought up their troops, which checked the enemy, and at the same time, however, succeeded by great exertions in bringing across Sedgwick and Richardson's divisions, who drove back the enemy at the point of the bayonet, covering the ground with his dead.

This morning the enemy attempted to renew the conflict, but was everywhere repulsed.

We have taken many prisoners, among whom is General Pettigrew and Colonel Long.

Our loss is heavy, but that of the enemy must be enormous.

With the exception of Casey's division, the men behaved splendidly.

Several fine bayonet charges have been made. The Second Excelsior made two to-day.

GEO. B. McCLELLAN,
Major-general Commanding.

After reading this and knowing that General Birney was present when "Kearny most gallantly brought up his troops," his friends were somewhat surprised by the announcement in the papers of the next day, that General Birney had, on the 31st of May, "halted his command a mile from the enemy," for which he had been put under arrest by order of General Heintzelman. They did not believe the charge, but the fact of the arrest they were compelled to admit. What General Birney did on that day is written in the official reports of Generals Kearny and Birney, for which see Appendix. Why he was arrested and subjected to the ordeal of a court-martial needs some explanation. His men were under arms all night, and he and they were all under the impression that their whole duty had been performed. The next morning, (Sunday,) at daybreak, he received the order placing him under arrest. Knowing there was some misapprehension, (which General Heintzelman subsequently admitted in his official report of the battle,) he at once rode over to General Heintzelman's headquarters, and sent in his name by an orderly. He was answered by a staff-officer that the general was not out of bed and could not be disturbed, and was reminded that being under arrest, his duty was to await further action. This he knew well, but he insisted on seeing the general for the purpose of explanation, and while he admitted the irregularity of the application, according to the strict rules of regular military usage, he asked that his message be taken in. He received for answer, that all communication with General Heintzelman must be in writing.

He returned and did not resume the command of his brigade until after the court-martial had passed upon the charges preferred against him. He made one more effort, however, to make explanation, and this time the rules of military etiquette were complied with, and the application was in writing. A note from General Birney was sent to General Heintzelman by Major J. F. Tobias, of Philadelphia, a volunteer aide on General Birney's staff, and enclosed the following from General Kearny:—

HEADQUARTERS THIRD DIVISION, THIRD CORPS, *June* 2, 1862.

SIR:—I am positive that General Birney has never disobeyed orders, intentionally, nor by any want of either courage or intelligence. I look on him as a superior officer.

I am positive that if you would accord him a hearing, or enable him to answer any categorical demands, it would be perfectly satisfactory to you.

In a wooded country orders apparently conflict. The fact of his saving Couch's division seems a proof of his effecting what was intended. As for myself, with Berry's brigade, I retook Casey's lost ground, and the *consequence* was, that my troops were *completely cut off* from the enemy, forcing in other troops of Keyes' corps.

I take the liberty of bringing this to your notice, knowing your kindness, as well as generosity of disposition towards all under your command.

Most respectfully,

P. KEARNY,

Brigadier-general, commanding Third Division.

To CAPTAIN MCKEEVER,

For General Heintzelman.

This, however, produced no result, and General Birney quietly awaited the receipt of charges and the action of the court to be constituted. As the army was in motion the court could not be assembled until June 14th, and its duty was performed in a day.

General Heintzelman was called as a witness before the court, and said he had given General Birney no orders, but they were conveyed through General Kearny. Of the circumstances which led to this arrest, General Heintzelman thus speaks in his report, dated June 7, 1862:—

"Early in the afternoon (three o'clock, P. M.) an order was sent, on the application of General Keyes, to General Kearny, to send a brigade up the railroad to his assistance. The order sent to General Kearny was to send a brigade up the railroad to the front, and General Birney's was ordered up. I learned, after I arrived on the field of battle, that the brigade was halted on the railroad a very short distance from the camp. * * * * Through what misunderstanding or counter orders it was kept back, I am unable to say. I have since learned that General Kearny gave the orders. After the battle General Birney was placed under arrest, by my order, and brought before a court-martial, for disobedience of orders. The court honorably acquitted him."

General Birney managed his own defence before the court, and interposed no objection whatever to any witness or question. When the case of the Government was concluded the court was cleared, and on its reopening General Birney was informed that the court did not consider it necessary for him to offer any defence. Under this intimation he called no witnesses, and was the same day "honorably acquitted" by a finding, which, with the charges, &c., will be found in the Appendix.

Thus ended this prosecution, which had been gazetted throughout the land. Its result in the army and on the general public was highly advantageous to General Birney. His conduct as a soldier was made the subject of investigation by a tribunal composed of gentlemen of the regular army, to whom he was a stranger. It terminated by eliciting their admiration for him as a man and a soldier, and established his position among them as nothing else could have done. The public, as well as General McClellan, approved the finding; and General Birney "resumed his sword and his command" with the sympathy which human nature always bestows on those who have had to pass through such an ordeal without cause.

After General Birney's return to his brigade the following letter was addressed him by Colonel (now Major-general) Egan, of the Fortieth New York volunteers, and is an evidence of the feeling which was entertained for him by the officers and men of his brigade:—

HEADQUARTERS FORTIETH REGIMENT N. Y. V.
June 19, 1862.

BRIGADIER-GENERAL D. B. BIRNEY,
Commanding Second Brigade, Kearny's Division.

GENERAL:—It is with heartfelt pleasure that, on behalf of the officers of my regiment, as well as myself, I offer you our congratulations on your return to the command of your brigade, after so speedy and triumphant a vindication from the charges made against you.

As for our part, on the morning of the 31st May, not a heart beat but with joy at the prospect of encountering the enemy, and with implicit confidence in the bravery, energy, and skill of our leader. We were, as we all knew, in a position of incalculable importance, the very key of the whole line, and all looked forward eagerly to a renewal of the scenes of Williamsburg, and to the addition to our laurels already gained of new ones, which should shed lustre on the whole brigade.

What was our surprise, therefore, on the next morning, to find that you had been relieved from your command on charges known to us to originate in mistake, and to involve offences utterly foreign to your nature? The news fell upon us unexpectedly, and with painful effect. But we knew the valor and worth of your successor, and determined that the discipline and self-devotion of your command should that day refute the slanderous charges made against you.

We were soon at our task—that of saving from capture and destruction a whole division of our forces. The scanty numbers of your brigade, after the fight, and the appalling weight of the fire poured upon us by overwhelming odds, you know well. We leave to our commander to say whether we merited your approbation.

General, we welcome you among us, and we are ready, though with decimated numbers, to follow you again, and trust that the next battle will afford you an opportunity of convincing every one, as thoroughly as us, that in the willingness to obey, you are second to none.

I am, General,

Very respectfully,

Your obedient servant,

T. W. EGAN,

Lieut.-Colonel, command'g Fortieth N. Y. V.

FAIR OAKS, OR SEVEN PINES.

FTER discussing the court-martial which passed upon the charges preferred against General Birney for his supposed misconduct at the battle of Fair Oaks, it will be pertinent to show what he did and under what orders. The whole movement was unexpected by our commander-in-chief, and his report of it to the War Department was eventually modified so as to relieve some of our soldiers from the censure which they encountered from his first telegram to Washington, which has been published in full in the foregoing history of the court-martial. It appears now that General Casey's men had been permitted to advance too far beyond the Chickahominy. There they were encamped against the remonstrances of some of their general officers, who saw that the position they had taken was not tenable. The anxiety of these officers is not *now* misunderstood, though at the time the criticisms were neither flattering nor complimentary. They saw that it was impossible to hold the position they had assumed, unless their support was invincible. This it could not be, for our army was spread over a large territory, and to throw the columns to any one point in a given time was a physical impossibility. So the result proved. Casey's men were attacked by overwhelming numbers, and were driven in upon the command of General Keyes. These men in their turn required support, and at three o'clock, P. M., on the 31st of May, 1862, General Birney received an order from General Kearny to move his brigade up the line of the railroad, and report to General Keyes. Within ten minutes after the receipt of the order, the brigade, which had been in the rifle-pits, was in motion, led by the Fourth regiment of Maine volunteers, followed by the Fortieth New York, the Third Maine, and a part of the Thirty-eighth New York; the remainder of the Thirty-eighth having been detailed early in the day for picket duty. Soon after the brigade had begun its march, General Kearny rode up and ordered General Birney to return to the Williamsburg and Richmond road, and place his men in rifle-pits thrown up there. This order was obeyed, General Kearny himself superintending the disposition of the men of the Fortieth New York volunteers. In peremptory tones he ordered General Birney to obey no order unless it came through him, saying that the enemy had possession of the first line, and the only hope of success was the second line; part of which General Birney's men held. When the men were driven back General Birney succeeded in rallying some of the fugitives, and with the aid of Captain Cavada's company of the Twenty-third Pennsylvania volunteers, (part of his old regiment,) attached them to the Thirty-eighth New York. In this he was aided by "Captains Gwyn and Cavada, and Lieutenant J. B. Fassitt of the Twenty-third Pennsylvania volunteers," who actively assisted him in his efforts to reform the fugitives and attach them to Captain Cavada's company, which had been on picket duty, and in the confusion of the battle willingly joined and did their duty faithfully under his command.

At five o'clock a staff officer from General Heintzelman, who commanded the Third Corps, came to General Birney with an order to advance to the support of General Keyes. He moved without delay—the Third Maine being in the advance—and sent his aids, Major J. F. Tobias and Captain Mindil, to withdraw the Fortieth New York and the Fourth Maine from the positions in which they had been placed by General Kearny, and order them to follow. As General Birney moved, Colonel Campbell, of the Fifty-seventh Pennsylvania volunteers, reported to him that he too had been ordered up the railroad. General Birney assumed command of this regiment and placed it in his column. After advancing about a mile up the railroad the firing became very heavy upon the left of the column. General Birney led the Fifty-seventh Pennsylvania and Fortieth New York into the woods on the left and drove back the enemy, from the attempt to turn the right flank of our troops, and in this effort Colonel Campbell was severely wounded and the major of his regiment killed.

During this struggle, one of General Couch's staff officers rode up to General Birney, and said that he had come direct from General Couch, with word that his command had been cut off, but he had found a road through the swamp, by which he could escape if General Birney could hold the railroad. General Birney answered, that he could and would hold the railroad. In a few moments Captain Sydam, of General Keyes' staff, rode up to General Birney and told him that General Heintzelman ordered him to still advance up the railroad. General Birney asked the messenger whether General Heintzelman knew where he was, and was told that General Heintzelman was two miles in the rear, and that he (the messenger) knew nothing beyond the order. General Birney at once commenced to throw out skirmishers and withdrew his regiments. While doing this Captain Hassler, of General Kearny's staff, rode up and ordered him to return with his brigade to the position he had occupied at three o'clock. General Birney at once sent Captain Linnard, of his staff, to General Kearny, explaining his position. He received in answer a repetition of the order to return. He then went himself to General Kearny, explained his position, and was directed to retain it. He did so, and in a short time his men were connected with those of General French. During the night General Birney's men bivouacked behind the railroad embankment, with the enemy in their front, under arms and prepared for an attack. At daylight the next morning he was placed under arrest, by order of General Heintzelman. For what reason this arrest was made he never knew beyond what transpired during the court-martial, before referred to, and during his subsequent career he was too much engaged to inquire into the reasons.

AN ELOQUENT ORDER.

ON the 5th of June, 1862, General Kearny issued to his troops the following characteristic and eloquent order, which is introduced as one of a series by which he gave to his men credit for what they had performed, and animated them with spirit for the future:

HEADQUARTERS THIRD DIVISION, THIRD CORPS,
CAMP NEAR RICHMOND, *June* 5, 1862.

[GENERAL ORDER, NO. 15.]

BRAVE REGIMENTS OF THE DIVISION:—You have won for us a high reputation. The country is satisfied; your friends at home are proud of you. After two battles and victories, purchased with much blood, you may be counted as veterans.

I appeal then to your experience, to your personal observation, to your high intelligence, to put in practice on the battle-field the discipline you have acquired in camp. It will enable you to conquer with more certainty and less loss.

Shoulder Straps and Chevrons! you are marked men; you must be ever in the front.

Colonels and Field Officers! when it comes to the bayonet, lead the charge; at other times be among your men and supervise. Keep officers and men to their constituted commands; stimulate the laggard; brand the coward; direct the brave; prevent companies from "huddling up."

Marksmen! never in the fight cheapen your rifles. When you fire make sure and hit. In wood or abbattis one man in three is to fire, the others reserve their loads to repel an onset, or to head a rush. It is with short marches and this extra fire from time to time, such ground is gained. Each man up in first line; none delaying; share danger alike; then the peril and loss will be small.

Men! You brave soldiers in the ranks! whose worth and daring unknown, perhaps, to your superiors, but recognized by your comrades, influence more than others, I know that you exist. I have watched you in the fire. Your merit is sure to have its recompense; your comrades at the bivouac will repeat your deeds; it will gladden your families, and in the end will be brought before your country.

Color-bearers of regiments! Bear them proudly in the fight; erect and defiantly in the first line. It will cast terror into your opponents to see them sustained and carried forward. Let them be the beacon-light of every regiment. The noblest inscription on your banners are the traces of the balls.

Again, noble division, I wish you success and more victories, until—the cause of our sacred Union being triumphant—you return honored to your homes.

By order of Brigadier-General Kearny,

W. E. STURGESS,

Acting Assistant Adjutant-general.

THE SEVEN DAYS.

N the 19th of June, 1862, the finding of the court-martial, before which General Birney was tried, was made public and approved by General McClellan, by whom General Birney was ordered to "resume his sword and the command of his brigade." During the time he was relieved from command there was no fighting. On June 25th, our bridges and entrenchments being at last completed, an advance was ordered preparatory to a general forward movement. Between eight and nine o'clock of that day the advance was begun by General Heintzelman's corps. On the following day General Birney received from General Heintzelman, the officer by whose order he had been arrested and subjected to the ordeal of trial by court-martial less than a month previous, the following note:—

HEADQUARTERS THIRD CORPS, SAVAGE'S STATION, VA., *June* 26, 1862.

BRIGADIER-GENERAL D. B. BIRNEY,

Commanding Second Brigade, Kearny's Division.

GENERAL:—The Brigadier-general commanding desires me to express to you his thanks for the prompt and energetic manner in which you brought forward your brigade to the support of General Hooker, yesterday morning.

I am, sir, very respectfully,

Your obedient servant,

(Signed) CHAUNCEY McKEEVER,

Chief of Staff.

General Birney.

This action has been called the battle of Glendale, or Nelson's Farm; and though in his report of it General Heintzelman does not mention the name of General Birney, he speaks in terms of the warmest commendation of the conduct of Kearny's division. The foregoing note is evidence of his appreciation of General Birney's services.

On the 26th of June the battle of Beaver Dam Creek was fought. In this the Third Corps was not engaged. On the evening of the 26th it was evident that, on the following day, there would be a general engagement, which took place, and is known as the battle of Gaines' Mills. In this desperate fight the Third Corps took no part, but were placed in the entrenchments on the banks of the Chickahominy ready to move when ordered. The engagement having, however, resulted disastrously to our arms, General McClellan determined to change his base, and on the morning of the 28th the change began. On the night of the 28th the Third Corps received orders to withdraw from the advanced position they had taken on the 25th, and to occupy the entrenched lines about a mile to the rear. This movement was executed the next day in good order, though the troops were followed closely by the enemy, who took possession of our camps as soon as the men left them. On the morning of the 30th the Third Corps destroyed the bridge at Bracket's Ford, and felled trees across the road to impede the progress of the enemy. This duty having been successfully performed a halt was ordered, but was not of long duration. The next morning, the 31st of July, General Franklin was compelled to fall back, and General Heintzelman, commanding the Third Corps, and other corps commanders were ordered to fall back also.

The positions occupied by the different corps were those assigned by the Commander-in-chief to resist the further advance of the enemy. This resulted in the battle of Malvern Hill, or, as it is sometimes called, Turkey Bend, which the *Richmond Examiner* described, on July 4, 1862, as the fiercest and most sanguinary of the series of bloody conflicts that signalized each of the previous seven days. The division of General Kearny was on the left, connecting with the right of General Couch's division, who was supported by General Hooker on the right of Kearny. Against this part of our line the enemy massed their troops, but to no purpose. During the day the Fourth Maine, one of the regiments of General Birney's brigade, was particularly distinguished for its coolness in holding a ravine and repulsing the enemy's skirmishers.

This was the last of the fighting of the famous seven days on the Peninsula. The enemy followed no further, having been defeated in the engagement at Malvern Hill more thoroughly than during any engagement which up to that time had been fought. Our army was then permitted to rest, and never was rest more welcome. The men were exhausted by fighting during the day and marching during the night. From the 26th of June to the 1st of July inclusive, the Army of the Potomac suffered and endured as much as it was possible for men to undergo. During these days many general officers, and among them General Birney, had not their horses unsaddled, nor had they time for repose or refreshment, either day or night, except such as they took by the wayside. All their personal baggage was lost, with papers, memoranda, &c., which would be invaluable in writing the story of these engagements. The absence of official documents has caused great variety of opinion and much discussion in regard to the campaign on the Peninsula. Its failure has, of course, elicited considerable criticism, which probably will never be quieted. The causes of the failure will be explained by different writers, according to their personal and political prejudices, during the life of the present generation; but when time shall have destroyed these prejudices, history will record the almost unprecedented sacrifice of life and of treasure on the Peninsula, without censuring the policy which Abraham Lincoln, or any of his cabinet, adopted in their determination not to risk the Capital of the Nation.

HARRISON'S LANDING.

THE order was given on the 1st of July, 1862, for the movement of the army to Harrison's Landing, on the north bank of the James river, which had been selected as the new position for the army. The Fourth Corps, under General Keyes, was ordered to cover the movement, by the left and rear. One of the divisions on the left was not able to move as early as was anticipated, and it was found necessary to place a rear guard between this division and the enemy. This delicate duty was entrusted to the Third Pennsylvania Cavalry, under Colonel (now Major-General) Averill, the only cavalry attached to the Third Corps. By judicious use of the resources at his command he deceived the enemy so as to cover the withdrawal of the left wing without being attacked, remaining himself on the previous day's battlefield until seven o'clock of July 2d. Aided by this movement General Keyes was able to cover the movement of the entire army and protect the trains, the last of which arrived in safety at Harrison's Bar after dark on the 3d of July.

It was during these dark days that Colonel (now Major-General) Robert O. Tyler, then in command of the First Connecticut Artillery, displayed those qualities which have since made him so distinguished, and have enabled him to render such valuable services to his country during her troubles.

At Harrison's Landing the army rested until the middle of August, 1862. On the 14th the Third Corps received orders to retire to Yorktown. The next morning, under orders from General Heintzelman, General Birney marched his brigade to Jones' bridge, on the Chickahominy, which he was ordered to hold, and cover the movement of the troops from their old camp at Harrison's Bar. This was done, and on August 16th General Heintzelman moved the corps to Barhamsville, thence to Williamsburg, where he united with the main body of the army, and was there joined by General Birney.

POPE'S CAMPAIGN.

STOPPING one day at Williamsburg, the corps moved to Yorktown on the 17th, and on the 20th General Kearny's division embarked for Acquia Creek. Here they were met by orders to continue up the Potomac to Alexandria, where they arrived at thirty minutes past one, P. M., on August 21st, and received orders to hurry forward to the support of General Pope. General Birney's brigade left Alexandria that afternoon and arrived the next morning at Warrenton Junction, where they were soon joined by the Third Corps on August 26th; and on the 27th the entire corps advanced to Bristow Station and thence to Greenwich. On reaching Bristow Station the troops encountered a part of General Ewell's corps, which, after a sharp engagement, retreated towards Manassas Junction. The next morning General Kearny's division, followed by General Hooker's, advanced to Manassas Junction, where they found the railroad trains, fired by the enemy, still burning.

After the halt, General Birney, with part of Companies H and K, of the Second Pennsylvania Cavalry, under command of Captain Charles Chauncey, of Philadelphia, made a reconnoissance towards Centreville. Upon his arrival in the town videttes were thrown out, and he endeavored to ascertain from the inhabitants the direction the enemy had taken. While in conversation with one of the citizens, a vidette rode in and reported that a regiment of cavalry, displaying the United States flag, was approaching the place, at a gallop, with drawn sabres. General Birney inspected the newcomers through his field-glass, and seeing they were in rebel uniform, decided that it would be expedient for him and his escort to return without delay to our lines. They started immediately, and the chase began towards Manassas Junction. Birney and his men being well mounted, soon left their pursuers behind them. The chase was kept up until Birney and the escort were within our lines, when the majority of the pursuing regiment halted at a respectful distance from a battery which General Kearny had planted in the road. One rebel, better mounted and more daring than his comrades, had, from the start, made an effort to ride up to General Birney, and came near him when approaching our lines. When almost near enough to strike the general with his sabre, he called out, "Surrender! you're my prisoner!"

Birney, though riding at a run, replied, "I guess not," and raising his revolver, which he had carried in his hand from Centreville, fired, and unhorsed his captor, who fell to the ground, and was never again able to raise his sword against a soldier of the Union.

During the afternoon it was ascertained that the enemy had fallen back on Centreville and were about thirty thousand strong. Kearny pushed on, Birney's brigade being in the advance, and when they reached Centreville found but one regiment of rebel cavalry, which fell back with the main body on the Warrenton Turnpike. Here Birney's men encamped on August 29th, and it was their first attempt to rest for fifteen days, but the halt was of short duration. At one, A. M., of August 30th, they were ordered to advance until they met the enemy's pickets.

Of August 29th and 30th, General Kearny, in his official report, dated Centreville, August 31st, speaks as follows:—

"On the 29th, on my arrival at this place, I was assigned to holding the right wing on the turnpike. I posted Colonel Poe with Berry's brigade in my first line; General Robinson with the first brigade on his right partly in line and partly in support, and kept Birney's most disciplined regiments reserved and ready for emergencies. During the first hours of combat, as tired regiments in the centre fell back, General Birney, of his own accord, rapidly pushed across to give them a hand to stimulate them to a renewed fight.

"On the morning of the 30th, General Ricketts, with two brigades, relieved me of the charge of the left of the road, and I again concentrated my command. We took no part in the fighting of the morning. About five, P. M., a sudden and unaccountable evacuation of the field by the left and centre was made. Under orders from General Pope, I massed my troops at the indicated point, but soon reoccupied with Birney's brigade, supported by Robinson, a very advanced block of woods. The key-point of this new line was held by regiments of other brigades. On being attacked they ceded the ground without warning us. I maintained my position until ten, P. M., when I retired and reached Centreville at two, A. M., this morning. My loss has been over seven hundred and fifty, about one in three. None were taken prisoners excepting my engineering officer.

"It makes me proud to dwell upon the renewed efforts of my generals of brigade Birney and Robinson."

* * * * * * *

On August 31st an incident occurred which is worth narrating. General Kearny had on his staff at that time Second Lieutenant J. C. Briscoe, a tall, soldierly-looking Irishman, who, after graduating as a civil engineer at Dublin University, came to America to seek his fortune, without friends, without influence, and without money. He soon obtained employment as an engineer in the construction of a railroad in Pennsylvania, and on its completion, in the fall of 1860, sought other employment. He soon obtained an engagement to go to Brazil as one of the constructing engineers of the "Don Pedro Railroad," which the Emperor was then building from Rio Janeiro to the western part of Brazil. To qualify himself the better for this position, Briscoe sought and obtained employment early in 1861, in one of the machine shops of the city of New York. When the rebellion broke out he was working in this shop for day's wages, but had engaged his passage to Rio in a vessel advertised to sail about May 1, 1861. The President's Proclamation calling out troops interfered with his plans for engineering. The next morning, having settled with his employers, who released him from his contract, he presented himself at one of the recruiting offices of the First New York volunteers, and asked to be enlisted as a private. His appearance and bearing was such that the officer in charge offered to at once make him a non-commissioned officer.

"No," said the new recruit, "I know nothing about the science of war, and until I learn something, do not wish to accept any position except that of a private."

When the regiment left New York, he, being in the color company, was appointed by the colonel color-bearer of the regiment. The regiment was at first in the brigade of General Mansfield, where Briscoe volunteered to act as a scout. While scouting he gained valuable information about the enemy's works, and planned the surprise of a number of rebels, whom with a squad of men he captured and brought to camp, before daylight one morning. This exploit converted him into a sort of hero with his comrades, for at that time rebel prisoners were very scarce, and these were the first that had been seen by that portion of the army. His regiment took part in the celebrated battle of Big Bethel, and, though he was one of the few who were wounded in that engagement, he retained possession of the colors and brought them safely from the field.

During the fall, General Mansfield procured his promotion to the rank of second lieutenant. In the spring of 1862, his regiment was put in the brigade of General Hamilton, and during the Peninsular campaign was part of General Kearny's division. On May 30, 1862, Lieutenant Briscoe was superintending the digging of rifle-pits, and his overcoat concealed his shoulder-straps. General Kearny, riding up, criticised in rather severe terms the plan of the works, and inquired for the officer in charge. Lieutenant Briscoe answered, and gave his reasons for constructing the works as he had. General Kearny at once admitted that he was wrong, and apologized, addressing Briscoe as colonel.

"I am not a colonel," said Briscoe.

"Well, then, major."

"I am not a major."

"What the d—l are you?" asked Kearny.

"A second lieutenant, sir."

"Do you want to go on my staff as engineer officer?" said the general.

"Yes," said Briscoe, "I should like it very much."

When Briscoe returned to camp he found the order for the detail on the staff of General Kearny, where he remained until August 31, 1862, when he went to Libby Prison. On his return, General Kearny having been killed in the mean time, he went upon General Birney's staff, whose fortunes he faithfully and gallantly followed until August, 1864, when, at the instance of General Birney, he received authority to raise the One-hundred-and-ninety-ninth regiment of Pennsylvania volunteers. This regiment was at the front within twenty days after Briscoe had received authority to raise it, and constituted part of the Tenth Army Corps, which General Birney commanded until his death. From that time until the surrender of General Lee, Colonel Briscoe, with his regiment, one thousand strong, was continually in the field, and though wounded during the assault on Fort Gregg, was pushed forward by his men, and was one of the first to cross the parapet. In the pursuit of Lee the regiment took part, and was engaged in the battle of Appomattox Court House, so that from one of the earliest until the last battle of the war, Briscoe has taken part in every engagement in which the Army of the Potomac or the Army of James has participated.

The writer apologizes for this digression by saying, that it gives him pleasure to speak of the conduct of such men. Briscoe's is not an isolated case. There are hundreds in our armies who, without patronage or favoritism, have, by their own talents, worked their way up from the ranks to the positions to which their merits have entitled them. Without the aid of such men the armies of the Union never would have been victorious. May the day never come when the country will cease to do honor to men like Briscoe.

The incident of August 31, 1862, to which reference has been made, illustrates Briscoe's coolness, without which no soldier can gain the admiration of his comrades. About noon he had been sent by General Kearny to carry an order to a remote part of the lines. When returning, about four o'clock, he met the general riding with General Birney. After hearing Briscoe's report, Kearny directed him to accompany him to a house at some distance from the point where they were standing, which he had selected as his headquarters for the night.

Briscoe replied, "That house, general, is in possession of the enemy; when I rode by it I narrowly escaped being taken prisoner."

"Nonsense," said Kearny, "you are timid, lieutenant; come ahead."

"Well, sir," rejoined Briscoe, "if you think I am mistaken, let me ride in advance; if our men hold the house

I will fire my pistol; if I do not return you may know I am a prisoner."

"All right," replied Kearny; and Briscoe rode forward into the rebel lines, was taken prisoner and sent to Libby Prison, of which he had the honor of being one of the first inmates. He thus saved Kearny and Birney from capture, for the same rashness which would have impelled Kearny to have gone to the house which he proposed, led him forward the next day within the lines of the enemy, where he fell mortally wounded.

CHANTILLY.

SUNDAY, August 31st, the men had some rest at Centreville, but the next day, September 1st, General Pope sent for General Heintzelman, informed him that the enemy were threatening our rear, and ordered him to fall back on the road to Fairfax Court House to aid General Reno in driving back the enemy. General Kearny's division was again sent forward, Birney's brigade in the advance. At three, P. M., General Reno made an attack. "A portion of his troops gave way, but General Birney's brigade of General Kearny's division gallantly supported them."

On reaching the field, near the village of Chantilly, General Birney, by orders from General Kearny, reported to General Reno, and was ordered to the front. When he arrived, a portion of the division of General Stevens was retiring in disorder, the officers of the regiments stating that their ammunition was exhausted. Birney ordered forward the Fourth Maine, and then took forward the One-hundred-and-first New York, Third Maine, Fortieth and First New York. These regiments engaged and drove back the enemy, though greatly inferior in numbers. As the regiments were going forward, General Kearny came up with Randolph's

Battery, which was at once put in position to sustain the brigade. General Birney pointed out to General Kearny a gap on his right, caused by the retiring of Stevens' men, and asked that Berry's brigade be ordered up to fill it. Kearny insisted that it was impossible for such a gap to exist, and said he would ride forward to see what troops were there. Birney warned him, and urged him to remain, saying he would ride into the enemy's lines, but Kearny retorted a jesting remark about Birney's caution, and dashed ahead. This was the last Birney ever saw of his friend. In the words of General Heintzelman, he pressed "forward to reconnoitre in his usual gallant, not to say reckless manner, and came upon a rebel regiment. In attempting to escape he was killed. The country has to mourn one of its most gallant defenders. At the close of the siege of Yorktown he relieved General Hamilton in the command of the division, and led it in the various battles on the Peninsula, commencing with Williamsburg. His name is identified with its glory."

As General Kearny did not return, General Birney supposed he had been taken prisoner, and assumed command of the division, being the ranking brigade commander on the field. Though a violent thunder storm was raging, our men fought desperately, and the enemy were driven from our front. Their retreat was hastened by the Thirty-eighth New York and Fifty-seventh Pennsylvania, which Birney ordered up "to complete the victory." Afterwards Robinson's and Berry's brigades were ordered forward to relieve the tired and decimated regiments, and Birney remained in possession of the field until three, A. M., the next day, when he followed, with the division, the corps of General Reno to Fairfax Court House.

During the night our men were busy in removing the wounded and burying the dead. About ten, P. M., the officer in command of the enemy's lines sent a flag to General Birney and made himself known as a former correspondent of Birney's at Columbia, South Carolina. He said he had within his lines the body of General Kearny, and would forward it if General Birney wished him to do so. Of course General Birney requested that the mangled body be sent him, and when the troops moved they carried with them the remains of their gallant and beloved general. That midnight march was a sad one for officers and men. They had gained a victory, and an important one, but their brave leader had fallen, and his death caused grief which prevented any exultation over their success. Birney was not the least of the mourners. Though for months he had been in the midst of carnage and slaughter, he could not restrain his feelings, and had the enemy during the darkness made an attack upon those lion-hearted men who a few hours before had won a victory at the point of the bayonet, they would have found them unmanned and almost incapable of resistance.

The success of our arms at Chantilly was of great importance to our army. General Pope, disheartened by the want of co-operation on the part of some corps commanders, was on the retreat towards Washington with exhausted troops, who had become dispirited by frequent reverses. The rebel commander, with troops flushed with success, attempted to out-flank General Pope. Had this movement been a success, such of our men as succeeded in regaining Washington would have entered it as a disorganized mob and not as an army. Besides this, the wounded and sick were suffering for want of care and medicine. One large train of medical stores had been captured, and the movement which Chantilly had frustrated would have resulted in the loss of the second train, which was then on its way to General Pope's army. General Pope, in his official report, on pages 18 to 27, gives to the success at Chantilly its real importance. He says, (p. 27:) "The main body of our forces was so much broken down and so completely exhausted, that they were in no condition, even on the 1st of September, for any active operations against the enemy, but I determined to attack at daylight on the 2d of September, in front of Chantilly. The movement of the enemy had become so developed * * * * and was so evidently directed to Fairfax Court House, with a view of turning my right, that I made the necessary disposition to fight a battle on the road from Centreville to Fairfax Court House.

"Reno was to push forward to the north of the road in the direction of Chantilly, Heintzelman's corps was directed to take post immediately in the rear of Reno. * * * Just before sunset on the 1st, the enemy attacked us on our right, but was met by a counter attack by Hooker, McDowell, Reno and Kearny's division of Heintzelman's corps. A *very severe action occurred in the midst of a terrific thunder storm,* and was terminated shortly after dark. The enemy was driven back entirely from our front."

THE KEARNY PATCH.

AFTER the battle of Chantilly the army retired to the defences of Washington. General Birney retained the command of the first division of the Third Army Corps, which had devolved upon him on the death of General Kearny, by right of seniority. General Kearny, before his death, had issued an order requiring the officers and men under his command to wear a badge or mark, by which they would be known wherever met. This badge was a piece of scarlet cloth, worn on the cap or hat, so as to be visible at all times. This was the first attempt to designate officers or men in our army by any distinctive mark or badge. The evident object of this order was to individualize the members of this division, and to designate the officers and men should they lag on the march or straggle in action.

General Birney and his men reached the defences of Washington after a tedious march, on the 3d of September, 1862. On the next day he issued the following order:—

HEADQUARTERS KEARNY'S DIVISION,
FORT LYON, VA., *Sept.* 4, 1862.

[GENERAL ORDER, No. 49.]

The Brigadier-general commanding this division announces with deep sorrow the death of Major-general Kearny, its gallant commander. He died on the battle-field of Chantilly as his division was driving the enemy before it.

The entire country will mourn the loss of this chivalric soldier, and officers and men of this division will ever hold dear his memory.

Let us show our regard for him by always sustaining the name which, in his love for the division, he gave it, viz.: the "Fighting Division."

As a token of respect for his memory, all the officers of this division will wear crape on the left arm for thirty days, and the colors and drums of regiments and batteries will be placed in mourning for sixty days. To still further show our regard, and to distinguish his officers as he wished, each officer will continue to wear on his cap a piece of scarlet cloth, or have the top or crown-piece of the cap made of scarlet cloth.

By command of Brigadier-general D. B. Birney.

J. B. BROWN,
Acting Assistant Adjutant-general.

The scarlet patch referred to in the foregoing order was soon converted into a piece of red cloth or flannel, cut in the form of a diamond, and this for some time was known as the "Kearny patch." After General Hooker was put in command of the Army of the Potomac, late in January, 1863, the propriety of designating the officers and men of each corps by some distinctive mark was recognized in a general order from headquarters, and since that time each corps has had its badge; the first division of the corps wearing it in red, the second in white, and the third in blue.

By this order, which at first affected only the Army of the Potomac, but which was subsequently confirmed by the War Department, and extended to all the Union armies in the field, the Third Corps badge was a diamond, and the first division of this corps, which General Birney commanded from the death of Kearny until the middle of July, 1864, wore a red diamond.

When, in the spring of 1864, the Third Corps was disbanded and its divisions annexed to other army corps, General Birney was fortunate enough to procure an order by which his division, though annexed to the Second Corps, as the third division, was permitted to retain the Kearny red patch; and throughout the campaign of 1864, and during the war, the officers and men of this division, whether in camp, in hospital, or on leave, wear this badge, and are proud of it. Let any one converse with those who wear it, and he will find in their hearts as noble a monument of General Birney as can be erected to his memory. These officers and men followed him for nearly two years, during the severest trials to which the Army of the Potomac was subjected, and they are always ready to communicate to any stranger their appreciation of his worth as a soldier, and as a man. They have, under his lead, stormed earth-works, captured fortifications, and have often driven the rebel forces opposed to them from their chosen positions. Always in the advance, they have done their whole duty; and though their ranks have been thinned by the cannon-ball, the musket, the bayonet and the sabre of the enemy, they have always preserved their organization, and have ever been ready to march or to fight, as occasion required. The writer has met them of all grades, from that of brigadier-general to private. They all bear the same testimony. They were willing to serve anywhere under Birney, and to undergo privations with him; for they have felt that he loved his men, and would not order them where he was unwilling to go himself. These men are the sincere eulogists of Birney, and, while their hearts beat, his fame will never die.

When the division, with the rest of the army, retired to the fortifications of Washington, General Birney established his headquarters near Fairfax Seminary, about three miles from Alexandria. He occupied the residence of Bishop Johns, the Episcopal Bishop of Virginia, for the use of which he paid rent to the agent of the Bishop. Instead of permitting his men, who had been accustomed to the most active duties of a soldier's life, to remain idle, he kept them busily engaged in throwing up earthworks around the seminary, to instruct them in what he believed would be an important element of their success in the future. The experience thus gained was afterwards of great advantage to them and their future comrades, though the works themselves were of little value. Besides educating the men, this employment promoted contentment, and accustomed them to endure the long days of inactive camp-life which they subsequently encountered.

General D. E. Sickles, who was afterwards in command of the Third Corps, was at that time encamped near General Birney. Though these men subsequently became firm friends, at that time they were not known to each other except officially. One Sunday morning General Sickles sent over an orderly to General Birney with his compliments, asking the loan of a copy of the Constitution of the United States. General Birney made search for a copy, but could not find it among the Bishop's works. He returned word accordingly, and added, that he found a great many editions of the Bible in all languages in the library, and if General Sickles wished a copy, in the absence of the Constitution, he should have it for his Sunday reading. The orderly did not return, and it is fair to presume that on the day in question General Sickles did not study the Constitution or the Bible.

FANCY DUTY.

SOON after General Birney returned with the division from Pope's campaign to Fairfax Seminary, a gentleman of Philadelphia, with whom he had little if any previous acquaintance, but who brought with him letters and endorsements from the leading men of Pennsylvania, applied to him for a position on his staff as a volunteer aid. As General Birney was in favor of all men serving their country, and especially those who did so without pay and paid their own expenses, which was the case with volunteer aids, he took him on his staff. This rule he observed until the War Department issued an order abolishing the system of volunteer aids altogether, and the result was, that General Birney was never at a loss for officers to perform staff duty. The applications to go on his staff were numerous, and he granted them all, and every man appointed did his full duty except one, who, after procuring his appointment, in 1863, found that the exigencies of his business compelled him to stay at home, which he did. Soon after the gentleman referred to had taken his place on the staff, an enemy of his, who held an official position in Philadelphia under the Government, wrote to the War Department protesting against allowing such men to hold positions as staff officers, and alleging that the officer in question was not fit for his duties by reason of his sympathy with the enemies of the Government. The writer of the letter (whose name and letter are not published for obvious reasons) referred to certain citizens of Philadelphia to corroborate his statements. This letter was referred to General Birney by the War Department, and his reply was as fine a piece of epistolary writing as can be produced. He offered to make an inquiry about the truth of the allegations of the accuser, and on doing so it was found that they all melted away like snow before the summer's sun.

In consequence of his reply to the War Department, as he was told by the officer who had its organization, he was ordered to act as the member of a court of inquiry in Washington. He made an unsuccessful effort to be excused from complying with the order, for this was the only "fancy duty" ever assigned to him. He was unable to obtain relief, being told that the court was one of great importance, and his letter referred to had convinced the Department of his fitness for the duty, which would not interfere with his field duties, as it was probable the army would be quiet during the fall. This, however, did not prove to be the case. Soon after his appointment as a member of the court, General Lee began his movement up the Shenandoah Valley, which culminated in the battle of Antietam. The army under General McClellan moved to meet him. The Third Corps remained for some time in the defences of Washington, but eventually moved; and, Birney being unable to get relief from the court, General Stoneman was assigned to the command of the division, on September 15, 1862, and moved up the Potomac. This irritated Birney beyond measure. He wanted to be in the field whenever active campaigning was going on, and could not content himself with other duties. As soon as the division moved, leaving him behind, he sent in his resignation, and put it in the hands of Secretary Chase, hoping thus to have it accepted at the earliest possible moment. In this, however, he was mistaken, for the Secretary wrote him as follows:—

WASHINGTON, *September* 15, 1862.

MY DEAR GENERAL:—I shall not present your resignation until I have seen you and you insist upon it. I will try to visit you to-morrow. If I cannot, you must call on me the next day. We cannot spare our truest men.

Yours, truly,

S. P. CHASE.

BRIGADIER-GENERAL BIRNEY.

This letter and the remonstrance of friends had its effect. General Birney withdrew the resignation, and the Secretary returned it with the following note:—

WASHINGTON, *September* 20, 1862.

DEAR GENERAL:—I enclose to you with great pleasure your resignation.

It is still my hope to visit your camp. Should you come to the city I shall be glad to see you.

Wishing and expecting for you a brilliant and successful career,

I remain sincerely yours,

S. P. CHASE.

BRIGADIER-GENERAL D. B. BIRNEY.

A PRESENTATION.

T this period of his career the friends of General Birney, stimulated by what they considered his success at Chantilly, raised in Philadelphia a subscription to a testimonial for his use. The subscriptions in a few hours amounted to fifteen hundred dollars, with only sixty names. They were then reduced to ten dollars, and in a few days they comprised about one hundred and twenty of the leading men of the city, whose names will be found in the Appendix. When the fund was raised, the contributors, at a meeting held September 22, 1862, resolved to purchase a horse, equipments and a sword. The orders were given, and the testimonial was ready for transmission in a few weeks. The articles being procured were forwarded with the following letter:—

PHILADELPHIA, *October* 30, 1862.

GENERAL D. B. BIRNEY:

DEAR SIR:—We have been requested by a number of your fellow-citizens to present you, in their behalf, the horse, equipments, and sword which will be handed to you with this note. They are intended as a testimonial of the estimation in which your services in the field are held, and we hope that they will not only prove useful to you in the discharge of your duty in future, but will serve to remind you that we have attentively watched your career and approve of the course you have pursued.

When we first took leave of you in April, 1861, and wished you success in your efforts to aid in sustaining the laws of the land, we did not think you would be compelled to make the sacrifices you have made, or to encounter the privations you have endured, and hoped that, with your fellow-soldiers, you would soon return to your usual avocations. As the rebellion gradually assumed the proportions of the most formidable civil war in which any nation has ever been engaged, in common with others we awaited with anxiety the selection to be made from the army of the men who were to lead our soldiers in the field.

Knowing the natural energy of your character, and that you had determined to devote yourself to your new profession, to the exclusion of every thing else, we were not surprised when the Government called you from the ranks to take command. We believed the selection well made, and were gratified when subsequent events proved that the confidence reposed in you had not been misplaced. Your conduct at Yorktown, Williamsburg, Fair Oaks, Malvern Hill, in the battles of the seven days, and at Centreville, has amply proved this, though in the chances of war you were, after the battle of Fair Oaks, subjected to an ordeal trying to every soldier, but which resulted in your complete justification, and proved that your readiness to obey is equal to your ability to command.

We need hardly add that the part you took at Chantilly gave us additional gratification. It was under your command that the battle was won, and a large train and stores were saved, which, but for the success on September 1st, would have fallen into the hands of the enemy, and the retreat of our division intercepted. We have fully counted the cost to the Government of a reverse in the engagement, and, in forwarding the accompanying testimonial, do all in our power to recognize your services and urge you to renewed exertions in the future.

O. W. DAVIS,
A. D. JESSUP,
JOSEPH F. TOBIAS,
EDWARD J. MAGINNIS,
JNO. H. CHAMBERS,
C. H. CLARK,
L. J. LEBERMAN,
GEORGE BULLOCK.
} *Committee.*

General Birney acknowledged the receipt of the testimonial as follows:—

CAMP ON RAPPAHANNOCK RIVER,
November 1, 1862.

To Messrs. O. W. DAVIS, A. D. JESSUP,
JOSEPH F. TOBIAS and others:

GENTLEMEN:—Permit me to heartily thank my friends and the citizens of Philadelphia who have, through you, in such flattering terms, presented to me the noble horse, handsome equipments and superb sword, received with your note. My brigade feels that the compliment to its commander is also to it, and have greatly admired the gift.

To my brigade has been awarded by the Military Commission appointed by the General-in-chief, the proud privilege of wearing on its banners the names "Williamsburg, Fair Oaks, Orchards, Glendale, Malvern, Manassas and Chantilly." It was our good fortune to have been engaged in all these actions, and in all were successful.

I trust, gentlemen, when this unnatural rebellion has been crushed by the use of all the means that a gallant and free nation can use, and the army of volunteers return to peaceful pursuits, you will be able to say that your sword was not presented in vain. I shall continue my efforts to sustain the Constitution, encouraged by your handsome testimonial and kind words, and shall try to equal your expectations and prove that I am worthy of a city that has given so liberally of her men and treasure to sustain the Government.

So long as it is in my power to render service in the field, in whatever position I am placed, under whatever general or rule I may be, I shall continue to struggle for the unity of our people, the supremacy of our laws; and hope the time is not far distant when the good old flag will again wave from gulf to lake, and from ocean to ocean. I have never been so hopeful of the success of our army as now.

Your obedient servant,

D. B. BIRNEY.

The equipments were worn out by hard service, and the horse was in the same condition when General Birney died, but he has since recovered by kind treatment. The family presented him to a friend, who has had him treated with the tenderest care, and prizes him beyond any price which could be offered for him. He will never be sold or bartered away, but kept as a memorial of his deceased master, and respected as a veteran who has taken part in the battles of Fredericksburg, Chancellorsville, Gettysburg, and the campaigns under General Grant. The sword and its service and dress-scabbards are fine specimens of the handiwork of the artizan, and are prized by the family beyond description.

IN THE FIELD.

FTER the Court of Inquiry had been adjourned, General Birney was ordered to the command of his old brigade. This order he willingly obeyed, and mounting his horse rode seventy miles to join the Army of the Potomac. On November 16, 1862, the day that General Burnside assumed command of the Army of the Potomac, General Birney reached his old brigade and was ready to resume its command. But a day or two previous to his arrival General Stoneman had been assigned to the Third Army Corps, thus leaving the old division vacant, to which he was assigned, and immediately took command. From that day until about the middle of July, 1864, when he was ordered by General Grant to command the Tenth Army Corps, he retained command of this division, except at intervals during the temporary absence of the commander of the Third Corps. This command he preferred to any which could be assigned him, and between him and the gallant and dashing Stoneman, relations of the most agreeable character were soon established, which continued to the time of General Birney's death.

Soon after he resumed command of his division the Army of the Potomac moved under General Burnside towards Falmouth, where they remained until the early part of the spring of 1863, when they followed Lee into Pennsylvania, and won the battle of Gettysburg. Until December 13, 1862, General Birney was constantly engaged with the reorganization and discipline of his division, never leaving it for a day on any pretext whatever. His efforts here, and his previous efforts during the fall, while near Fairfax Seminary, were amply rewarded when the division was called into action. At Fredericksburg and Chancellorsville, the division won for itself honors that will remain fresh so long as the history of the Army of the Potomac is remembered.

During this period General Birney started in his division the organization, eventually known as "The Third Corps Union," of which more will be said hereafter. The "Union" was not dissolved when the Third Corps was broken up, but will probably be continued as a means of reviving the memories of the past so long as any of its members are alive.

THE BATTLE OF FREDERICKSBURG.

HE writer approaches with pleasure the recital of the part taken by General Birney in the battle of Fredericksburg. His conduct in that action has been severely commented upon by those who have attempted to make him the scape-goat of their failure. General Burnside has not yet (May, 1865) made his official report of this action, but his testimony before the Committee on the Conduct of the War, and that of General Franklin, who commanded the left wing of the army; that of General Reynolds, who commanded the First Corps of this wing, to whom General Birney reported directly; and the official reports of General Stoneman and General Birney, furnish ample material to describe with impartiality the movements of General Birney and his division. Even the testimony, before the Committee on the Conduct of the War, of the present commander of the Army of the Potomac, does not, except by implication, condemn General Birney. He says, it is true, that three times he sent back to General Birney—twice a request and the third time a command—for him to advance to his support; while General Birney testifies that he received but one request, and referred the staff officer to General Reynolds, who was in command of the corps, of which both Meade's and Birney's divisions formed a part—General Reynolds at the time being on the field and within a short distance of General Birney and staff, who were then executing an order which had been issued by General Reynolds a few moments before. Before any answer was returned from General Reynolds, General Birney saw that Meade's troops were beginning to fall back, and without waiting for a revocation or modification of the order which he was obeying, when General Meade's condition became known to him, he at once ordered up four regiments, under General Ward, to support General Meade. While these regiments were moving forward, he rode up to General Reynolds and asked permission to bring up his batteries. This permission was granted, and the batteries were placed so as to cover the movement of General Meade, whose troops were pursued so closely that the enemy (part of Early's division) came within fifty yards of General Birney's guns. General Birney then opened upon them and drove them back. This position General Birney held until eleven o'clock on Monday night, the 15th of December, when he received orders from General Stoneman, who had by that time resumed the command of his corps, to retire across the Rappahannock river, which he did.

Let us follow General Birney's movements critically, and see whether it was in the power of any one to do more than he did. It must be remembered that the Army of the Potomac had, for three months, been taunted by the press of the country with its failure to prevent Lee from recrossing the Potomac, and for three months the men had been inactive. It is natural to suppose that they partook of the feeling of their new commander, General Burnside, and were anxious to be led against the enemy.

Preparatory to this movement, a new organization of the army had been effected. The brigades, divisions and corps remained as heretofore, but the army itself was divided into three grand divisions, the right commanded by General Sumner, the centre by General Hooker, and the left by General Franklin. The Third Corps was part of the centre division, under General Hooker, and was encamped near Falmouth, opposite Fredericksburg.

During the night of Friday, December 12, 1862, General Birney received orders from General Stoneman to move his division to the Rappahannock, and be ready to cross on the bridges constructed by General Franklin. This he did without delay, and at two, A. M., the division was at the bridges awaiting orders. At ten, A. M., he received written orders from General Stoneman to cross the division, and proceed to the left and report for orders to General Reynolds. This he did by eleven o'clock, and was told by him that General Meade was to begin the attack, and Birney was ordered to deploy his division in the rear of General Meade's. The field in which he was directed to take position was separated from the road by a high embankment, and a ditch next to the road, about six feet deep. Over this ditch and through this embankment were two narrow wagon-ways, along which a regiment could only be moved by the flank. The right was occupied by Ward's brigade, the left by Berry's, and Robinson's coming up last, was kept in reserve, the men being deployed in two lines. As soon as the division took position, the enemy opened upon it from a number of batteries, which commanded this open field, and the fire was very destructive. General Reynolds, commanding the corps, who was near General Birney, personally ordered him to retire his men behind the embankment. Before this movement was half completed, General Birney received word from General Meade that his men were severely pressed, and he needed assistance. General Birney, as has been said, pointed to General Reynolds, who was near by, and said that he would advance as soon as he received an order.

As the officer left him he saw that General Meade's troops were commencing to fall back. He "*immediately*," and without waiting for an order, reversed the movement of Ward's brigade, placing the Ninety-ninth Pennsylvania volunteers, Colonel Leidy, the Fifty-seventh Pennsylvania volunteers, Colonel Campbell, and the Fifty-fifth New York volunteers, Colonel (now Brigadier-general) De Trobriand, in support of General Meade's batteries, and ordered forward the Thirty-eighth and Fortieth New York, and the Fourth Maine volunteers to the support of the troops in the front, and this order was executed at the "double quick."

Berry's brigade was ordered to resume its position on the left, in the field from which the men were moving, and this was done without delay. Seeing that General Meade's batteries had exhausted their ammunition, Birney ordered up Randolph's and Livingston's, the only two in his command, which immediately went into action under Captain Randolph, of the Rhode Island artillery, and Chief of Artillery of the division. He then ordered Colonel Campbell, of the Fifty-seventh Pennsylvania volunteers, to again advance and report to General Meade, and the Third

Maine and Fifty-fifth New York volunteers to the support of one of Gibbon's batteries on his right.

The enemy pressed General Meade's men and were in full force on General Birney's front, with a brigade deployed in line and one doubled on the centre on each flank. This was part of the rebel Early's division, and the movement was intended to take the four batteries on the crest of the hill, two belonging to General Birney's division and two which had been posted there by General Meade, of which General Birney had assumed the command. While the enemy was making his dispositions, General Birney was not idle. By his order General Berry brought up a part of his brigade and extended to the right, to the point occupied by General Gibbon's batteries. These having withdrawn, the Ninety-ninth Pennsylvania volunteers, Third Maine and Fifty-fifth New York volunteers, formed the extreme right, the remainder of General Ward's brigade being in advance of this line. Then the contest became exciting. The rebels, flushed by their success in driving back General Meade's men, rushed forward to a second victory. Captain Randolph kept his guns quiet until the rebels were within fifty yards, and then opened on them with canister. Still they were not repulsed, until General Berry, whose men bore the brunt of the attack, poured a galling fire into the ranks of the approaching enemy, and aided by the oblique fire from that part of Ward's brigade which was on the extreme right, soon stopped the advance. Never were Birney's men more resolute than on that day. The officers of the division saw that it was part of the rebel plan to mass their troops at this point of our line, and to force their way to the bridges over which General Birney had that morning crossed his men. Had this movement been successful, the rest of our line would have been flanked, and one of the crossings of the river lost to our army. But no such disaster occurred, for Birney's men stood firm, and though their ranks were thinned by the fire of the enemy, there was no disorder or retreat. By one o'clock the enemy began to fall back, when General Robinson arrived, and the One-hundred-and-fourteenth and Sixty-fifth Pennsylvania volunteers came immediately to the front and hastened the retreat of the enemy by an effective and galling fire.

This work being accomplished, General Birney received an order from General Reynolds to hold the crest of the hill, as the enemy were making an effort to get through the line to attack General Doubleday's division, which was on Birney's left, and forming an angle, connecting with the Rappahannock. General Birney immediately made a new disposition of his troops; Berry's brigade being on the left, Robinson's in the centre, and Ward's on the right, with four batteries on the crest of the hill, two being those of General Birney's command already mentioned, and two which had been sent by General Reynolds as reinforcements, under Captains Cooper and Lefevre.

The enemy were within three hundred yards, sheltered by woods, the railroad embankment, rifle-pits and ditches, in Birney's front. As this proximity was not desirable, General Birney, about three o'clock, sent out a line of skirmishers to capture a ditch running parallel with his front. This order was gallantly executed, and some sixty prisoners taken. Preparations were in progress for similar movements, but at half past four o'clock, the enemy, uncovering ten guns on a hill opposite the left of his line, opened a deadly fire on Doubleday's division. These were soon replied to, and in less than thirty minutes silenced by the fire of the two division batteries and that of Captain Lefevre. The enemy then opened upon the left a battery of Whitworth guns, but night soon threw her mantle over the scene and put an end to the fierce combat.

This was the work which Birney's men performed on Saturday, the 13th of December, 1862, though they began their march at two o'clock in the morning of that day. Such was the service they rendered the country on the first day of the memorable battle of Fredericksburg, which was not a defeat at this part of the line. Colonel Campbell, of the Fifty-seventh Pennsylvania volunteers, went into action with his arm in a sling, still suffering from a wound he had received at the battle of Fair Oaks on May 31, 1862, and paid the penalty of his heroism by another wound from a rebel bullet, which felled him to the ground and unfitted him for service for many long months. So great was the loss of the division that General Birney asked for a new regiment to replace it, and for the consolidation of the old regiments, whose ranks had been so thinned as to reduce them far below the minimum.

The following description is from a private letter, written by an eye-witness, which found its way, in the latter part of December, 1862, into the columns of the "*Courrier des Etats Unis*:"

"The much-regretted General Kearny could not have had

a worthier successor than the brilliant General Birney, the present commander of the division. Under his orders the troops have rivalled each other in dash and intrepidity to sustain the reputation of a corps which had already so greatly distinguished itself on the several fields of battle. But no brigade had as great a task as the second, commanded by General Hobart Ward.

"After the division had crossed the Rappahannock to reinforce the grand division of the left, (General Franklin's,) we were immediately led upon an intermediate point between the division of Pennsylvania Reserves (Meade's) and Gibbon's division, who were actually engaged with the enemy, trying to dislodge him from a formidable position, which was covered by the artillery and defended by three rows of rifle-pits raised above each other on the sward, and in the woods.

"After an obstinate contest, these two divisions, repulsed with loss, recoiled across the plain, leaving Birney's division the only one in line of battle, unsupported on the right, and attacked on the left.

"This perilous position, far from intimidating our veterans, rather seemed to inflame their ardor. General Ward, at the head of four regiments—the Thirty-eighth and Fortieth New York, the Fourth Maine, and the Fifty-seventh Pennsylvania —threw himself forward to meet the foe, and, supported by a part of Berry's brigade, crushed back the rebels to their intrenchments.

"To give an idea of the obstinate fury of the fight at this point, it is only necessary to say that the four regiments which I have just mentioned each lost more than one-third of its complement, and number among the killed and wounded two colonels and two majors.

"During this time the three regiments on the right, the Fifth-fifth New York, the Third Maine and the Ninety-ninth Pennsylvania, had remained under orders to cover and defend a battery of artillery, which was in a position so exposed that, being threatened both in front and on the flank, the artillerymen would have been soon obliged to withdraw their pieces to the rear. Colonel De Trobriand, of the Fifty-fifth New York, on whom the command of the three regiments had fallen, while General Ward bravely conducted the three others to the attack on the left, maintained his line of battle, even after the retreat of the battery; and being covered by a line of riflemen, kept the enemy busy enough to oblige him to remain at a distance, and finally to find shelter in the wood. Thanks to the precaution taken in making the men lie down in the furrows, the losses have been relatively inconsiderable in that quarter, although projectiles of every kind had full play among them.

"After the battle, which had, nevertheless, cost him so much in officers and men, General Birney was not relieved from his post on the field. The whole division remained two days and nights deployed near the enemy, who did not attempt to force it back any further. And we only left our position on Monday night, to recross the river."

After dark General Reynolds personally ordered General Birney to remain in command of that line, and hold the position he then occupied until further orders. This he did, and the tired regiments of the division, with fixed bayonets and loaded guns, awaited the return of the enemy they had so successfully repulsed—all that night, all Sunday and Sunday night, all Monday and until Monday night at eleven o'clock, when, under orders from General Stoneman, who had resumed command of the Third Corps, they returned to their camp across the Rappahannock, having lost in killed and wounded nine hundred and sixty-one out of seven thousand men. During their absence from camp, from two, A. M., of Saturday, the 13th, until eleven, P. M., of Monday, the 15th of December, both officers and men were without blankets. From Saturday at eleven until dark they were in action, and on Sunday and Monday they were exposed to the fire of sharp-shooters and pickets until late on Monday afternoon, when, at the suggestion of the rebel General Ewell, an informal arrangement was made, in pursuance of which this mode of fighting ceased.

In his report of this action, the rebel General Lee says that at no part of his line were his men driven from the ground they had captured from our troops, except at the point where Birney's division drove back Early's division of Ewell's corps.

So much for the facts and the testimony of an enemy. Now let us call disinterested witnesses, and hear their testimony. Up to May, 1865, General Burnside's official report of this battle has not been made to the Adjutant-general at Washington, and the only official reports to which the writer has had access are those of which copies were sent him at the time, and which the Adjutant-general of the United States army has permitted to be published. In part first of the report of the Committee on the Conduct of the War can be found the testimony, before the Committee, of General Burnside, who commanded the Army of the Potomac at that time; of General Franklin, who commanded the left grand division; of General Reynolds, who commanded a corps in that grand division, to whom General Birney reported during the battle, and of General Meade. Added to this is the official report of General Stoneman, who commanded the corps of which General Birney's division was a part.

By examining these critically the following result is obtained: General Burnside, in his testimony, says not one word about General Birney or the movements of his division. General Franklin says that after receiving a telegram from General Burnside, dated December 13th, 5.55 A. M., but received by him about 7.30 A. M., he directed General Reynolds to carry out so much of the order as related to the attack with one division, and General Meade, who commanded the division composed of the Pennsylvania Reserves, was ordered to make the attack. He was soon in motion, General Gibbon's division supporting him on the right, and General Doubleday's division being held in reserve. General Meade began to move on December 13th before eight o'clock A. M., supported as has been stated. The divisions of Birney, Sickles and Newton were subsequently ordered up, and, as General Franklin testifies, it required at least four or five hours to bring these divisions into position so as to render assistance. It is not surprising that General Birney was not on the ground at eight o'clock, when General Meade began his movement, as he did not receive until ten o'clock of that day the order from General Stoneman to advance and report to General Reynolds. On receipt of this order his division crossed the river and reported to General Reynolds by eleven o'clock; making in one hour the movement which General Franklin testifies "would have taken from three to five hours."

When the movement of General Meade began, a large force of the enemy was on his extreme left, and in such a position that they could fire into Meade's rear as he advanced. "General Reynolds stopped Meade, and sent Doubleday's division to drive off the enemy. While he was stopped, and Doubleday was advancing, I (General Franklin) sent for one of General Stoneman's divisions, *which was on the other side of the river at the bridges.* This division—General Birney's—I (General Franklin) sent an aide-de-camp to direct to report to General Reynolds. General Birney did so report, but *before* he got up General Meade had advanced into the woods. He had a severe fight with the enemy, and drove them so that his men were on the crown of the hill, when they were attacked by an immensely superior force and driven back."

"*By this time* two regiments of Birney's division had arrived on the field, and General Reynolds *immediately* put them in. They were also driven back, and it was not until the main body of Birney's division came up that they were able to retrieve themselves, so as to hold any part of the woods."

General Reynolds testifies that the attacking force under General Meade did not reach the point which it was desired they should take and hold. "They were a little short of it." Had that point been taken and held, the enemy would have been obliged to vacate their position. When asked whether General Meade sent to him at any time for help, he said that General Meade did send word "to say that Gibbon was not advancing on his right." He further says, "I sent Gibbon orders, and also went over myself and urged him on. I sent two aides-de-camp, and they were with him doing the best they could to help him on. They did not advance so vigorously as they should have done, I think." When speaking of Birney, he says that his and Sickles' divisions "must have commenced crossing (the river) before Meade made his attack," but he did not know whether they had crossed before the attack was made. He nowhere censures Birney for not having been up in time.

General Meade, in his testimony, says that "General Birney did come up just in time for me (General Meade) to get the men out, and prevent the enemy from following any further than the edge of the woods in front of the batteries." He also says, "The division of General Birney *I think* might have come up sooner than it did." In his official report of the battle, he says the column of attack was formed between nine and ten o'clock, and the disposition of the troops had scarcely been made when the enemy began the attack. As has been shown, General Birney did not receive until ten o'clock the order to cross his division over the Rappahannock. Is it any wonder that he did not support an attack made between nine and ten o'clock, more than three miles from the point from which he moved? The man who "*thinks*" that he might have come up sooner has surely not taken the trouble to ascertain the hour of the day when Birney received the order to advance.

Between the testimony of General Meade and that of

General Birney there is a discrepancy which a faithful historian cannot fail to note, notwithstanding the fact that he thus places side by side the statement of a dead man with that of a General who has lived to see the end of the rebellion, and who by good fortune has occupied so conspicuous a place in the Army of the Potomac. General Meade says he sent three times to General Birney, twice requesting him to advance to his support. To these "requests the answer was that General Birney was under the order of General Reynolds, *sustaining General Stoneman*, and could not move without their orders." The third time, General Meade says, he "assumed the responsibility, (though it was an assumption on his part,) and *ordered* Birney up." General Birney, on the other hand, testifies that he received only "a request from General Meade to advance to his support," with which request he immediately complied, though by doing so he disregarded an order from General Reynolds, his immediate commander. Both the statements of these officers are under oath, and the reader must judge between them. The only comment the writer will make is, that if General Meade's messengers, who carried the first two requests, are reported correctly, they must have misunderstood General Birney, for he was not at any time "sustaining General Stoneman."

In calling General Stoneman as a witness, we will let him testify in his own words, and submit the following extracts from his official report of the battle:

"The state of affairs when Birney's (First) Division arrived on the ground, followed soon after by Sickles' (Second) Division, was any thing but promising. Their opportune arrival, however, first checked and then drove back the advancing enemy, who, with their peculiar yell, were in hot pursuit of the two exhausted and retiring divisions of Meade and Gibbon, and also were able to save each and every gun belonging to the latter division, which had in the confusion been abandoned by their support. Nor was this all the results of the timely arrival and gallant conduct of the two first-named divisions; for they succeeded in not only preventing Doubleday's command from being cut off and taken in reverse, the left of Smith's corps (which had not been engaged) from being turned, but possibly, if not probably, saved the entire left wing from disaster.

"But in doing this valuable service, this First Division lost upwards of a thousand as brave men as ever pulled a trigger.

"Of the conduct of this division I cannot speak too highly. Composed, as it is, of regiments from almost every State from the Penobscot to the Mississippi, the entire country may justly feel proud of its well-earned fame.

"Amongst the stragglers and skulkers the *Kearny badge* was in no one single instance observed, while the new regiments, then and now belonging to this division, appeared to vie with their veteran brothers in arms, in coolness, courage and efficiency.

"Where all did so nobly and well, it is difficult to distinguish. I must, however, be permitted to compliment Brigadier-general D. B. Birney upon the handsome and admirable manner in which he handled this, his now present division, and, at the same time, cannot omit to give all due credit to his able Brigadier-generals, Berry, Robinson and Ward, for the splendid manner in which they led and fought their separate brigades."

General Birney's report of the part taken by his division in this battle will be found in the Appendix to this sketch.

An explanation is perhaps requisite to show why so much has been said about General Birney's conduct at the battle of Fredericksburg. It has so often been made the subject of criticism by officers of the army who had only heard one version of the story, and of comment in social circles, where General Birney and his accusers are both known, that the writer has thought it but fair to the memory of General Birney that the whole story should be told, and when this is known he is willing that an intelligent public shall decide whether Birney was or was not in fault. Conscious of having done his entire duty, Birney never attempted to justify his conduct either in public or private, but such indifference would be criminal on the part of any one who undertakes to sketch the military life of any man who served his country so faithfully as did General Birney.

EMANCIPATION PROCLAMATION.

AFTER the defeat of the Union forces at Fredericksburg, the indignation of the country was unbounded. It was doubtful, for some time, with whom rested the responsibility of the movement and its failure. Vague and painful charges were made against officers of the army and of the administration. A bad feeling prevailed in the army, and the friends of the different prominent general officers were engaged in warm discussions about the part their several friends had performed in the movement upon Fredericksburg. Besides the destruction of mutual confidence among the general officers in the army of the Potomac, there were also dissensions at Washington. General Burnside had determined upon another movement of his army, and on the 30th of December it had actually begun, when the President telegraphed to General Burnside that no general movement should be made without letting him know of it. The movement was suspended, and General Burnside went at once to Washington, when the President told him that some general officers of his command had represented that the contemplated movement, if made, would be disastrous, and, General Burnside understood the President to say, that no prominent officer of his command had any faith in the proposed movement. After a consultation with the President, the Secretary of War, and General Halleck, General Burnside returned to the army without any definite instructions, and the movement was abandoned.

These differences in the councils were soon known to the general public, and increased the dissatisfaction already existing throughout the country. The removal of General McClellan from the command of the Army of the Potomac, in November, 1862, had caused great discontent among his friends, who were then numerous, both in and out of the army. General Burnside's failure at Fredericksburg proved that the change in the commander of the Army of the Potomac had not been an improvement, and General McClellan's friends did not fail to impress this upon the public mind, hoping thus to have him replaced. When it was known that differences existed between General Burnside and members of the administration, the general public feared a repetition of the dissensions and want of co-operation which, from the commencement of the Peninsular campaign, had existed between the civil and military power of the country, and which had done so much to paralyze its strength.

These, to the patriot, were the gloomiest days of the rebellion. At that time, it must be remembered, the Western armies had not begun their brilliant movements, and every general officer who had been entrusted with an important command in the field had proved a failure; some because they were incompetent, and others because they had been fettered by orders, which prevented them from accomplishing any important results. Even the honesty, the strength of purpose, and common sense of Abraham Lincoln, who eventually proved to be the sheet-anchor in the storm, could not unite the discordant elements of the North. The radicals pelted him with "paper bullets," because he was not progressive enough to suit their views, and the conservatives abused him, because he did not wage the war as they wished it "for the restoration of the Constitution, the laws, and the Union." Thus stood the politicians; the camp followers, who sought the loaves and the fishes; and the jobbers in contracts, who, like jackalls, were fattening by robbing the soldiers. It soon happened, however, as it always has where a nation has been really in trouble, that the middle men of the country—men who had all at stake, and whose trade was not office or power—rose up in their strength and rallied to the support of those officers of the Government and of the army, who really wished to end the rebellion by hard blows.

Nothing contributed so much to elicit this latent element of power as the publication of the Emancipation Proclamation by President Lincoln, on the 1st day of January, 1863. This document, which will hereafter stand side by side with the Declaration of Independence, in the history of the United States, will be found in full in the Appendix. No soldier hailed its appearance with more joy than General Birney. He had long hoped for it, and believed that its publication would strengthen the strong man and animate the weak. He had buckled on his sword, because he believed that this rebellion was begun by men whose principal object was to perpetuate the curse of slavery upon our land, while he had determined that, so far as lay in his power, as a man and a soldier, the curse should be removed. It is sad to reflect that after he had endured so much, and suffered so long, he was not permitted to see the results he had aided to bring about.

A single incident will illustrate his feelings in this regard. During the three months' campaign, while he was division officer of the day, the commanding general sent him word that a fugitive slave was in camp, and requested Lieutenant-colonel Birney to have the fugitive apprehended and sent to headquarters. Birney replied that, "after a careful examination of the articles of war, he found nothing that required him, as an officer of the United States army, to aid in catching runaway slaves," and he declined to perform the duty. No further efforts were made to apprehend the fugitive, who probably never returned to his master.

CAMP LIFE.

ON Monday night, December 15th, 1862, General Birney received from General Stoneman, his corps commander, an order to leave that portion of the field of Fredericksburg which his division had held for three days and three nights, and retire across the Rappahannock. This order was obeyed, and on Tuesday, the 16th of December, they occupied their old quarters near Falmouth, opposite Fredericksburg, until the 22d day of January, 1863, when the famous "Mud Campaign" began. This movement was undertaken by General Burnside on his own responsibility. After his contemplated movement on the 30th of December, 1862, had been checked by the authorities in Washington, General Burnside had some correspondence with the President and General Halleck, in which he expressed his opinion that a forward movement should be made, and solicited authority to make it. General Halleck replied, that he had always favored a forward movement of the army, but he would not take the responsibility of directing when or how it should be done. General Burnside went to work to make it, but his plans were frustrated by a severe winter storm and the condition of the roads, which were almost impassable, even for infantry. When the impossibility of advance became manifest, the men were ordered back to their original encampments. Here they remained until the 27th of April, 1863, when they moved forward under General Hooker, who had been appointed to succeed General Burnside in the command of the Army of the Potomac on the 26th day of January, 1863.

Shortly after General Hooker assumed the command, the President sent to the Senate a number of names for promotion; among them Generals D. E. Sickles and H. G. Berry, who were promoted to be Major-generals. General Sickles had commanded the Second Division of the Third Corps, while General Birney had commanded the First Division, and General Berry, who as a Colonel had commanded a regiment in Birney's old brigade, had for several months commanded a brigade in Birney's division. While Birney did not deny the merits of either of these officers, or their right to their reward for distinguished services, he felt that he was equally entitled to promotion, and the omission of his name in the list which was forwarded by the President to the Senate, early in 1863, was mortifying to himself and his friends.

To the credit of "Joe Hooker," be it said, that he participated in the disappointment, and did all in his power to secure Birney's promotion. After he had been placed in command of the Army of the Potomac, he wrote to the President a letter, of which the following is a copy:

HEADQUARTERS ARMY OF THE POTOMAC,
CAMP NEAR FALMOUTH, VA., *February* 3, 1863.

TO HIS EXCELLENCY
THE PRESIDENT OF THE UNITED STATES:

MR. PRESIDENT:—Permit me to recommend to your favorable consideration Brigadier-general D. B. Birney. He is an applicant for promotion, and if service and qualifications are of weight, he is richly deserving of it.

He has been in command of Kearny's old division the greater part of the time since the death of that officer, and I know of no better division commander in this army, or one that I would prefer to have in my command. He is an ornament to any service.

Very respectfully
Your obedient servant,
JOS. HOOKER,
Major-general Commanding.

In this application General Hooker was joined by the Hon. Wm. D. Kelley, Hon. A. K. McClure, Hon. Edgar M. Cowan, Hon. David Wilmot, (the last two then being Senators from the State of Pennsylvania;) by Judges Casey and Carter, of Washington; by Major-general S. P. Heintzelman; by Hon. John M. Read, of the Supreme Court of Pennsylvania, and by a number of the leading citizens of Philadelphia. But all these were of no avail. General Birney's time had not come. In the additional list of names sent by the President on the 2d day of March, 1863, General Birney's name did not appear.

This omission elicited from General Hooker the following telegram:

HEADQUARTERS ARMY POTOMAC, *March* 4, 1863.

HON. E. M. STANTON:

DEAR SIR:—I am informed that Brigadier-general David B. Birney has been dropped from the roll as arranged for promotion. This is not as I was led to believe.

There is no better division commander in the army I command than General Birney, and I beg to insist upon his nomination. The influence which is brought to bear in opposition to his being promoted is of a character entirely detrimental to the good of our cause and the country.

JOSEPH HOOKER,

Major-general commanding Army of Potomac.

In spite of the efforts of superior officers and of political friends the promotion was not made, but these efforts elicited from Mr. Lincoln the following remark:

Late in March, 1863, while General Birney was in Washington to appear before the Committee on the Conduct of the War, he called upon President Lincoln to pay his respects, and after the usual salutations, the President said, "Birney, why do your friends remind me of the newsboys about Washington?"

"Indeed, sir," said Birney, "I cannot tell."

"Why," answered Old Abe, "they are always crying out 'Extra' Star."

The point of this joke consists in the fact that the most enterprising daily paper in Washington is called the "*Evening Star*," and the newsboys about the city have, since the rebellion, been in the habit of selling the "EXTRA STAR" whenever any news prompted the publication of an extra.

About the middle of February, 1863, General Hooker placed General Stoneman in command of the cavalry of the Army of the Potomac, and Major-general D. E. Sickles was, by the President, assigned to the command of the Third Corps. He retained this command until he was wounded at the battle of Gettysburg, and during those four months and a half the relations between him and General Birney were of the most intimate character. They soon formed a friendship for each other which broke down the barrier of official intercourse, and lasted until General Birney's decease. They united and cultivated an *esprit du corps* among their men which made the Third Army Corps celebrated for the unity of feeling that existed among its officers, and the devotion of the soldiers to their officers and to each other. Their head-quarters soon became noted for hospitality, and during the spring of 1863, the Third Corps established a popularity in the army, and with the visitors to the army, which will long be remembered. During this period the foundation was laid of the "Third Corps Union," which is believed to be the only association of the kind organized in any of the Union armies. Its object was to preserve the history of the brigades and divisions of the corps, to promote good fellowship among the officers, and to provide assistance for its members and their families in case of need. The several members were under an obligation, in the event of any officer of the corps being taken prisoner, to make exertions to procure his release, or if he fell in battle the officers of the Union were bound by the by-laws of the association to have his body properly embalmed and sent to his friends for interment. The members of this "Union" were designated by a badge which the association had adopted, and this mark of distinction they all wear, and prize beyond any designation conferred upon them as a reward for services rendered the country. In the future, when these men shall have returned to the pursuits of peace, they will value the "Third Corps Union" medal, and the recollections of this association will be one of the most pleasant reminiscences of their life in the field. Its members and their descendants will find the "Third Corps Union" as strong a badge of union as has for ninety years united the society of the Cincinnati.

The efforts of the general officers of the Third Corps to create a good feeling among its members were extended to the private soldiers, and during the spring of 1863 the monotony of camp life was varied by such entertainments and amusements as could be extemporized in the field, and the correspondents of the press during the dearth of army news, which it was their business to collect, amused the public by long descriptions of the amusements prepared for the soldiers by thoughtful commanders. General Birney, as usual, was foremost in these efforts to employ the thoughts of the soldiers during the dullness of camp life. These entertainments were so successful that they were frequently repeated, and each time with more and more eclat. The most successful occurred on the 28th of March, 1863. The correspondent of the *Philadelphia Inquirer* writes as follows:—

"OPPOSITE FREDERICKSBURG, *March* 28, 1863.

"In one of our letters of this week we alluded to a grand jollification which was to take place in the division commanded by General Birney, and that because of the bad condition of the roads it had been postponed from Tuesday to Friday of the present week.

"Yesterday, in the usual course of events, rolled round, and a brighter, more lovely and glorious day could not have been accorded us had it been 'made to order.'

"The site selected for the performance was a large open field, near the headquarters of the division. During the week the staff connected with headquarters, under guidance of Lieutenant Briscoe, had been busy in perfecting such arrangements as would render the whole affair a success.

"The race-course, about one mile and a quarter in length, passing over a country with but slight diversification of hill and dale, had been during the week put through such a 'course of training' as to render it admirably adapted for the purpose. Upon the highest part of the ground and overlooking the entire field a stand of some one hundred and twenty feet long and sixteen wide was erected, a portion of the same being appropriated to the Judges. In front of this Judges' position a small flag marked the starting point, and following the course, some thirty yards distant, was a deep ditch, eight feet wide. Continuing along the track the next obstruction was a hurdle some six feet high, and made of brush; further on was another similar hurdle, then another eight feet ditch, and again two other hurdles, the last home-stretch up to the main stand being perfectly level and about a hundred and fifty yards long.

"The crowd to witness the exhibition began to assemble early, and by ten o'clock the entire track was hemmed in by the gallant soldiers of this and other divisions. General Hooker granted a general holiday to the army, with the exception of those doing picket-duty.

"The stand was occupied by some fifty or more ladies, who are visiting us, together with almost all our major and brigadier-generals.

"Just before the initiatory exhibition was commenced, the entire ground encircled by the track was cleared of all parties occupying it, except such commissioned officers as were mounted. The regiments selected to do guard duty was the Thirty-eighth New York, Colonel De Trobriand, and the One-hundred-and-fourteenth Pennsylvania, Colonel Collis. Much credit is due to this body of troops for the admirable manner in which they performed their duties.

"The Judges were Generals Birney, Owens and Ward, the latter being the Master of Ceremonies. Major-General Berry was referee, while Captain John Gossin, chief of General Meagher's staff, was selected as the starter of the races. Lieutenants Lee and Raphael, of General Ward's staff, were selected to have charge of the comical portions of the programme.

"Major Brevoort, Captains Fassitt, Tallman, Markle, and Lieutenants Briscoe, Graves, Moore and Clarke, together with Surgeon Lyman, of General Birney's staff, were all, during the entire day, actively engaged in attending to the wants of the assembled guests, and helping to make the day one long to be remembered with pleasure by all assembled.

"The first thing on the programme arranged for the occasion, was a Hurdle Race and Steeple Chase, best two in three; entrance fee, twenty dollars, open to all officers, the winner to pocket the stakes. The second best entitled him to his entrance money. Seven horses were entered for this race, viz:—

"Captain Kurshow, bay mare 'Queen,' ridden by Count Blucher. Colonel Van Schaick, sorrel gelding 'Faderland,' ridden by owner. Quartermaster Martin, bay mare 'Kathleen-Mavourneen,' ridden by Dr. Reynolds, of General Meagher's staff. General Meagher, bay gelding 'Napper Tandy,' ridden by Captain Whiteford. Colonel McKnight, bay gelding 'Billy,' ridden by Lieutenant McHenry. Lieutenant Seibric, bay mare 'Zella,' ridden by owner. Prince Salm Salm, bay horse 'Fasco,' ridden by owner.

"At the given word, the horses started off fair and evenly, came dashing past the grand stand almost simultaneously, going splendidly over the first ditch, and keeping well together over the first hurdle. The horses 'Faderland,' 'Kathleen Mavourneen,' 'Fasco,' and 'Zella,' in the same order began to take the advance. It was evident, however, that Prince Salm Salm was not urging his steed, and doubtless would have won the race had not his horse stumbled and thrown him. The injuries he sustained are mostly internal, but he is fast recovering; the horse, however, was seriously injured.

"In the order above-named the horses came up to the winning post, time 3·15.

"The second heat was similar to the last, with the exception that no accident occurred; time made, 3·10, the decision of the Judges awarding the prize to Colonel Van Schaick, his horse, 'Faderland,' winning in two straight heats.

"It was in contemplation to have the next race run by 'taking' only the hurdles, and not the ditches. The competitors were to have been Prince Salm Salm, Generals Birney, Averill and Meagher, but owing to the unfortunate accident to the Prince the race was deferred.

"After the lapse of half an hour the bugle was sounded, and when quiet was obtained, General Owen announced the next race to be one open to all officers, entrance fee five dollars, one straight heat, the winner to take the entire stakes.

"For this race only four horses were entered, Major West, of the Seventeenth Maine, entering a horse to be ridden by Lieutenant Samuel McHenry. Major Burns, Fourth Excelsior, bay mare, ridden by owner. Assistant-Surgeon Daniel E. Kelsey, Sixty-fourth New York, entered a dark bay horse, ridden by himself. Captain A. P. Hill, Fourth Excelsior regiment, horse, ridden by Captain Shine.

"At the word 'go,' the horses got off together, and had a close race until after passing the first hurdle, when all the horses but that of Major West bolted the track, leaving the latter to make the balance of the track at an easy gait, and winning the race, coming in at an easy walk.

"Again, another race was instituted, the orders for governing it being of a peculiar nature, and confined to horses belonging to officers of the first brigade only. Each horse to be ridden by its owner's antagonist, the last horse to win a purse of one hundred and forty dollars. The owner of the first horse to reach the starting point to receive fifty dollars, and the rider of the same an equal sum. Twelve horses were entered for the race, viz.:—

"Colonel Kirkwood entered 'Archy,' ridden by Colonel Watkins. Colonel Collis entered 'Zoozoo,' ridden by Lieutenant Dennison. Colonel Watkins entered 'Yankee,' ridden by Lieutenant Boyle. Colonel McGenahan entered 'Tommy,' ridden by Major Spalding. Major Spalding entered 'Ned,' ridden by Lieutenant Kimple. Colonel Madill entered 'Little Billy,' ridden by Lieutenant Garretson. Lieutenant Dennison entered 'Robin Hood,' ridden by Lieutenant Searle. Lieutenant Searle entered 'Stumbler,' ridden by Lieutenant Moorhead. Colonel McKnight entered 'Pete,' ridden by Colonel Madill. Colonel Sides entered 'Billy,' ridden by Colonel Collis. Major Danks entered 'Boston,' ridden by Colonel Crawford. Lieutenant Collis entered 'Homicide,' ridden by Colonel Gamble.

"This was a flat race, no ditches or hurdles were to be gone over, and to be decided in one straight heat.

"The horses got off well together, and so continued untll on the last turn, when wind began to tell, and as they came around on to the home-stretch the speed was awful, Colonel Kirkwood's horse being in the advance. Colonel Collis, riding Colonel Sides' horse, had evidently been riding what is called in jockeying parlance a waiting race; but, just before coming to the last turn, he began to leave some behind and decrease the distance between himself and those in the advance. As he came up to the guide flag that marked the turn, the horse he was on was going at a slashing pace, when down went horse and rider, rolling over and over. The fall was occasioned by turning too short in the mud, the horse's feet slipping out from under him. The horse recovered his foothold before its rider, and came up to the stand without a guide, thereby coming in last and winning the one hundred and forty dollar purse. At the pace Collis was going when this mishap occurred, it is fair to presume he would have come in first best. As it was, Colonel Kirkwood's horse, ridden by Colonel Watkins, came up to the stand first, and secured the prize above-named for the first horse in.

"Another race was then established, to be ridden on the same course as the last, entrance fee twenty dollars, open to all officers, one straight heat; the winner to take the pool. For this race Captain Fassitt entered 'Black Diamond,' ridden by Colonel Welch. Colonel Vincent entered 'Rodney,' ridden by Lieutenant Chambers. Colonel Berdan entered 'Hunter,' ridden by Lieutenant Shoup. Count Blucher entered 'Independence,' ridden by himself.

"After two false starts they got off, Colonel Berdan's 'Hunter' baulking at the last start, and withdrawing from the race. Colonel Vincent's horse came in the winner, time 2·55.

"Next came the comicalities, in which the privates indulged. First a foot race, prizes, ten dollars, five dollars and three dollars; next, climbing the greased pole; then a sack-race; next, wheel of fortune; another foot race; yet another sack race, and winding up with a cock fight—two men personating roosters, and bucking against each other in the same manner as do the bipeds.

"After this performance was over the invited guests adjourned to the headquarters of General Birney, where for an hour or two they indulged to their hearts' content in all the convivialities usual upon such occasions, eating, drinking and making merry. The festivities were ended by an Ethiopian concert gotten up by members of General Ward's brigade.

"After the Ethiopian performance, the guests quietly retired to their several camps, and thus ended a day which will long be remembered by all connected with the Army of the Potomac.

"Prominent among the participants of the amusements were Governor Curtin and General Hooker. General Birney's headquarters were decorated handsomely with evergreens.

"With the exception of the accidents referred to, nothing occurred to mar the enjoyment of the day."

The correspondent of the *New York Herald* sent his description of the sports in the following language:—

"It was Friday, March 27, 1863. So the sun rose and cut up sundry shines, and annihilated the mud, and behaved generally as if he had been on a special detail to clear up the roads and get matters ready for sport. He did his part of the business well, and then the indescribable imp, yclept Mat, who attends to the chronicler's horse and boots, saddled our noble Rosinante, and we rode towards the scene of the promised fun—the field of the cloth of gold.

"On every hand, wherever there were cedar trees, the birds came out, and, as Pierre Vidal or some other amiable troubadour hath it, 'trilled richly their notes of golden latin,' and made the way very pleasant as we rode; and from every direction, also, there rode gayly out from among the 'lazy tents' troops of gallant fellows in all the bravery of rich attire, and all rode the same way; and that is how it was that we came, without any trouble to find it, upon the very scene of the festivities, in the open plain near Falmouth.

"For a perfectly natural, free race, the course was just exactly what it should be. From the grand stand it stretched in a circuit of one mile out into the open country, and had sufficient inequality of surface to make the ride a hard one. At two points in the course the horses were out of sight from a position in the field near the grand stand, on account of the hills. About a hundred yards from the stand was the first ditch, some six or seven feet in width, and two or three hundred yards further on the first hurdle. There were, I believe, four hurdles; but they were very innocent affairs; for if a horse did not quite clear them his heels broke through, and he went on just as well.

"In two or three places on the course there was considerable mud; except in these few spots the ground was in good condition. In the absence of stakes to define the course, its direction over the wide plain was marked out by a line of men drawn around its whole extent. There they stood, at order arms, impassive as the posts they stood for, and this gave a picturesqueness and character of order and regularity to the scene very pleasant to behold on a race course. Thus every post was light blue below and dark blue above; and each post, too, was a blaze of sun-beams, 'a wreath of radiant fire,' as from every musket-barrel the sunshine was reflected, broken in a thousand splinters of light.

"The grand stand was upon a hill that commanded a full view of the course, and was formed of part of a bridge train built upon wagons. Over the stand fluttered the colors of General Birney, (first division, Third Corps.) Three excellent bands were on the stand, and played admirably all the airs that one knows and loves to hear, and all the airs that one don't know and wishes he did—exquisite and delicious music—

> "Music that more gently on the spirit lies
> Than tired eyelids upon tired eyes.

It tempered to a proper degree the mirth that without it might have been on the over-boisterous order.

"On the stand was the Judge, and the herald (in the form of a bugler) blew thrice the summons to the various encounters of the day. Up and down the track in front of the stand a strong guard was drawn up, part of which was in the brilliant uniform of the Zouave, and these, with the blue of other uniforms, the brilliant dresses of officers and the colors of the ladies' dresses—all seen in strong relief against a clear blue sky—made a very animated *coup d'œil.*

"'Fighting Joe' was there in his usual trim. Sickles was there, as suave and courteous as Sickles always is. Meagher was there, in a black coat and on a white horse. White horses have become quite the style in the army, and General Birney himself was mounted on a very handsome one. Officers from every part of the Army of the Potomac were there.

> "Bated like eagles, having lately bathed;
> Glittering in golden coats like images;
> As full of spirit as the month of May,
> And gorgeous as the sun at midsummer,

These wanton fellows galloped up and down and admired one another in the open plain inside the course.

"So it was a scene of chivalrous pomp and pageantry, and all was gayety and good humor, when, exactly at eleven, A. M., the field was called for the first race.

"Five horses were entered. One of these was a beast of special note—a perfect beauty—said to be owned by Colonel Von Schaick, of the New York Seventh. He was ridden by a German artillery officer. Another horse was ridden by the Prince Salm Salm. There were two riders in this race gotten up in the showy colors of the course. This was a tolerably 'soft' race, and was won by Colonel Von Schaick's horse with ease in two straight heats. He went over the obstructions like a bird. The Prince Salm Salm was badly thrown at a ditch, and it is said had some ribs broken. As for the men 'in motley,' their appearance was very lively, if their movements were not.

"'Now, then, gentlemen, this is your time,' said a clear voice with the Irish accent or patois. 'This is your time—sweepstakes—entrance five dollars—open for any horses—to be ridden by officers of the Army of the Potomac.' And the speaker rode on and made his announcement up and down the field—a sort of *marechal de champ* and crier in one. He hadn't the baton that the marshals have in the illustrated Froissarts, and he had better clothes than the town criers are apt to have anywhere. Beautiful were his clothes! Behold him brilliant in blue and gold, with a black belt wide as a baldric over his left shoulder, and the ends of his moustache dressed with pomade Hongroise. Beautiful were his clothes—and he was an Irishman, and formerly, some one said, in the Austrian service. What soldiers they are, those sons of the Emerald Isle, with their liquid and musical voices, and how very fond they are of gold lace! Fighting cocks fond of their feathers.

"But here is the field for the next race—only four horses. They are to run over the same track—hurdles, ditches and all—and there they go; not much of a start, not a jockey in the party. Never mind what is ahead or what behind; and every horse pushed to his utmost from the word go. Of course the pace soon gave out.

"The race was won by a distance. Horse No. 2, far behind, came to the last ditch and put his rider into it handsomely, and went down himself in an easy, safe sort of way. But the rider was game. He was up and on again in no time, and still came in second. So you may judge where the other two were.

"As the last of these four horses came to the last of the hurdles he refused to rise, but broke his way right through the hurdle. But his rider was too conscientious to ride a race in that way, and so, though already a quarter of a mile behind, and sure to come in last, he determined to come in 'on the square,' and therefore took his horse back around the hurdle and brought him over it in very fair style.

"So there was another interval of gossip and of gallops up and down. And then came the third race, open only for officers of General Birney's division. There were six or seven competitors for this race, and they got away any how, with no start at all, and dribbled all down the track for some hundreds of yards.

"Now, in this race there was a certain horse full of fire and fine points, and ridden by a colonel. Horse and colonel were both disposed to show what could be done, and, though in the long, drawn out kite-tail sort of start, the horse and the colonel were the last knot but one in the kite-tail, they soon came to the front, and by the time half the course was made they had a fair lead of the field. But toward the end of the run there was a very short turn, which the horse, 'lost in the labyrinth of his fury,' didn't appreciate. He was now disposed to show what he could do without the colonel, became a wilful beast and went his own way all over the field, and everywhere but towards the stand. After some minutes of that sort of conduct, he concluded that he and the colonel couldn't agree; so he deposited the colonel in the ditch, and had a career on his own account. By all of which arrangements his speed was wasted, and the horse that had been second went in winner.

"In this race there was an officer who, having scarlet pants as part of his uniform, had also mounted a scarlet shirt and scarlet night-cap, and shone out an airy red rider of the most grotesque appearance. But it happened that, as his horse ran on, this *homme rouge* lost his seat just at a point where the mud was very yellow, and so it transpired that, though he started in the full bloom of brilliant red, he returned to the stand in very dirty yellow.

"Then there was a foot-race between soldiers. No swift-footed Achilles was present on the occasion, and perhaps it is to the honor of these soldiers of the Army of the Potomac that they did not run particularly well. Then came the fourth race, run, like the third, on a flat track. It was contested by three good horses and was the best race of the day. All three of the horses were right together for half the length of the course, when two went in alone; for to the third it happened that, at the rise of a little hill, he stumbled and went forward on his head, and his rider went over on his head; and then, as the rider staggered to his feet, the horse partly regained his feet, and again fell with his rider under him. And yet the rider came out apparently unhurt.

"Another foot-race followed, then a race of boys tied in sacks, and sundry lusty fellows made ineffectual attempts to climb a greased pole, for the sake of a bank note at the top—entertainment admirably calculated for those of the men and boys who chose to participate; 'youths who thunder at a play-house and fight for bitten apples.'

A private letter, published in the *Salem* (Massachusetts) *Gazette*, describes the amusements as follows:—

"This morning, having leisure, I thought that I would sketch the events of yesterday, that the good folks at home might have thorough information concerning the last and the greatest movement in this army, one before which all former reconnoissances fade away, and cavalry raids grow 'small by degrees and beautifully less.' I refer to a 'hurdle-race and other festivities,' under the management of General Birney, similar to but on a more extended scale than those which celebrated St. Patrick's Day in the Irish brigade.

"'The morning was glorious,' and about ten, A. M., you might have seen the representatives of the brigade staff, in common with hundreds of others, *en route* for the course. You know how the road looks in the country on a muster day, when everybody's nose points in the same direction, and moves forward according as their good fortune has provided them with swift feet or fast horses. Even so was it here, save that girls and boys, women and babies were *not* the largest proportion of the living stream. The equestrians of course outnumbered the pedestrians, and the number of wheeled vehicles was small, being for the most part ambulances, although there were several which were evidently improvised for the occasion. Hence, thoroughbreds, half-breds and mules filled the road, bearing everybody, from major-generals to 'contrabands.' Equality, if not fraternity, seemed to be the order of the day, and privates elbowed officers, splashed mud over them—no matter, all right so long as neither has his neck broken and both arrive on the ground before the performances commence.

"Arriving there we found the course encircled by a string of vigilant sentinels, in the picturesque uniform of the Zouave. Being mounted, we were permitted to pass through and join the already large number who were dashing hither and thither, running and jumping, or making an inspection of the track. Following the example of the latter, we found there were three ditches and three hurdles, the former about six feet wide, the latter not quite so high; and then took our stations nearly opposite the platform, which was built on army wagons for the Judges and 'distinguished visitors,' and listened to the music of the two brass bands, which alternately vied with each other as to which should produce the oldest and most doleful tunes suitable to the occasion. While waiting we surveyed the crowd and commented thereon. If you wished for style, it was there; for beauty, it was at hand; for elegance and grace, you need go no further; for any language under the sun, from *parlez vous* to the *argot* of a New York fireman, you had but to listen. There were shoulder straps from the size of a Poor Man's Plaster to the regulation; gold lace by the yard; clanking sabres and rattling spurs; gorgeous housings and elegant equipments. Beside them were uniforms 'tattered and torn,' ill-shaped and ill-fitting, and splashed with Virginia mud, looking as if the wearers put them on when they enlisted 'for three years or during the war,' and did not intend to take them off until they were discharged. Noticeable above all others were two, a colonel and surgeon in jockey suits of red and white. They were both Irish, and I presume good riders, but as my knowledge of their style is derived from the *pictures* of Derby day and fox hunting, I do not consider myself competent to judge, but will venture the remark that it was neither elegant nor graceful.

"Meanwhile General Sickles and staff reached the ground, and the platform commenced to fill. Prominent in the foreground were several *real live* women, be-silked, be-furred, and bonneted like those of a more civilized state, showing us at once they were not indigenous to the soil. Another equally curious curiosity was a citizen, with a tall black hat, who the crowd said was his Excellency Governor Curtin. Knowing he was here 'expressing his satisfaction at the discipline and efficiency of the army,' (which he probably knows as much about as you do,) I was content to believe, and gazed and wondered how Pennsylvanians could be unhappy while Heaven left them Governor Curtin. A faint cheering was heard in the distance, and in a moment General Hooker and staff dashed down amid what newspaper correspondents will doubtless call a 'storm of huzzas.' They dismounted their horses and mounted the platform, and soon General Stoneman and his crowd appeared and did likewise. But to enumerate all the generals who were there would be to tell over half the sins of the administration, and besides there is not time, for the first race is about to begin.

"General Meagher, Colonel Von Schaik, Prince Salm Salm, and several other officers, entered horses for the first heat, best two in three. After several notes from a bugle, they started and rushed by, taking the first ditch and hurdle splendidly, but not running at a very rapid rate. On they went, and when, by stretching our necks forward, we could see them no longer, we turned about and they soon came in view behind us. One was missing. Hip, hip, they went, over ditches and hurdles, until at the last ditch one went down and the rider went over, but was up again before we could see it, saving his distance and coming in second best. Colonel Von Schaik won easily, for he rode a splendid English hunter. The second heat but four started, and Salm Salm, who came down slam slam and broke a rib or two, wished to be excused. This time there were no accidents, and again the colonel won easily. The second race was open to all officers. Four or five entered, two being first-class specimens of the New York Mose, not caring if they broke their necks if they had their fun, and with horses which they never tried at jumping, and, perhaps, which they never mounted before. One pulled off his coat, exhibiting a shirt slightly torn, which a brother officer importuned him to cover, without effect; for 'don't I look good enough without a coat, sa—ay?' Well, they started: some went round and some did not, but luckily none met with any accident. The next race was a straight one—no jumping—in which one of the riders was thrown and at first reported killed. Colonel Collis, of Philadelphia, also came down, his horse falling and rolling completely over. The horse came in alone, and raised a storm of yells, which were not diminished when the colonel arrived on another animal, his Zouave uniform covered on one side, from head to foot, with mud, showing he had measured his length. Then there was a sack-race, which you know is a very funny affair, and a foot-race between three men; after which there was some shinning a greased pole, for a greenback which was fixed at the top, which would have done credit to a Wall street broker. The man who reached it took something which he had tied around his neck, and, when he reached the spot where the former aspirants failed, rubbed off the grease and made good his hold. The whole concluded with an encounter the like of which is not spoken of in any of the books of history, so far as my reading has progressed and my knowledge of the Grecian games extends. Shades of the Gladiators! did ye witness it? Two men were pinioned in the manner which is known among soldiers as bucking, and is used as punishment, and which was, in my boyish days, familiar under the name of 'rotten egg.' Thus pinioned they were set to butting each other, looking very like two enormous Shanghaies fighting; when one tumbled over they set him up again, until he was satisfied. From pit and private boxes alike the contest was greeted with shouts of laughter, and watched with intense interest.

"We scattered pell-mell. If ten thousand times ten thousand 'greybacks' had been after us, the distribution could not have been accelerated. Some adjourned to General Birney's headquarters to eat, drink and be merry, but you must be content to gallop back to my humble tent, (for I have no invitation,) talk over the events of the day there, and wonder at the glory of a soldier's life, especially of the superlative glory attending those who are so fortunate as to have their names enrolled as 'soldiers of the Army of the Potomac.'"

The foregoing descriptions have been inserted at length, because they were prepared by eye-witnesses, and form part of the current literature of the day. They are part of the history of the first division of the Third Army Corps, which would be incomplete if nothing but its conduct in action were narrated. The descriptions may seem trivial to the general reader, but the scenes they portray were great events to the soldiers who witnessed them. Few men understood better than General Birney how to appeal to the weak side of human nature, and to elicit from his men a ready response to his commands, in return for what the severely practical commander would designate as trifles.

CHANCELLORSVILLE.

THE amusements of the Army of the Potomac were soon interrupted by a forward movement of the army, which, under the direction of General Hooker, who had succeeded General Burnside, commenced on the 27th of April, 1863, when the Fifth, Eleventh and Twelfth Corps, broke camp and marched westward from Falmouth towards Kelly's ford. On the 29th the Third Corps struck their tents and marched by a route through ravines to a position about five miles below Fredericksburg, on the Rappahannock river. Here the men bivouacked for the night, and on the 30th of April General Birney received an order to advance his command to a bridge over the Rappahannock, in rear of the Sixth Corps, which had just passed over the river. Here the division remained until two o'clock, P. M., when General Sickles sent an order to General Birney to march the division to the United States ford, some fifteen miles distant, and cross the river by half past seven o'clock the next morning, Friday, May 1st, taking care to move through the ravines, thus concealing the movement from the enemy. By half past eleven o'clock, P. M., the division reached Hammets, on the Warrenton turnpike, and there bivouacked. At half past five the next morning, the march was resumed, and at half past seven, as per orders, the division crossed the bridge over the Rappahannock, and marched on to Chancellorsville, which they reached about eleven, A. M., and awaited orders.

Around Chancellorsville was fought one of the most memorable battles of the rebellion. The Army of the Potomac was under its third commander, and since its success at the battle of Antietam its movements had been reverses. The country watched the preparations for the movements which culminated in the battle of Chancellorsville anxiously and attentively, hoping and believing they would result in the surrender or destruction of the rebel army. General Stoneman, with his cavalry, had been sent to General Lee's rear, to intercept his retreat, and the press of the country predicted the end of the rebellion. But the end was not yet. General Hooker, like General Burnside, was compelled to recross the Rappahannock after the battle, and the army again went into camp. The sacrifice of life during the action was fearful, and the mortality among the officers was greater perhaps than in any preceding one. The rebels, remembering their success at Fredericksburg, fought with desperation, and our troops were eventually compelled to fall back. Among others who fell during this battle were Major-general Berry, of Maine, who commanded the second division, and Brigadier-general Whipple, who commanded the third division, of the Third Corps. When the telegraph announced the death of General Berry, by a slight alteration in the letters of the name, the telegrams to the different cities throughout the Union announced that General Birney had been mortally wounded, and his friends for one day suffered under the painful belief that he had fallen a prey to some rebel missile. Their relief was great when they learned the next day that Birney had been spared. The writer on that day was in Boston, and remembers well the sensation in the community which this report caused, for Birney, even at that time, was one of the most prominent of the division commanders of the Army of the Potomac, and his reputation extended far beyond the circle of his own personal friends and acquaintances.

The clearing in the woods called Chancellorsville takes its name from the principal landed proprietor in the vicinity. It is located at the intersection of the Fredericksburg and Orange Court House plank road, leading from Fredericksburg to Gordonsville, and the Wilderness road, leading from the Rappahannock river southwardly, towards Spottsylvania Court House. From Chancellorsville there is a road leading northeasterly to Banks' ford on the Rappahannock, and another leading north to the United States ford, over which General Birney had crossed with his division. General Hooker's headquarters were in the large brick house at the intersection of the roads.

When General Birney came up with his division, the line of battle was being formed, and the officers were getting their men in readiness for the conflict which, for three days, took place between the contending armies. General Birney formed his division immediately in rear of General Hooker's headquarters, and at one o'clock, under orders from General Sickles, sent Lieutenant Briscoe, of his staff, with Graham's brigade and Turnbull's battery, about two miles out the plank road to report to General Howard, who commanded the Eleventh Corps. When they arrived, General Howard told General Graham that the sending of the brigade and battery was certainly a mistake, as his own force was ample, and their presence would interfere with the disposition of his own troops. This was reported to General Sickles, who ordered the troops to remain for the time being where they were. About five o'clock an attack was made by the enemy along that part of the line, in front of General Hooker's headquarters, held by the Twelfth Corps, under General Slocum. General Birney at once ordered back Graham's brigade and Turnbull's battery, and led forward Ward's and Hayman's brigades of his division up the plank road. When General Graham rejoined the division, his brigade was assigned to the support of one of General Slocum's batteries, and there subjected to a heavy artillery fire without the power of resisting it.

General Birney went further up the plank road, to the line occupied by the Twelfth Corps, and learning from Generals Williams and Knipes, of General Slocum's command, that the right of their line was weak, he replaced two of their regiments with the Twentieth Indiana and Thirty-seventh New York volunteers, of his command, dislodged the enemy from a house in a field in his front, and lay under arms all night.

At daylight on Saturday, May 2d, after consultation with General Howard, commanding the Eleventh Corps, which was on his right, General Birney occupied the line south of the road, through the woods, and connected with the left of the Eleventh Corps, and at this time General Graham coming up with his brigade, the division was again complete. About eight o'clock, Birney ascertained that a continuous column of infantry, with trains and ambulances, was passing to the right, along his front. Ordering up a section of Clark's rifled battery, he opened upon the column. The shots fell with telling effect, causing the column to double-quick, and throwing it into confusion. The other section of the battery was then ordered forward, and soon stopped the further passage of the trains. The rest of this movement is well-described by T. M. Cook, Esq., the *New York Herald* correspondent, in a letter written from the scene of action, and published May 7th, 1863:—

"When the train was stopped, General Sickles conceived the idea of obtaining possession of the road over which it had been moving, and thus preventing any further operations of the enemy in that direction. With this purpose in view he ordered Birney to advance and take possession of the hill on the south side of the ravine running out back from the farm, and opposite to the heights over which the road occupied by the rebels ran. The Berdan Sharpshooters were placed in the advance of this movement, supported by the Twentieth Indiana regiment. These deployed as skirmishers, advanced across the farm, and then up the hill through a densely tangled mass of underbrush, skirmishing with the enemy at every step, who were found to be in considerable force on the slope as well as on the summit. As soon as the skirmishers had crossed the field, the main column was ordered to advance, General Birney placing himself at their head. Before crossing Scott's run, it became necessary to throw a bridge across it, in case artillery should be needed on the heights. This work was so rapidly done by the sappers and miners of Graham's brigade as to cause but a few minutes delay, and before the enemy could prepare for them the whole force was on the top of the hill. The summit was found to be covered with a bushy second growth of timber that was extremely difficult of passage, and rendered observation entirely out of the question. The force was liable to be ambuscaded at every moment in this tangled thicket. There was, it is true, a little winding country road leading through this brush, but nothing more, and that scarcely wide enough for an ox-cart to pass through. Still the column was pushed forward, constantly skirmishing with and driving back the enemy, until at last they came upon a system of rifle-pits, in which the enemy made a desperate stand. At this point, too, the enemy were strengthened by a field battery, planted at some point back, which our forces could not then discover, and from which they continued to throw shells into the woods, though, fortunately, hurting no one. Still the shelling was excessively annoying, and a battery was ordered up to reply to it. Lieutenant Turnbull's battery, United States artillery, and one section of Captain Randolph's First Rhode Island battery, were quickly in position three-quarters of a mile out on the little road over the hill, and entered into a brisk duel with the rebel artillery, though neither party was able to see the other. Unfortunately, when this battery was ordered up the hill there was no time allowed it to procure a supply of ammunition. It could, therefore, work but a short time, and in twenty minutes was obliged to retire to replenish its caissons. During the short time it was engaged six of its men were more or less wounded.

"At this juncture General Birney ordered a charge upon

the rebel rifle-pits, which were quickly cleared, about a hundred of their occupants falling into our hands as prisoners. With the annoyance of musketry thus stopped, our men found less difficulty in advancing, the enemy's artillery doing but little damage to us. But even this was destined to be quickly ended. Colonel Berdan had worked his little sharpshooter brigade close up to the battery under cover of the bushes, when, ascertaining its exact position, he disposed his little force to capture it. Dividing them quietly into three parties, he moved a party forward to either side of the battery, and then charged it from in front with the third party, himself leading them. The battery was supported by the Twenty-eighth Georgia regiment, all of whom that were to be seen, about two hundred and seventy in number, threw down their arms at the first challenge to surrender, and were marched to the rear as prisoners. In the excitement of securing so considerable a body of prisoners, the battery was for the moment lost sight of, an opportunity which the rebel gunners improved to fly, taking every thing with them but a single caisson.

"We had now reached the extreme brow of the hill, and had driven the rebels back fully a mile. We had obtained a commanding position, overlooking the opposite range, across which the rebel road ran. At this point there was quite an opening in the timber and a large frame building, recently erected by the rebels for a foundry, at which it was evident they had recently been casting shot and shell, manufacturing gun-carriages, limbers and caissons, and doing other handy jobs in that line essential to warfare. It was a good point gained, and one that ought to have been held. But it was by no means a pleasant position at that particular time. The woods covering the face of the opposite hills were filled with rebel sharpshooters, who lost no opportunity of picking off any one who chanced to show himself. Berdan posted a portion of his famous command about the foundry and behind the trees in that vicinity, and commenced duelling at long range—a practice in which, if the rebels did not suffer more than we, their loss was very immaterial.

"Another party of our sharpshooters, together with the Twentieth Indiana, moved forward, still pressing on farther away from our main line. They skirmished along up the easterly slope of the hill we had gained until the road crossed the ravine and entered the road that had been used by the enemy, at a little white farmhouse full half a mile from the foundry. This was the limit that it was desirable to reach at that time, and General Birney ordered Colonel Hayman to advance his brigade—the third—to that position. A battery was also ordered up to take position at the foundry and shell the opposite woods. General Sickles, at this time, was present on the hill, directing operations generally, and while standing by the foundry in conversation with General Birney had a very narrow escape. The two generals, with a squad of their respective staffs, were standing out upon the brow of the hill in plain sight of the rebels, when one of their sharpshooters marked them and fired. The ball whizzed through between the two generals, narrowly escaping General Sickles, as indicated by the sensible puff of wind it produced in passing.

"During the progress of the movements that I have

attempted to describe above, General Sickles had kept General Hooker constantly acquainted with his position and advances. The latter frequently, during the afternoon, sent up word that Sickles was going too fast and venturing too far; he should move slower. General Sickles had applied for support for his movements, but had not succeeded in getting any, even from his own corps, until the eleventh hour, when permission was accorded him to advance General Whipple to General Birney's support. Application had been made to have General Berry also moved up; but General Hooker replied that the enemy were massing a strong force in front of the headquarters, and he needed Berry in that vicinity in case of an attack. But when it was reported at headquarters that Birney had really gained the heights and was in possession of so desirable a situation, General Hooker immediately consented to ordering up all the support needed.

"The Eleventh Corps, lying in the rear of Birney's right, was thereupon directed to advance and join its left flank to Birney's right, and the Twelfth Corps was also ordered up on the left. General Whipple, who had arrived on the ground with his division, was directed to charge simultaneously with the others, moving up the ravine. General Williams' division of the Twelfth Corps, in moving up, would come directly on to the hill from which Birney had been so much annoyed by sharpshooters. There appeared to be no greater obstacle in their way than this, and the column was deployed at the crossing of Scott's creek and moved into the woods, taking proper precautions in keeping a good line of skirmishers in advance. They had not advanced a hundred yards into the woods when their skirmishers became engaged with those of the enemy, the latter, however, gradually falling back. The main line pressed hard on after the skirmishers, keeping always within close supporting distance, although the nature of the country was the most impracticable that could be selected for the advance of a column in line of battle. But still they went forward, and had advanced about half way up the hill, when they came face to face with the rebels drawn up in two lines of great strength. An engagement ensued at once, our men charging boldly on the rebel lines. Then commenced the first real action of the day. The enemy held their ground obstinately, replying to volley with volley, and contesting the ground with perfect desperation.

Wherever we came in contact with them they outnumbered us greatly; but the brave men who attacked them never stopped to consider the heavy odds that existed against them. Rapidly they loaded and quickly fired their pieces, taking care always that their aim was not wild, but effective. Under their sure aim, the enemy quailed, and finally the first line gave way and fell back upon the second. Our men gave a shout of triumph and pressed on anew, determined to carry the heights. But the enemy were as determined to hold them, and with a powerful line of fresh troops their advantages were greatly increased. Our men, borne down with heat and fatigue, began to show evidences of faltering, which was promptly observed by their commander, and the column was ordered to fall back. It was manifestly an impossibility for them to carry the position in that condition by a direct attack, and to hold the men under fire after they were persuaded of their inability to accomplish the task would only prove disastrous. By ordering them back at the first indication of discouragement, General Williams displayed his good generalship and saved his fine division, bringing them off in the most perfect good order. It is probable that, had Whipple been a little more prompt in advancing his column upon Williams' right, both divisions would have accomplished the task assigned them. But for some unexplained reason Whipple's division did not get fairly in motion before Williams was hotly engaged, and the enemy were enabled to throw all their available force in that vicinity directly in his front; and afterwards, when Williams had retired and Whipple advanced, the same powerful combination of force met him and drove him back.

"But the climax of the disaster was not yet reached. The Eleventh Corps had been ordered to advance on the right of Birney, and moved forward to take the position assigned to them on Birney's flank. One brigade succeeded in getting up the hill, and reported, by its commander, to General Birney. The rest of the corps met the enemy in force when about two-thirds of the distance up. Here they had a short engagement, in which it does not appear that they had even so large a force to contend against as that which Williams, with his single division, had fought so bravely. Headed by their commander, the gallant Howard, the German corps charged boldly up to the rebel lines. Here they were met, as the rebels always meet their foe, with shouts of defiance and derision, a determined front and a heavy fire of musketry. The German regiments returned the fire for a short time with spirit, manifesting a disposition to fight valiantly. But at the time when all the encouragement to the men was needed that could be given, then some officer of the division (one at least, as I am informed) fell back to the rear, leaving the men to fight alone. At the same time General Devens, commanding the first division, was unhorsed and badly wounded in his foot by a musket ball. Thus losing at a critical moment the inspiriting influence of the immediate presence of their commanders, the men began to falter, then to fall back, and finally broke in a complete rout. General Howard boldly threw himself into the breach and attempted to rally the shattered columns; but his efforts were perfectly futile. The men were panic-stricken, and no power on earth could rally them in the face of the enemy. Information of the catastrophe was promptly communicated to General Sickles, who thus had a moment given him to prepare for the shock he instantly apprehended his column must suffer. The high land of the little farm that formed the base of his operations was parked full of artillery and cavalry—nearly all the artillery of the Third Corps, together with Pleasanton's cavalry, being crowded into that little fifty-acre enclosure. But Sickles was not to be thrown off his guard by a trifle, and any thing short of a complete defeat seemed to be considered by him in the light of a trifle. With the coolness and skill of a veteran of a hundred campaigns, he set to work making his dispositions. He had not a single regiment within his reach to support his artillery; Whipple was falling back, and must meet the approaching stampede with his own force in retreat; Birney was far out in the advance, in imminent danger of being completely surrounded and annihilated; the rebel forces were pressing hard upon the flying Germans, who could only escape by rushing across his lines, with every prospect of communicating the panic to them. It was a critical moment indeed, and one that might well stagger even the bravest-hearted. But it did not stagger the citizen soldier. Calling to one after another of his staff, he sent them all off, lest any should fail of getting through, to warn Birney of his danger and order him to fall back. Then turning to General Pleasanton, he directed him to take charge of the artillery, and train it all upon the woods encircling the field, and support it with his cavalry, to hold the rebels in check should they come on him, and himself dashed off to meet Whipple, then just emerging from the woods in the bottom land. He had scarcely turned his horse about when the flying Germans came dashing over the fields in crowds, meeting the head of Whipple's column and stampeding through his lines, running as only men do run when convinced that sure destruction is awaiting them. At the same moment large masses of the rebel infantry came dashing through the woods, on the north and west, close up to the field, and opened a tremendous fire of musketry into the confused mass of men and animals. To add to the confusion and terror of the occasion, night was rapidly approaching and darkness was beginning to obscure all things.

"I must frankly confess that I have no ability to do justice to the scene that followed. It was my lot to be in the centre of that field when the panic burst upon it. May I never be a witness to another such scene. On one hand was a solid column of infantry retreating at double quick from the face of the enemy, who were already crowding their rear; on the other was a dense mass of beings who had lost their reasoning faculties, and were flying from a thousand fancied dangers, as well as from the real danger that crowded so close upon them, aggravating the fearfulness of their situation by the very precipitancy with which they were seeking to escape from it. On the hill were ten thousand of the enemy, pouring their murderous volleys in upon us, yelling and hooting, to increase the alarm and confusion; hundreds of cavalry horses, left riderless at the first discharge from the rebels, were dashing frantically about in all directions; a score of batteries of artillery were thrown into disorder, some, properly manned, seeking to gain positions for effective duty, and others flying from the field; battery-wagons, ambulances, horses, men, cannon, caissons, all jumbled and tumbled together in an apparently inextricable mass, and that murderous fire still pouring in upon them. To add to the terror of the occasion, there was but one means of escape from the field, and that through a little narrow neck or ravine washed out by Scott's creek. Towards this the confused mass plunged headlong. For a moment it seemed as if no power could avert the frightful calamity that threatened the entire army. That neck passed, and this panic-stricken, disordered body of men and animals, permitted to pass down through the other corps of the army, our destruction was sure. But in the midst of that wildest alarm there was a cool head. That threatened calamity was averted by the determined self-possession of Major-general Daniel E. Sickles.

Spurring his horse forward he forced his way through the tangled mass and entered this narrow neck. Across this neck there runs a strong brick wall, behind which the forces of Generals Williams and Berry had already thrown themselves preparatory to meeting the enemy. On one flank of the wall was the deeply sunken bed of the creek, impassable for any species of vehicle, and scarcely safe for men. At the upper end of the wall was a narrow gateway, the only opening to be found. To this point General Sickles picked his way, and there, drawing his sword, blocked the passage with himself and horse. On came the panic-stricken crowd, terrified artillery riders spurring and lashing their horses to their utmost; riderless horses dashing along regardless of all obstacles; ambulances upsetting and being dashed to pieces against trees and stumps; men flying and crying with alarm—a perfect torrent of passion, apparently uncontrollable. But against all the brave General threw himself, and, by his determined action, brought the first heavy mass—a cannon drawn by six horses, well-mounted—to a halt, and blockaded the passage. Others dashed up behind and crowded upon the first, their drivers cursing and swearing and calling to the foremost to go on. The loose horses jumped the stone wall, and the flying men scrambled over it, utterly oblivious to the fact that the opposite side was crowded with men whose lives were thus doubly endangered. But by the blockade of the main passage the stampede of the artillery and cavalry had been principally checked. Once halted, reason began to return to those who had previously lost it, and much of the artillery, properly manned, was quickly brought back upon the field.

"In the meantime, Pleasanton, in obedience to the orders received from General Sickles, had mustered two or three of the batteries, and was busily employed pouring grape and canister into the woods that were filled with the rebels. Every moment his effective force of pieces was increased by cannoniers recovering from their fright and returning to duty, so that, by the time the stampede was finally checked, he had at least twenty-five pieces bearing directly upon the enemy in all directions about the field, and at so close a range that every discharge took effect, not upon one or two, but upon dozens. The slaughter here must have been beyond count. We have reason to believe that nearly the whole, if not the entire body, of Hill's force was in the attack upon that little field, which must have filled the woods. Such an incessant fire from so many pieces, and into so dense a mass, could not have produced any ordinary limit of a slaughter. But it being now quite dark, and as we never regained entire possession of the woods, where the enemy were the thickest, we have no means of knowing how great the slaughter was. It was sufficient to know that the enemy was held in check, and Sickles' gallant corps had an opportunity to rally from the disastrous effects of the shameful stampede of the Eleventh Corps.

"Let me here finish with the Eleventh Corps. They did not all fly across Sickles' line. They dispersed and ran in all directions, regardless of the order of their going. They all seemed possessed with an instinctive idea of the shortest and most direct line from the point whence they started to the United States ford, and the majority of them did not stop until they had reached the ford. Many of them, on reaching the river, dashed in and swam to the north side, and are supposed to be running yet. As soon as General Hooker heard of the panic, he established a line of guards across the roads and stopped all who were to be seen upon the highways; but by far the greater portion never thought of the roads, but dashed on through the woods until they reached the river. It was no worse with privates than with officers. The stampede was universal; the disgrace general. The fugitives were picked up the next day wherever found, and the corps was reformed, but has not since been taken into action.

"In the midst of the confusion incident to this panic the brave Birney and his gallant division have been forgotten. Almost simultaneously with the reception of the information sent him by General Sickles of the rout of his supports on the right, he began to have practical evidence of it; and before he could prepare to retire his force, he found his line of retreat cut off by the repossession by the rebels of the road by which he had advanced. In this dilemma he had no other recourse but to make a road out. His column was therefore ordered to leave the lane and move quietly down into the ravine. This was successfully accomplished, even the battery that had been taken up to the foundry being brought down the hill. In the ravine he had a slight skirmish with a portion of the rebels who had been pursuing Whipple, put them to flight, and then moved his column out through the ravine in the most perfect order."

At midnight of Friday, May 2d, General Birney received

an order from General Sickles to make the necessary dispositions to drive the enemy from the woods in his front, and retake the plank road and earthworks near it. Ward's brigade was placed in the advance, and Hayman's in support, one hundred yards to the rear. General Birney ordered every piece to be uncapped, and none discharged until the plank road was reached. Upon the left a wide road had been cut perpendicular to the plank road, along which the Fortieth New York, the Seventeenth Maine, and the Sixty-third Pennsylvania marched by column of companies. Slowly and cautiously the men moved along this road at midnight. No officer uttered words of encouragement; no drum beat; no colors waved; no cheer rose from the ranks; not a sound could be heard except the footsteps along the new-made road, as they advanced to the intrenchments the enemy had deliberately thrown up. The pale light of the moon, beaming at intervals from between the clouds, increased the effect of the scene and photographed it upon the memories of those who beheld it, in characters never to be forgotten.

Add to this the flash of the guns from the batteries stationed in the rear of the line, which, in the early part of the evening, concentrated their fire upon a point on the plank road to deceive the enemy as to the real character of the movement. As the batteries belched forth their flames and lighted up the landscape with a death-like hue, which the flash of powder at night always imparts to surrounding objects, the scene was grand beyond description.

At a given signal the fire of the batteries ceased, the men rushed forward upon the intrenchments, and their object was accomplished. The enemy abandoned the position without a struggle, and soldiers and officers rested upon their arms until daylight.

The importance of this success is well described by the army correspondent of the *Boston Journal*, who, under date of May 7th, says: "A hundred shots a minute were thundered from those thirty cannon—one unbroken roll of thunder, sweeping away the rebels as a housewife an army of insects into the fire! They quailed, halted, fell back—the torrent was stemmed. The grand movement of Jackson had been checked. Coolness, nerve, pluck, endurance, had won the day, and apparently had turned the tide of destiny. It was a fierce and successful assault. Our men recovered a portion of the lost ground, and gave Hooker time to reform his line for the great contest of Sunday."

The loss the rebels sustained by this attack, in killed, wounded and prisoners, in loss of trains and stores, was, in their estimation, insignificant compared with the loss they suffered in the death of General Jackson, generally known as "Stonewall Jackson." According to the *Richmond Enquirer*, General Jackson was in command of the line in Birney's front. When he was wounded, on Saturday night, May 2d, General A. P. Hill assumed command of his corps, "but he in turn being compelled to quit the field, with a flesh-wound, the command devolved upon General Rhodes." This arrangement, it appears, did not suit the enemy, for the correspondent of the *Enquirer* goes on to say that "General Stuart was at once sent for, and on his arrival upon the field assumed control of the movement of Jackson's corps." Thus this corps had, during the midnight attack, four different commanders. The loss the enemy sustained by Jackson's death, according to the same correspondent, was keenly felt by General Lee. The messenger who carried him the information of Jackson's misfortune found him at four o'clock in the morning on a bed of straw, and when he was told of what had happened he exclaimed, "Thank God it is no worse! God be praised that he is still alive! *Any victory is a dear one that deprives us of the services of Jackson, even for a short time.*"

It is claimed that Jackson was wounded accidentally, by one of his own men. This may be so. It is possible that the truth may never be known, but of one thing there is no doubt: the hand that fired the gun that wounded Jackson, whether that of a friend or of a foe, would probably have been quiet on May 2, 1863, had it not been for the midnight attack which has just been described.

There was still work for the division to do, and on Sunday morning, at daylight, though the men had not had more than two hours rest, they were again on the march. While changing their position, Graham's brigade was attacked by the enemy with both infantry and artillery. But this attack did not prevent the veterans from falling back in good order. The rest of the story is well told by the correspondent of the *New York Herald*, already alluded to, who was an eye-witness of the movements he described.

"A little before sunrise, while General Sickles was removing his two divisions, the enemy fell upon him in great force, the attack coming from the woods on the northwest of the field. The bulk of the corps had been withdrawn from the field, and were already in position at the designated point. A single brigade each of Birney's and Whipple's division remained, and these set their faces bravely towards the enemy, and returned the fire which was so unceremoniously poured upon them.

"Simultaneously with this attack, the rebels pushed on down the plank road and fell upon Berry's division at the edge of the woods, and then upon French, lying on Berry's right flank, and almost in a moment the fighting became general and intensely hot all along the entire left wing of the army. The position in which the two divisions of Sickles' corps were placed, so far in advance of the rest of the army, and with no breastworks to shelter them, was delicate in the extreme. The enemy, for the first time, brought up several pieces of field artillery, with which they opened upon that little body of brave men with a vigor that threatened their annihilation. They were assailed by not less than twenty thousand of the enemy, against whom they could oppose scarcely more than five thousand men in both brigades combined. Fortunately there were one or two batteries yet remaining on the field, which were so efficiently worked as to check the advance of the rebels. Gallantly they fought, many of their number falling upon the field under the merciless fire of the sheltered foe; but they would not run, however severe that fire might be. But it was impossible that they could stand long against such odds as assailed them here. For half an hour they held their ground, and then fell back in good order to the shelter of the stone wall that divides this field from the Chancellorsville opening, dragging their cannon after them. And here they made another glorious stand. If some of them were left upon the upper field, ten times the number of the foe, who now advanced from his shelter and occupied the ground they had vacated, were laid there to keep them company. The position was now changed. The weaker party had the shelter, while the stronger was forced to fight in the open field. And coming into this field the rebels also exposed themselves to a most severe raking from several field batteries planted on the other side of the neck, close by the position of Whipple's division. It was truly astonishing how lavish they were of human life and blood. Regiment after regiment was completely swept away by our musketry and the grape and canister of our artillery, and yet fresh regiments were as often pushed forward to take their places. At last, gaining possession of the woods on the right of the stone wall, they got an enfilading fire upon our little band of heroes, who were compelled to abandon their position. But if the enemy had driven them back it had cost him dearly. The little field was strewn all over with the mangled corpses of the slain rebels, telling the silent story of the desperation of the struggle.

"The determined obstinacy of this little band of two small brigades, in holding the rebels more than an hour in check, had given General Hooker opportunity to perfect the formation of his main line of battle on the line he had intended to take, and with the exception of these two brigades, who were too much exhausted to renew the action immediately, the line was formed precisely as desired. The two brigades which had thus far done the severe fighting fell back to the rear, leaving the field open for the enemy to advance up to our rifle pits.

"Along the rear of the line of infantry we had a large number of field batteries planted. These were protected by earthworks which had been thrown up during the previous evening and night. Our front line of battle was formed in rifle pits and behind breastworks of timber and brush, hastily thrown up, but affording some shelter to the men. The second or reserve line lay upon the open field, and was intended to advance to the breastworks when the first line should become exhausted. The line was formed upon either side of the plank road leading to Orange Court House, and close up to the woods. We had a section of Dimmick's famous battery planted directly in this road on a line with our reserves, which swept the road to prevent the enemy advancing down it. But the enemy had also brought around a quantity of field artillery, with which they opened upon Captain Dimmick with great earnestness. The duel fought between these batteries was a hard one. The brave Dimmick fell during its progress, and many of his gunners were carried wounded to the rear.

"But the enemy had advanced through the woods close up to our lines, and were attacking us in great force, despite our artillery. We filled the woods with shell, crossing fires in all directions, but still the masses of the enemy crowded on. It seemed as if they were a dense mob, those in the rear being ignorant of the carnage going on in front, crowding their companions on to sure destruction. They appeared in front of our lines for at least a mile, along the front of the entire third and second corps, coming up in dense masses, climbing over the heaps of the fallen, firing heavy volleys, and going down among the slain as the response broke from our ranks. It was frightful to contemplate the slaughter to which these men were forced. Whole brigades were swept away in the determined effort to force our lines, and still other brigades sprang up to take their places. And so they fought us, and so we continued to fight, until the cartridge boxes of our men began to grow light, and their powers of endurance to flag under the constant exertion.

"In this frightful life-and-death-struggle the whole plain of Chancellorsville was swept by the missiles of one or the other party, and, heart-sick and weary of witnessing such sacrifices of human life, I turned my horse's head away and moved down the road towards the ford. And here other scenes equally affecting met my eye. Long trains of ambulances were continually coming down the road, depositing their loads of suffering, mangled men at impromptu hospitals, hastily fitted up beneath the shelter of the woods, where a large force of surgeons was busily occupied in dressing the wounds. The road swarmed with those not sufficiently wounded to require carriage in an ambulance, yet for whose sufferings, as they went hobbling, groaning along, the stoutest-hearted must bleed.

"And still the carnage went on. It was nine o'clock. Since five o'clock that deafening, horrible roar of musketry had known no cessation, and the loud booming of a hundred cannon sent the sound only to a greater distance without adding to its volume. And yet our men held their position. Could human endurance stand more? They, too, were suffering; not slain so lavishly as the enemy, because sheltered, but their ranks were sensibly thinning. Half-past nine o'clock—our column is growing weak; ten o'clock—the work of death still goes on. Twenty thousand brave men have been killed or wounded during the past five hours—four thousand an hour! The ratio of deaths to the simply wounded was never equalled in war. We mowed the enemy down by brigades. Could we endure the exertion long enough, even though they did so greatly outnumber us, we could finally destroy them. But our men were exhausted.

"Half-past ten o'clock—our ranks are broken. From sheer fatigue our men have given way. One entrance into those rifle pits and the still dense masses of the enemy make but short work of clearing them. But though repulsed, we are not disordered. Like veterans, every column falls back in order, and the line is re-established at the old brick house, Chancellorsville.

"The old house had been taken early in the battle for a hospital, and was now crowded with wounded. Our lines were reformed in front of it, to hold, if possible, the cross roads. The enemy halted on the edge of the woods, as if to breathe, and there was a moment of silence. That horrible roar had ceased. The quiet was painful. But it lasts only a few seconds. The enemy brought forward his guns and commenced to shell our new position.

"Here General Hooker met with a very narrow escape. He was standing on the porch of the old brick house, leaning against one of the pillars, when a shell struck the pillar, shattering it to splinters. The general was thrown down and somewhat stunned, but was otherwise unhurt. He had been on the field throughout the battle, everywhere present where the fight was the hottest, encouraging his men to renewed efforts, and had escaped without a scratch. His safety seemed miraculous.

"The vigorous shelling of the enemy riddled that old mansion in all directions, and some of the wounded whose wounds had already been dressed were killed. At last an incendiary shell burst within the building, and it soon was enveloped in flames.

"Between eleven and twelve o'clock the enemy mustered their forces and renewed the assault. They came down upon us in solid masses, against which it seemed like folly for our comparatively small force, wearied and exhausted as they were, to contend. But they accepted the challenge of battle and, though overpowered, fought like heroes, contesting every inch of ground back to the White House, half a mile on the road to the ford, and here the contest ceased. Here we had a powerful array of artillery that drove the rebels back as rapidly as they advanced, and they were glad to accept the opportunity of resting from the fierce struggle."

This was the end of the fighting at Chancellorsville. Our troops, however, still retained possession of the line they had reached, and the first division of the Third Corps, after intrenching themselves as well as they could with the tools at their command, were exposed to the fire of sharpshooters and artillery of the enemy until Wednesday at four o'clock, A. M., when, in obedience to orders, they started for their former camps, near Falmouth, where they remained until they followed General Lee into Pennsylvania, and did their full share of the fighting at the memorable battle of Gettysburg.

General Birney's conduct during the battle of Chancellorsville and the movements which it involved, won the most unqualified praise from all who knew what he had done, from subordinates as well as superiors. Every movement of which he had charge was a success, and he did his entire duty faithfully and without hesitation. In a few days he was rewarded with promotion to the rank of major-general, to rank from May 5, 1863. Why this date was chosen instead of May 2d, the date of Major-general Berry's death, whose place Birney was appointed to fill, the uninitiated reader may be unable to explain, but when he is told that, by this postponement, officers of the regular army, whose promotions were to rank from Chancellorsville, would thus take precedence of Birney, he can understand the reason. This marked injustice for a time depressed Birney, but his sense of duty and love for the cause he had espoused soon gained the ascendancy, and all other motives were subordinate to these. He had not gone into the army for place or for promotion, nor did he ever seek either, or permit his friends to do so, until he considered that he was fully up to the standard by which others were judged. He asked only for fair play and the rank to which his services entitled him. These he eventually obtained by his own merits, and without the intervention of friends.

INCIDENTS OF CHANCELLORSVILLE.

THE following is extracted from the *Philadelphia Inquirer* of June 19, 1863:—

"THE GENERAL AND THE DRUMMER BOY.—Last winter the wife of one of our Philadelphia generals, who was with her husband in camp, paid daily visits to his division hospital. She brought to her husband's attention the needs of his men, and he was prompt to send to Washington for such articles of comfort as could not be obtained nearer. Among those cases which especially interested her was that of a little drummer boy, about sixteen years of age, who was lying very low with typhoid fever, and who, but for a woman's presence and attention, might never have been restored to health again. The young lad appreciated the cooling drinks and kind nursing, and became devotedly attached to the general's wife. She returned to her home previous to the battle, scarce expecting ever to hear from her little charge again. But after the battle of Chancellorsville, this humane general visited his hospital to look after his wounded men, and was greeted by the bright face of the lad, who lay on his back in his cot, as he said:—

"'Oh, general! how glad I am to see you again!'

"'Why, are *you* here?' answered the general; 'how came that about?'

"'I went into the fight, general; I could not help it, and I lost one of my legs; but that is nothing now that you are safe. Why, we thought that we had lost you at one time.'

"Is it any wonder that at such a manifestation of self-forgetfulness and heroism, the general was obliged to turn away his head to hide his emotion? Brave as a lion, collected under all circumstances, singularly reticent, he was not equal to that emergency. General Birney will not thank us for this notice, for he is not an ostentatious man; but the spirit manifested, creditable alike to the general and the drummer boy, should be recorded for others to emulate and to stimulate the women of the country to work early and late for the comfort of our brave soldiers. Only those who have visited the field hospitals can testify to the destitution that too often exists there.

"At this hour the women of Philadelphia have an urgent call made upon them. The comforts and luxuries that they provide may minister to the necessities of their own husbands, sons, or brothers. Yesterday demands were made upon the Women's Pennsylvania Branch of the United States Sanitary Commission, No. 1307 Chestnut street, for medicines, stimulants, nourishing food, etc., etc., to be sent without delay to the border. Special agents have already been despatched by them."

Soon after the battle of Chancellorsville General Birney and some of his friends in Philadelphia, at their own expense, had manufactured about five hundred "Kearny Crosses," for presentation to non-commissioned officers and men who had distinguished themselves in battles in which the division had been engaged. These were distributed by a General Order, issued May 16, 1863, which is published at length in the Appendix. The following description of this presentation is extracted from the army correspondence of the *New York Herald* of May 29th, under date of May 28th:—

"A very interesting ceremony occurred in General Birney's (late Kearny's) division, of General Sickles' corps, yesterday afternoon, being the presentation of upwards of four hundred medals to non-commissioned officers and privates of the division, distinguished for meritorious services in the battle of Chancellorsville.

"The presentation was made in the presence of the entire division, drawn up in a hollow square. Among the guests present were a number of distinguished Philadelphians, influential in getting the medals, together with Generals Sickles, Meade and Birney, with their staffs; a delegation from the staff of General Hooker and Brigadier-generals Humphreys, Graham, Crawford and Tyler, with their respective staff-officers.

"The presentation speech was made by General Sickles, and was pronounced one of the happiest impromptu efforts of the season.

"After the presentation of the medals, a beautiful stand of colors (the gift of the city of New York) was presented to the Thirty-eighth New York volunteers, whose term of service is about to expire. They were presented in an appropriate speech by Major-general Birney, which was replied to by Colonel De Trobriand."

GETTYSBURG.

THE period is now approached when the rebel army, under General Lee, made the grandest effort it attempted during the war. So long as American history continues to be written and read, the battle of Gettysburg and the gigantic movements which preceded it will stand forth in the panorama of events as the culminating point of the war. Had it resulted in the defeat of the Union forces, Philadelphia would have fallen; Pennsylvania, with its immense resources, would have paid tribute to the Confederacy; the city of Washington would have been isolated from the loyal States; the fate of the city of New York would have been within the grasp of the rebel army; foreign powers would have recognized the States in rebellion as a nation, and the restoration of the Union would not have occurred during the present generation. These calamities were, under a kind Providence, averted by the gallantry of our soldiers, who, after three days of hard fighting, gained a victory, which to our country was more important in its results than the battle of Waterloo to Europe.

If the description of the battle of Gettysburg and its incidents may appear tedious to the reader, the writer's excuse is, that he viewed the movements which culminated in this great battle from the same stand-point which every loyal Philadelphian occupied. The defeat of the Army of the Potomac, at Fredericksburg and at Chancellorsville, had not only given increased impetus to the efforts of those who sustained the rebellion in the Southern States, but had emboldened the sympathizers with secession in the North, who, too cowardly to avow their sentiments openly, did all in their power to encourage those who did the bidding of Jefferson Davis. The same fiendish and diabolical feelings that nurtured the conspiracy which resulted in the assassination of Abraham Lincoln, on the 14th of April, 1865, when, with "malice towards none and with charity for all," he yielded up his spirit, a martyr to the cause of self-government and human rights, prompted certain men in the city of Philadelphia, possessed of the spirit, but not the daring of the assassin who took away the life of the President, to publish, in one of the daily journals of that city, a list of the names, the residences, and the estimated estates of the leading Union men of the city, for the information of General Lee and his subordinates. It was very natural that the Union men of Philadelphia watched with anxiety the progress of General Lee and his army, when their intention of making Pennsylvania the theatre of action became manifest. For obvious reasons the Government withheld from the country at large all knowledge of the movements of the Army of the Potomac, and it was not until the first day of the battle of Gettysburg that the rebel army and the citizens of Pennsylvania discovered, simultaneously, the presence of our veteran soldiers to arrest the movement of the invader.

Since the battle of Gettysburg it has been customary, in other States, to taunt the citizens of Pennsylvania with the inefficiency of their State government, during this invasion, and to remind them, in terms not very flattering nor complimentary, that regiments of militia from other States came to their aid, before their own militiamen were in the field. For this, however, the citizens of Pennsylvania, as such, are not responsible. They did as men their full duty, but were not properly directed. Though at that time the rebellion had existed for more than two years, and the State of Pennsylvania had been twice invaded, the Legislature had made no provision for organizing the militia, nor did the State possess any field pieces, or arms, that could be used with safety to those who fired them, tents or equipments, for such citizens as were ready to respond to the call of the Governor. Besides this, there was mismanagement somewhere at Harrisburg. Among the first who went there and offered to the State their services, in any capacity, was a company of colored men, organized near Philadelphia. The general commanding the department, and the State authorities, both refused to receive them, and the company returned home, the men paying their own expenses. Companies of white men, both infantry, and cavalry mounted at their own expense, were, during the first few days, after the danger became apparent, sent home to Philadelphia again, because they could not be either armed or equipped. Many of these men, however, returned to Harrisburg in different organizations, and rendered such services as they were called upon to perform.

The Councils of Philadelphia, after the rebels had entered

the State, suddenly discovered that the city was without protection; and, embracing the opportunity to give some of their favorites a contract, appropriated money to be expended in fortifying the city. At some of the principal streets, within musket shot of Independence Hall, and on Lemon Hill, near Fairmount, on the east bank of the Schuylkill, earthworks were thrown up at an enormous expenditure of the public money, sufficient to have put in the field a number of regiments. As Councils, however, had neglected to make a "contract" with the rebels to march into the city by these most frequented streets, it was difficult to see how these hillocks would afford protection to a city whose natural line of defence is the banks of the Susquehanna. The action of the Army of the Potomac, however, saved Philadelphia from the necessity of relying on this sort of engineering for defence, but the earthworks still remain, beautifully sodded, and are monuments of the military knowledge of the city fathers of Philadelphia in 1863.

Though the State government may be amenable to the charge of inefficiency, and the City Councils may have been prodigal of public money during the crisis, many of the citizens of Philadelphia did their full duty. Early in May, 1863, President Lincoln had announced his intention of visiting the city on the 4th of July, as the guest of the Union League. This body was making preparations to honor him with a suitable reception and a dinner at the Academy of Music, the largest building in the city. Contributions to defray the expenses of this reception and entertainment had been made by the members. At a meeting of the League, held after the invasion was begun, the contributors unanimously placed this fund at the disposal of a committee, who expended it to organize and send forward two regiments, before the battle of Gettysburg; and who since that time have, with funds contributed by members of the League, organized and put in the field seven more regiments.

On Monday, the 15th of June, 1863, Governor Curtin issued a proclamation, apprising the citizens of Pennsylvania of the danger which threatened them, and calling upon them to take action. The response made by the First Troop of Philadelphia City Cavalry is thus described in the *Philadelphia Inquirer* of Friday, June 19th:—

"This company resolved on Tuesday, at eight P. M., to offer their services to the State. It was announced at the armory, during the meeting, that General Couch had asked that the Troop should be sent to Harrisburg, as he had not a mounted man in his command. The members who had resolved to go were at first told that they would be mounted at Harrisburg, but ascertained before midnight that this was doubtful, and accordingly resolved they would not leave the matter uncertain, but would go mounted, armed, and equipped at their own expense, and serve the State as long as they might be needed. The undress uniform which they resolved to wear, with the side-arms, etc., cost each member about three hundred dollars, but the members were determined to 'go the whole figure,' and made arrangements by which horses were purchased on Wednesday, and by five P. M. they could have started had they been able to procure transportation.

"They applied on Wednesday night to the officers of

the Pennsylvania Railroad Company, and were promptly met by the response that they could have a train at any time they might name on Thursday, and one was secured. Later in the evening they were informed by Colonel Ruff that, unless they were 'mustered in,' they could not have transportation, as he had received orders from Harrisburg during the afternoon to forward no men unless they were first mustered in. The members were willing to go at their own expense, and to serve as long as they might be wanted, under the orders of any one in command, and as they had resolved not to be mustered in, the officers in command could not offer to comply with the demand. On reporting to the members yesterday morning, they, without hesitation, resolved to pay for the train they had engaged, and if any thing should occur to prevent its use, because they were not mustered in, they determined to *ride* to Harrisburg.

"On application yesterday morning to the officers of the Railroad Company, they were told that the arrangements made the night previous would not be altered, and the train would be ready at one P. M. yesterday, at the siding near Hestonville, the question of pay being a future consideration. At eleven A. M. thirty-seven men were assembled on the lot at the rear of the Academy of Music, well mounted, armed and equipped, with cartridges in their boxes, and two days rations in their haversacks. An Adams' Express wagon, drawn by four noble horses, had been provided, and was loaded down with tents, picket ropes, valises, and provisions sufficient to last a week. At half past eleven the Troop, thus provided, rode out to

Hestonville, attended by many of the friends of the members, and by several of the 'can't-get-aways,' and reached the drove yard a few minutes before one o'clock.

"At one o'clock precisely the train came along under charge of Mr. Showers, who had come out from his office at Thirteenth and Market streets to see the boys off. The men dismounted, unsaddled their horses, put them in the cars, and, so complete were the arrangements, that in fifteen minutes the train was off, and by six P. M. yesterday as noble a set of men as ever mounted horses were in Harrisburg ready for any duty to which they may be assigned.

"Too much credit cannot be awarded M. Edward Rogers, the orderly sergeant, for the energy and intelligence he displayed in the absence of the commissioned officers of the Troop, some of whom are away in the service, and others were out of the city on business. The management of all the details—and they were not few—devolved upon him. Several members who have had experience in the service aided him most effectively, and they deserve all praise for their action in securing for the State so effective a company without a dollar of the public money being expended.

"Had it been possible to have obtained uniforms and arms, more men of the same sort could have been sent up, and the city would have seen as many troopers leave home after forty hours of preparation as went in the spring of 1861, four weeks after they first resolved to go. At least a hundred men, who have had experience in the cavalry service, and would make efficient soldiers, applied at the armory on Wednesday, and asked to be taken as recruits. It was impossible, however, to get them armed and equipped, and it was not deemed expedient to send them in any other way. Some members, who could not leave yesterday, went last night; others are yet to go, besides several recruits who have obtained arms and uniforms, and if the Troop should be needed for a week, they will number seventy-five or eighty men.

"The expenditures on Wednesday and yesterday for horses, tents, provisions, etc., amounted to about $6,500, and they will be increased should other members or recruits join the Troop in the field. It might be well for some of the Committees having in charge large funds for bounty and celebration purposes to consider whether they could not appropriate some money to repay to such soldiers their outlay. If this is not done, some of our citizens intend trying to raise a fund to be expended for keeping the horses the members now have for the use of the Troop during the war, and the members will hereafter hold themselves in readiness to march at six hours notice. If such a measure is not successful, it may well be said that Philadelphia has lost the liberality her citizens have heretofore displayed."

The suggestion made by the writer of the foregoing article was not acted upon by the citizens of Philadelphia. The entire amount expended for horses and for the subsistence of the Troop, while it was in the field, amounting to nearly twenty thousand dollars, was advanced by three members of the company. When the Troop returned home, as the efforts to make provision to keep the horses, for the use of the members during the war, were unsuccessful, they were sold, at a loss of about four thousand dollars, which was sustained by the three members who had advanced the money for their purchase. The expenditure for subsisting the Troop was subsequently refunded by the "Committee on Defence and Protection," principally through the exertions of S. A. Mercer, Esq., a prominent member of the Committee.

The recruiting for the Troop was continued until it comprised ninety men, all of whom furnished, at their own expense, their uniforms, arms and equipments. A number of efficient and experienced young men, who were unable to incur this expense, volunteered to go with the Troop. These were, within a few days, armed, uniformed, and equipped by the Government, and mounted at the expense of a number of citizens of Philadelphia. They were known as the Dana Troop, (in honor of Major-general Dana, who was then in command of Philadelphia,) and were in the service for six months.

Among other incidents of promptness may be mentioned the action of William B. Mann, Esq., for many years the efficient district attorney of the city and county of Philadelphia, who never deserted his country or his friends in an emergency. During Tuesday, the 16th of June, the day following that on which Governor Curtin issued his Proclamation, the neglect to respond to the call of the governor excited some comment. On Wednesday Mr. Mann excused himself from his duties at court, and using a table, placed in front of Independence Hall as a recruiting office, in a few hours enlisted a full company, and at two o'clock went with them to Harrisburg, where, during the emergency, and with such arms and equipments as the State had at hand, they performed provost duty.

These examples were not without their effect upon the people of Philadelphia, and regiment after regiment went forward from the city to the defence of the border. All that was needed was organization, and when this was effected thousands of the best young men of Philadelphia stepped into the ranks.

The City Troop remained in Harrisburg only long enough to rest and feed their horses, when, under orders from General Couch, they rode to Gettysburg, which was their headquarters until Friday, June 26th, when they vacated to give room to the rebel cavalry. During this time they acted as mounted scouts, under the direction of Major Haller, of the regular army, on General Couch's staff, who soon after was dismissed the service for "disloyal conduct and the utterance of disloyal sentiments." The Troop was under the immediate command of its only commissioned officer, Honorable S. J. Randall, member of Congress from the First District of Pennsylvania, who joined the company at Harrisburg. A large majority of the members had served during the "three months campaign," and by experience had learned the duties of soldiers. They performed services, and acquired information of the movements of the enemy, which were invaluable to General Couch, and were fully acknowledged by him.

The cavalry of the enemy, about two hundred strong, followed by five thousand infantry of Ewell's corps, came within sight of Gettysburg about three o'clock, P. M., of

Friday, June 26th. Their arrival had been anticipated by the Troop, and during the morning they made preparation to vacate. They made a rapid retreat towards York, in good order, saving all their baggage, with the loss of but one man, private Welsh, who was acting as an orderly to Major Haller. The major's horse was at some distance from his quarters, and Welsh, who was well mounted, insisted on Major Haller taking his horse, saying that it was better that a private should be taken prisoner than a major in the regular service. The Troop came the next morning to Columbia, and the loss of Welsh was soon known to his friends in Philadelphia. They felt considerable anxiety for his safety, as the Troop had not been mustered into the United States service, and the theory was started that its captured members would be treated as guerillas and not as prisoners of war.

On Monday, however, private Welsh returned home *via* Baltimore. After Major Haller left him he changed his uniform for citizen's clothes, and retreated from Gettysburg as fast as possible. After walking a couple of miles along a country road, he was overtaken by a farmer in a buggy, who kindly gave him "a lift;" and when the two had ridden some three miles, Welsh felt himself comparatively safe. Soon the travellers heard horses rapidly approaching, and in a few minutes two lads, mounted on the same horse, caught up with them, closely pursued by five rebel cavalrymen, who were firing their carbines. Welsh called to the boys to stop or they would be killed; they halted, and the cavalrymen soon came up, presenting a grotesque appearance, having on their heads straw bonnets, which they had confiscated at some store in Gettysburg. They soon seized the horses the boys were riding and the farmer was driving. After questioning the farmer they turned to Welsh, who represented himself to be John Merryman, a son of a farmer in the neighborhood, and located his father's house. His explanations seemed to be satisfactory to the soldiers, and they were about leaving him when one of them said, "John, give me your hat, and you can have this bonnet;" thus showing that, in 1863, some of the rebels, unlike Jeff. Davis, (who tried to escape in his wife's clothes,) preferred male to female attire.

Welsh, making a virtue of necessity, took off his hat to make the trade, and had no sooner uncovered his head when one of the "Johnnies" said: "Mr. Merryman, how long has it been since the farmers' sons in this neighborhood have had their hair cut in that style? You had better come along with us to headquarters and report."

Welsh put on the bonnet and rode back to Gettysburg. When he arrived he was taken before the colonel of a Georgia regiment, who was acting as provost marshal, and by him forwarded to General Ewell, who formerly lived in Philadelphia, and was a member of the City Troop. Welsh then gave a true account of himself, and Ewell asked him what other forces had been in Gettysburg. On being told by Welsh that the entire force consisted of the City Troop, Ewell laughed and said, "This is as good as a farce. I was informed that there was a regiment of cavalry here. If I had known who you fellows were, my men would have taken some of the starch out of you."

Welsh did not argue this point, but when asked whether

he would prefer being sent to Libby Prison, or being paroled, decided in favor of the parole. When it was made out General Ewell let him go into the town for his uniform and arms, and he returned home as quickly as possible thereafter.

The Troop reached Columbia about ten o'clock on Saturday, June 28th, where they found two regiments of militia. The next day General Early, whose command occupied York, from which he had driven the Union forces on Friday night, sent forward a part of his command to Wrightsville, on the south bank of the Susquehanna river, opposite Columbia. Our troops maintained their position until Sunday morning, when Early's men appearing at Wrightsville in large force, the City Troop burned the bridge over the Susquehanna. Preparations had been made, before the arrival of the Troop, to destroy a single span of this bridge, but, when tried, it was found that the arrangements were imperfect, and no alternative remained but to burn the entire structure. The Troop remained at Columbia under orders until after the battle of Gettysburg, when they moved to Harrisburg, and were there until about the 15th of July, when, by direction of the general commanding the department, they returned to Philadelphia, and were on duty for about twenty days before they were finally disbanded.

On Sunday, June 28th, while the members of the City Troop were burning the bridge at Wrightsville, the rebel army, divided into four parts, were encamped at Gettysburg, Chambersburg, where General Lee had his headquarters, York and near Carlisle. On this day, according to the official report of General Lee, "preparations were made to advance upon Harrisburg, but information was received that the Federal army, having crossed the Potomac, was advancing northward, and the head of the column had reached the South Mountain." The communication of General Lee with the Potomac being thus menaced, he resolved to concentrate his army on the east side of the mountain. He accordingly ordered Generals Longstreet and Hill to proceed to Gettysburg from Chambersburg, and General Ewell to advance from Carlisle, while General Early brought up his corps from York. The march, however, towards Gettysburg, by three different divisions of the rebel army, was conducted more slowly than it would have been had General Lee known more about the movements of General Hooker, who, according to General Lee's admissions in his report, had, up to this time, completely deceived him.

On the same day, President Lincoln, under some mysterious influence, which induced him to violate a rule of his life, was persuaded to "swap horses while crossing a river," and relieving General Hooker from command of the Army of the Potomac, put General Meade in his place. On the same day General Sickles, who had been absent for several weeks, joined the Third Corps at Frederick, Maryland, and resumed the command, which, during the march from Falmouth, had devolved upon General Birney.

Leaving for a few moments the march of the two armies, which subsequently were engaged in so terrible a conflict, it may be worth the reader's time to learn a couple of incidents, never before published, that transpired on the memorable Sunday which witnessed so many important events. On that day General A. P. Hill's corps was in possession of Chambersburg. General Lee was with him, and on Saturday, June 27th, an order had been issued which prevented any of the citizens of Chambersburg from procuring supplies from any of the mills in the neighborhood. On Sunday morning, a lady of Chambersburg went to General Lee's headquarters near the town, to solicit from him a modification of the order, so that the poor of Chambersburg would be able to procure their daily supplies. General Lee received her courteously, and in a frank conversation discussed the relative positions of the two armies, and the duties which devolved upon them. His fair visitor, being intent on relieving the sufferings of the poor in Chambersburg, avoided all political discussion, and eventually obtained from the general a modification of the order, and thus procured the supplies necessary for the destitute during the rebel occupation of the town. Few women would have had the moral courage to have undertaken such a mission, but to this lady nothing was impossible where the interests of others were involved.

Another incident, worthy of record, illustrates the heroic conduct of the same lady. A relative of her husband, who was in his office, a student of law, not having the fear of the enemy before his eyes, induced a companion of his to join him in a raid upon the horses and equipments of two rebel officers as they stood hitched in front of the quarters of their owners in the town. The raid was successful, and the two young men carried their prizes in safety to a farm house, about five miles distant, in an unfrequented part of the country. The same night the captors returned to Chambersburg, and the student of law returned on foot to the house of his preceptor, which, during his absence, had been occupied by a rebel general and his staff, for their headquarters. The lady to whom reference has been made was, of course, much provoked by the hardihood of the young student, but her natural wit soon suggested an expedient for his safety. He was made to exchange his clothes for those of a laborer upon the farm, and in this disguise personated one of the hired men, and, while the rebel officers were in possession of the house, pretended to do the work of a laborer. During the visit of the enemy, his mistress, to keep up the delusion, frequently reprimanded him for his laziness, and, in the presence of the rebel officers, threatened to report his alleged remissness to her husband on his return.

This ruse was completely successful, and, though one of the officers had lost his horse and equipments by the movement referred to, the culprit was not suspected. When the loss became known, the authorities of Chambersburg were compelled, by the rebel provost marshals, to pay fifteen hundred dollars, to compensate for the theft of the horses and equipments. After the enemy had evacuated Chambersburg, the authorities called upon the law student and his companion either to refund the money the town had paid or give up their prizes. The friend of our hero turned over the horse and equipments to the borough, but the law student, having in his mind what he had learned from Blackstone's "rights of persons and rights of things," from "Coke upon Littleton," and from "Fearne on *contin-*

gent remainders," stoutly refused to give up his prize. The town council, however, brought an action against him, but never pressed it to trial.

In narrating the conduct of some of the citizens of Philadelphia, and a few incidents which transpired during the rebel possession of Chambersburg, the reader may think that we have lost sight of the subject of our sketch. Begging the reader's pardon for the digression, we now return to General Birney, who, owing to the absence of General Sickles, was in command of the Third Army Corps, from the commencement of the march of the army from Falmouth until June 28th, when General Sickles resumed command at Frederick, Maryland.

General Lee began to move his army on the 3d of June, 1863, hoping to draw our troops from the advantageous position they occupied opposite Fredericksburg, and thus break up the plan of our campaign for the summer. With this hope he moved Longstreet's corps northward and ordered Ewell to follow Longstreet, leaving the corps of A. P. Hill to occupy the lines near Fredericksburg. This movement was discovered by General Hooker as soon as it was begun, and he made a counter movement, which caused the Army of the Potomac to leave their camps at Falmouth and follow General Lee. On the 9th of June a large force of Union cavalry crossed the Rappahannock at Beverly ford and attacked General Lee's cavalry, under General Stuart. After an entire day of hard fighting the rebel cavalry retired; but this defeat did not arrest the progress of General Lee's army, which moved forward as fast as it could be marched. General Hooker, however, was not idle. During the fight at Beverly ford the Union cavalry captured General Stuart's private papers, which, upon examination, disclosed his orders for an invasion of Pennsylvania. Thus the Union generals were put upon their guard, and no time was lost in moving to oppose General Lee. The account of the march up the Shenandoah must be left to those who attempt to describe, in detail, the movements of the army towards Gettysburg. The march was a forced one, and involved the loss of many men, but the end justified the means. General Birney, in a letter to the writer, dated June 17, 1863, says, "We *may* be a little late, but I think we will be up in time. The Third Corps, which I now command temporarily, is here and in position from Manassas Gap to Bull Run, covering the roads and fords to Centreville. Yesterday was a terrible day, hot and dusty; men dropped dead by the road side. I never can forget the scenes of yesterday. The country is barren of good water, and men would gather on the road side, lapping up like dogs any thing like liquid. After the column had halted, I rode some twenty miles to get the men in position and provide for their comfort. I assure you my sleep was deep last night. This morning I am again ready for the tramp, though I do not know where, and do not ask. I am satisfied to obey orders promptly, and still have implicit confidence in the ultimate success of the right. I expect General Sickles back in a few days, and will be glad to see him, for the responsibilities of a command like this, to a temporary commander, are very great."

On the 18th of June he writes as follows: "We ought

to bag all those scamps who are threatening an advance on Harrisburg and Philadelphia. I hope we will meet the City Troop. Come down and see me; we will show you some good fighting in a few days. To tell the truth, you people in Philadelphia are unnecessarily frightened. The army wishes nothing better than to meet General Lee's men."

On June 22d General Birney writes from Gum Springs, near Aldie: "We are still here. The Third Corps is alone, hourly expecting that the brave militia-men of Pennsylvania will pitch into General Lee in front. This afternoon I had a brush with Moseby's guerillas with my escort. We took eight prisoners, and sent several of them to their long account. At the time, these brave men were engaged in burning one of our trains."

This communication was the last which General Birney made to his friends, until July 14, 1863. In the mean time the battle of Gettysburg had been fought, and the Army of the Potomac had relieved the State of Pennsylvania and city of Philadelphia from all apprehension of General Lee and his followers. During the march of the Army of the Potomac, under the command of General Hooker, the army of General Lee, as well as the citizens of the loyal States, were in utter ignorance of the locality of the Army of the Potomac. General Lee's army was led to believe that the only resistance they would meet with would be the militia of Pennsylvania, and this belief led them on to spread desolation to the fertile valleys of the border counties of that State. Knowing that such a foe would be like chaff before the wind, they marched boldly to the land of promise which their leaders had described to them. The people of Pennsylvania saw the armed hosts of Lee approaching, and, not knowing the whereabouts of the Army of the Potomac, began to realize that a rebellion existed in the land.

This belief of Lee's men and the gloomy anticipations of Pennsylvanians were soon put at rest by the presence of those brave veterans under the command of General Hooker. Though Lee's army had three days the start of the Army of the Potomac, General Hooker proved himself equal to the emergency, and under his direction, between the 11th of June, the day on which its march began, and the 28th of June, when the administration "swapped horses while crossing the river,"—relieving General Hooker and putting General Meade in his place,—the Army of the Potomac performed a march unparalleled in military history. The heroism of both officers and men was never displayed so fully as upon this march, and when its details are written, by some future historian, he will give due credit to the energy of the officers and the zeal of the men. The horrors of the battle-fields of Waterloo, the Crimea, Solferino, and Magenta are insignificant compared with the sufferings which the soldiers of the Union endured on this march.

Though men dropped dead by the roadside, from want of water and the common necessaries of life, their comrades pressed onward, and at the end of the march were ready to take their place in line, and compel the enemy to retreat.

On Sunday, the 28th of June, General Hooker was relieved from command of the Army of the Potomac, and on the same day General Sickles, having met the Third Corps at Frederick, Maryland, resumed command. General Birney was thus relieved from the command of the corps and resumed command of the first division. Up to this time he had, against his will, discharged the responsibilities of a temporary command, and he hailed the return of General Sickles as a relief from duties which, for more than two weeks, he had performed with reluctance. During this day (Sunday, June 28th) and on June 29th and 30th, the movements of both armies were such as to plainly point to a great battle in Pennsylvania. The new commander of the Army of the Potomac, unable, from the necessities of the case, to change the programme which had been laid out by his predecessor, marched onward to meet General Lee, who, seeing the foe who was preparing to meet him, gathered together the three columns of his army from York, Carlisle, and Chambersburg, and concentrated them in Adams county, near the peaceful village of Gettysburg. The march on Harrisburg was abandoned, and General Lee with deliberation made his preparations for the greatest pitched battle of the war. He succeeded in concealing his movements from the commander of the Union army, but they were gradually developed by events which subsequently transpired, and culminated in the battle of Gettysburg.

On June 30th, General Reynolds, commanding the First Corps, received orders by telegraph to assume command of the right wing of the army, consisting of his own, the First Corps, the Eleventh, General Howard, and the Third, General Sickles. The command of the First Army Corps thus devolved on General Doubleday, who, in his report of the battle of Gettysburg, has given one of the most intelligible and satisfactory descriptions of that battle which has yet appeared in print. The right wing of the army, thus organized, was engaged on the morning of July 1st, and it withstood the unexpected assault of the enemy, though in superior numbers. About half past eleven General Reynolds fell a victim to the ball of a rebel sharpshooter, and the command devolved upon General Doubleday, who was doing good work on Cemetery Hill, when the gallant Hancock rode up to assume command of both the Eleventh and the First Corps. This was surrendered by General Doubleday without hesitation; but soon after General Hancock appeared on the field, orders came from General Howard—who ranked General Hancock—which conflicted with the orders in execution at the time. This occasioned some little delay and confusion; but, owing to the tact of the officers in command, the embarrassment was temporary, and our troops retired in good order to Cemetery Hill and Gettysburg.

The contest of this day, which lasted from nine and a half A. M. to four and a half P. M., was a severe struggle for position. The Union army lost in killed and wounded more than the enemy, but at the close of the struggle, thanks to the ability of Generals Doubleday and Hancock, our position at night was stronger than that of the morning, and when the next day the remaining corps of the army took position, they were able to retain it and prevent the farther advance of General Lee.

Wednesday night, July 1st, was one long to be remembered by the Army of the Potomac. From sunset to dawn the different corps, each of which constituted an army within itself, were in motion. Before midnight General Slocum arrived with the Twelfth Army Corps, and took position on the right of the First and Eleventh, occupying Culp's Hill. Before one A. M. General Sickles arrived with the Third Corps, and occupied the extreme left, immediately north of Round Top Hill. The Second Corps, which was Hancock's immediate command, came up after General Sickles, and took position on the left centre.

This was the disposition of the portion of our army which had reached Gettysburg by sunrise of Thursday, July 2d. The morning was pleasant, the air calm, and nothing denoted the struggle which took place during the afternoon. "During the early part of the day the enemy was perfectly quiet, and not a sound was heard, except the picket-firing and an occasional shot from our guns, for the purpose of feeling the whereabouts and strength of the enemy." (*Narrative of Professor Jacobs*, page 32.)

At twelve o'clock General Birney, believing the enemy to be making a movement towards the left, asked and received permission from General Sickles to send out a detachment of the First United States sharpshooters, with the Third Maine regiment as a support, under Captain J. C. Briscoe of his staff, to feel the enemy's right. These were advanced from the Peach Orchard to the Middletown road, but were driven back, with the loss of about sixty in killed and wounded, demonstrating, however, that General Birney's suspicion was correct. Birney then formed his line, with Ward on the left, resting on Broad Top, De Trobriand in the centre, and Graham on the right, in the Peach Orchard. The batteries of the division were also placed so as to support the brigades, and Birney, seeing there would be a warm contest, sent an aide to Major-general Sykes, asking for the support which had been promised.

About one A. M., on July 2d, General Meade, whose headquarters had been at Taneytown, arrived for the first time on the battle-ground, having on the 1st of July, after hearing of the death of General Reynolds, despatched General Hancock to "represent" him on the field. When he arrived he approved of the positions selected and the disposition of the troops, which had been made under the direction of General Hancock by the different corps and division commanders. How General Meade was employed from his arrival until three P. M. of July 2d, does not appear from his official report. "About three P. M." he "rode to the extreme left, and found that Major-general Sickles had advanced" too far. "Having found Major-general Sickles," General Meade "was explaining to him that he was too far in the advance." when General Birney ordered his batteries to open fire upon the enemy, who was advancing towards him on a line parallel with the Emmetsburg road. The enemy immediately returned the fire and, bringing forward columns of infantry, made a most vigorous assault. According to General Meade, "the Third Corps sustained the shock most heroically," and, supported by the Fifth Corps under General Sykes, still kept up the contest. About four o'clock General Sickles was wounded in the leg, which was amputated upon the field. The correspondent of the *Cincinnati Gazette*, describing the battle of

Gettysburg, under date of July 8, 1863, says, in the narrative of the events of July 2d: "On a stretcher, borne by a couple of stout privates, lay General Sickles, with his right leg amputated, grim and stoical, with his cap pulled over his eyes, his hands folded across his breast, and *a cigar in his mouth.* For a man who had just lost his leg, and whose life was in imminent jeopardy, this was cool indeed."

After this disaster to General Sickles the command of the corps fell upon General Birney. The men were closely pressed, and, as General Meade says in his official report, "Notwithstanding the stubborn resistance of the Third Corps, under Major-general Birney, (Major-general Sickles having been wounded early in the action,) superiority in numbers and corps of the enemy enabling him to outflank its advanced position, General Birney was counseled to fall back and reform behind the line originally designed to be held."

The correspondent of the *New York World,* under date of July 4th, describes the fighting on the left as follows: "Silence, deep, awfully impressive, but momentary, was permitted, as if by magic, to dwell upon the field. Only the groans, unheard before, of the wounded and dying, only a murmur—a morning memory—of the breeze through the foliage, only the low rattle of preparation for what was to come, embroidered this blank stillness. Then, as the smoke beyond the village was lightly borne toward the eastward, the woods on the left were seen filled with dark masses of infantry, three columns deep, who advanced at a quick-step. Magnificent! Such a charge, by such a force,—full forty-five thousand men, under Hill and Longstreet,—even though it threatened to pierce and annihilate the Third Corps, against which it was directed, drew forth cries of admiration from all who beheld it. General Sickles and his splendid command withstood the shock with a determination that checked, but could not fully restrain it. Back, inch by inch, fighting, falling, cheering, dying, the men retired. The rebels came on more furiously, halting at intervals, pouring volleys that struck our troops down in scores. General Sickles, fighting desperately, was struck in the leg and fell. The Second Corps came to the aid of his decimated column. The battle then grew fearful. Standing up firmly against the storm, our troops, though still outnumbered, gave back shot for shot, volley for volley, almost death for death. Still the enemy was not restrained. Down he came upon our left, with a momentum that nothing could check. The rifle guns that lay before our infantry, on a knoll, were in danger of capture. General Hancock was wounded in the thigh, General Gibbon in the shoulder. The Fifth Corps, as the Third and Second wavered, went again into the breach, with such shouts and such volleys as made the rebel column tremble at last.

"Up from the valley in the rear another battery came rolling to the heights, and threw its shot into the midst of the enemy's ranks. Crash! crash! with discharges deafening, terrible, the musketry fire went on. The enemy, reforming after every failure, with wonderful celerity and firmness, still pressed up the declivity. What hideous carnage filled the minutes between the appearance of the Fifth Corps and the advance to the support of the rebel columns of another column from their right, I cannot bear to tell. Men fell, as the leaves fall in autumn, before those horrible discharges. Faltering for an instant, the rebel columns seemed about to recede before the tempest; but their officers, who could be seen through the smoke of the conflict galloping and swinging their swords along the lines, rallied them anew, and the whole line sprang forward, the next instant, as if to break through our own by mere weight of numbers. A division from the Twelfth Corps reached the scene at this instant, and at the same time Sedgwick came up with the Sixth Corps, having finished a march of nearly thirty-six consecutive hours. To what rescue they came their officers saw and told them. Weary as they were, hungry, fit to drop to slumber, the wish for victory so overcame the thought of exhaustion, that they cast themselves '*en masse*' into the battle, and went down upon the enemy with death in their weapons and cheers on their lips. The rebel's camel's back was broken by this 'feather.' His line staggered, reeled, and drifted slowly back, while the shouts of our soldiers, lifted up amid the din of musketry and over the bodies of the dead and wounded, proclaimed the completeness of the victory."

In the *New York Herald* of July 6th, under date of the 4th, appears the following:—

"Birney commanding the first division of the corps, consisting of the brigades of Ward, Graham and De Trobriand, the heroes of Chancellorsville, with Clark's New Jersey battery, were first in position and compelled to meet the first assault, alone and unsupported, although completely overwhelmed and subjected to a fire of musketry and artillery that never was equalled in this or any other war. This division held their ground bravely, and fought as veterans can fight; but they could not be expected to stand long against such fearful odds, and soon were forced to fall back. They were then joined by Ayres' division of the Fifth Corps, and Humphrey's of the Third—Berry's old division, formerly Hooker's—and being heavily reinforced with artillery, again advanced and renewed the contest. At this point the battle raged even fiercer than before. Closer and closer the lines drew together, until the engagement became an actual hand-to-hand encounter, the bayonet playing a conspicuous part, strewing the ground with Union and rebel troops in one common mass. * * * Out of this little corps nearly three thousand men were placed *hors du combat* in this short engagement. * * * The gallant Birney was twice struck by the bullets of the enemy, but happily only slightly injured. It is but proper to mention that this single action saved us the day, and for this the credit is due to General Sickles. Repeatedly he notified General Meade that the enemy were pressing to turn our left flank, which the Third Corps formed; but still he was required to hold the position, facing to the west, when he was convinced the attack was coming from the south. Against this he protested without avail, until three o'clock in the afternoon, when a council of corps commanders was called. While this council was in session, and before it had decided upon a plan of battle, the attack came. General Meade at once said to General Sickles, 'Your left is attacked; that determines our plan; make your dispositions accordingly.' "

It was during the afternoon of Thursday, July 2d, about

dusk, that General Hancock, perceiving the danger which threatened the Third Corps, gallantly dashed forward with a division of his own men, and, approaching General Birney, said:

"General, you are nearly surrounded by the enemy."

"I know it, General Hancock," replied Birney; "we have been contending against a superior force all the afternoon."

"I have seen this," said Hancock, "and have brought you these reinforcements. General Willard is in immediate command, and will fight the men."

In a few moments General Willard was shot dead, but his men, stimulated by General Hancock, moved to the position assigned them, and thus encouraged the tired men of the Third Corps to make another onset.

As stated by the correspondents already quoted, the battle at this point was more deadly than before. The rebels, disappointed in maintaining the advantage they believed they had gained, fought with renewed desperation; but to no purpose; our men did not yield an inch of ground, and when night threw her veil over the scene, the Third Corps maintained the position they had originally taken.

This day's fighting decided the battle of Gettysburg, and the Third Corps suffered more severely during this day than in any previous action. Its officers and men had met the enemy at Yorktown, Williamsburg, Fair Oaks, and during the seven days, at Manassas, Chantilly, Fredericksburg and Chancellorsville, but the hail storm of rebel shot and bullet had never fallen upon them so effectually as at Gettysburg, on Thursday, the 2d day of July, 1863. Thinned by previous battles, they went into the action about eight thousand strong, though in Fredericksburg in December, 1862, they numbered between sixteen and seventeen thousand, officers and men. After the battle of Gettysburg they could not muster more than four thousand. During the action of July 2d, the losses in Birney's division alone, in killed, wounded, and missing, were as follows:—

The first brigade, General Graham, ...	735
The second brigade, General Ward, ...	763
The third brigade, General De Trobriand, . . .	490
Total, ...	1,988

During the night of July 2d, the Third Corps rested on their arms, and though ready the next day to renew the contest, they took no active part. They were moved up under the heavy artillery fire to support General Newton, commanding a part of the First Corps, but the enemy was repulsed without their co-operation.

In the report of the Secretary of the Sanitary Commis sion, of the operations of the Commission, during and after the battle of Gettysburg, J. H. Douglas, the associate Secretary, writes: "The Third Corps hospital was on high ground, south of Swartz's house, about one hundred rods above the junction of White's creek with Rock creek, on Schwitzel's farm; it contained two thousand five hundred and fifty wounded." Besides the losses we have enumerated, not only did General Sickles lose a leg, but Brigadier-general Graham, commanding the first brigade of the first division, and Lieutenant-colonel F. F. Cavada, commanding the One-hundred-and-fourteenth Pennsylvania volunteers (in the absence of Colonel Collis) were wounded and taken prisoners. They were carried to Libby Prison, where they remained until March, 1864. During his absence, Lieutenant-colonel Cavada spent his idle hours in making pen-and-pencil sketches on such scraps of paper as he could command. These sketches he and some of his companions brought away, concealed between their stockings and their boots, and Lieutenant-colonel Cavada afterwards incorporated them into a book, entitled "*Libby Life; Experiences of a Prisoner of War in Richmond, Virginia*, 1863—1864," to which the reader is referred as one of the most entertaining and fascinating books which the rebellion has created. It will long remain as the "*Picciola*" of American literature, though written without the inspiration of the little flower which inspired Saintine during his confinement; for the "Libby," though productive of animal life, was fatal to the existence of any subjects of the vegetable kingdom.

During the night of the 3d of July, General Lee retired with his forces southward, repulsed, dispirited, and thwarted in their designs to pillage and destroy the principal cities of Pennsylvania. While Lee and his commanders were making ready for the retreat, the council of corps commanders of the Union army was held at General Meade's headquarters. What transpired during this council few know except those who participated in it. If the secret history of the rebellion is ever written, the discussions of this council and the opinions of its different members will be revealed. Already a part of its deliberations have been given to the public, but the writer will not dwell on them. Their repetition would be fruitless. Whatever may have been the opinions of the different corps commanders on the night of July 3, 1863, the world acknowledges that the battle of Gettysburg was a victory for the Union arms, and for this victory the people of Pennsylvania and the citizens of Philadelphia owe the Army of the Potomac a debt they can never discharge. Every officer and soldier, whether he comes from the North, the East, or the West, has a claim upon Pennsylvania, which, for the sake of humanity, it is hoped may never be dishonored.

CAMPAIGN AFTER GETTYSBURG.

S is well known, the pursuit of Lee's army, by General Meade, was fruitless. In this pursuit the Third Corps did its share, General Birney retaining command. He, his officers, his men, and his friends considered that he was justly entitled to the command, at least until the return of General Sickles. In this opinion the commander of the Army of the Potomac did not participate. He thought the exigencies of the service demanded that the Third Corps should be increased; and it was increased, but not by filling the decimated regiments or by adding to the corps new ones. An order was issued July 12, 1863, by which the independent command of Major-general French, which had been at Harper's Ferry during the Gettysburg campaign, was consolidated with the Third Corps as the third division. From this time the spirit of the Third Corps was broken, and its hallowed associations and strong bond of union could not preserve its identity, after the old members were overwhelmed by the tide of new-comers.

One of the last acts of the officers and men of the old Third Corps proper was to contribute about five thousand dollars from their pay, to procure a testimonial for General

Sickles, their old commander. Prompted by a desire for his return, they thought the most fitting testimonial would be a carriage suitable for campaigning, four horses, and their equipments; in which they wished to see their General once more at their head. This privilege, however, was denied them, for after July 2, 1863, the day on which he was wounded, General Sickles was never assigned to a command. He received, in due time, the testimonial, and the committee having the matter in charge complimented the writer by entrusting him with the selection of the carriage. As nothing suitable could be found in the market, he had one built, which met the approval, not only of the General for whom it was intended, but of all the contributors who saw it.

After General French's command had been added to the Third Corps, as he was the ranking officer, General Birney relinquished to him the command of the corps and resumed that of the first division.

After this digression, let us follow the Third Corps in the pursuit of Lee's retreating army. This retreat was first known to the Army of the Potomac from a reconnoitering party which General Birney had sent out under command of Lieutenant J. C. Briscoe, on the morning of July 5th, the enemy, on the 4th, having simply drawn back his left flank, with the intention, as General Meade surmised, of assuming a new line. The 5th and 6th of July were employed by the Union army in succoring the wounded and burying the dead, when, this sad duty being completed, a movement was begun towards Middletown, Maryland. After halting a day at that place to provide supplies, the army moved through South Mountain, and by the 12th of July was in front of the enemy, near Williamsport. The next day was occupied in making reconnoissances and preparing for attack, but on advancing, on the morning of the 14th, it was ascertained the enemy had retired the previous night across the Potomac, by a bridge at Falling Waters and a ford at Williamsport. The Third Corps, under command of General French, continued the pursuit without success by the following march: on the 15th, through Sharpsburg to Pleasant Valley, over a portion of the battle-field of Antietam, reaching the Potomac and crossing at Harper's Ferry on the evening of the 17th; on the 18th, to the vicinity of Snicker's Gap; on the 20th, to Upperville; on the 22d, crossing the Manassas Gap Railroad at Piedmont Station, to Petersburg and Linden, two little villages situated between the mountains which form Manassas Gap. On the 23d a skirmish occurred in the gap, which is known as the "Wapping Heights affair," in which the two divisions of the Third Corps proper were alone engaged, losing nearly a hundred men in killed and wounded. The next morning, the 24th, they moved towards Front Royal, when, finding the enemy had crossed the Shenandoah river and destroyed the bridges, they returned through the gap. On the 25th, they continued the march through Salem towards Warrenton; on the 26th, through Warrenton; and on the 27th, to the line of the Rappahannock,—General Birney's division occupying the right, and going into camp in the immediate vicinity of the White Sulphur Springs.

IN CAMP.

T White Sulphur Springs General Birney took for his headquarters, "and opened for the season," a part of the hotel of that once famous watering-place, which had withstood the ravages of war. Here the men enjoyed rest, after the hard marching and harder fighting in which they had been engaged from June 11th. General Birney had on previous occasions done all in his power to relieve the tedium of camp life for his officers and men. How well this was done is described in a letter published in the *New York Herald*, September 6, 1863, from which the following extracts are not inappropriate:—

"Really General Birney has cast his lot in pleasant places, and his truly veteran division has reason to be thankful that even a short season of rest is given it. The headquarters were pitched directly within the enclosure of the spring grounds. The numerous cottages attached to the premises, once the favorite summer residences of the fashionables of the South, are now made attractive by fair visitors from the North and the surrounding country. In the absence of more warlike amusements, the elegant young men of the staff make themselves agreeable by polite attention to the ladies. Beneath gigantic trees, stretching out their dense covers of foliage, to shut out the fierce August heat, behold these battle-scarred veterans reclining in quiet misery upon the tufted grass, or promenading the broad avenue in the spring grounds, supported in their severe affliction by the smiles and converse of fair ladies; the soft strains of music from the band of the Philadelphia Zouaves (detached for duty at headquarters) wafted through the groves and mingled with the voices of singing men and peals of laughter, full and free; fountains playing and cool springs offering continual refreshment; horseback riding, swinging, or walking for exercise, with occasionally a little dancing by way of amusement; tables, groaning under the choicest selections from the gardens of Virginia and the markets of Washington, set amid the ancient shades, inviting and tempting the appetites even of warriors: these are the dangers these valiant men are now called upon to brave. Every thing wears an air foreign to war and particularly suggestive of an immense pic-nic."

During this respite from active campaigning his headquarters were visited by a number of friends, whom he was always ready to make welcome. At this time it was proposed in Washington to fit out an expedition to Texas, under the direction of General Sickles as diplomatic agent and General Birney as military commander, his old division to be the nucleus of the force to be sent. After much discussion and negotiation this programme was abandoned, and General Birney remained in the Army of the Potomac.

At the same time he proposed to write the life of his friend General Kearny, and began to collect materials for the work. His labors, however, were soon interrupted by active campaigning, and he was never able to resume them.

CAMPAIGN UNDER MEADE.

BY the middle of September General Lee's army in Virginia, having been depleted to reinforce Bragg's army in Georgia, retired towards Richmond, and it was thought that, "if General Meade's advance was rapid and energetic, he would be able to strike a telling blow at the rebel army." Little, however, is known of the movements of the Union army during the fall of 1863, for no official reports have yet been made of this campaign, and at the commencement the War Department ordered the press to abstain from the publication of military movements. It was known, however, that a movement was begun about the middle of September, and a march was made to the Rapidan, where the army remained until the 12th of October, "like a horse fighting flies in summer time, with nothing heavier than guerillas to occupy its attention." On October 12th the army took up the line of March towards Washington, and before the 20th were encamped around Bull Run and Centreville. A correspondent of the *Army and Navy Journal*, writing from Warrenton, October 26th, says: "If there be any truth in the maxim of Marshal Saxe, 'that the secret of success lies in the legs of the soldier,' our late campaign should be a great success indeed, for we have performed as much leg-work, in the way of marching and countermarching, as could well be crowded into a fortnight."

General Birney, writing to a friend, under date of October 22d, said: "Do not believe newspaper correspondents, writing under the terror of expulsion, about the skill and daring displayed in this last movement of the army. It was a forced retreat, before an inferior force, offering us battle daily, on ground affording us the vantage. The army was never in better condition for fighting, but the men are tired of this wolf-and-dog strategy."

While retreating from the Rappahannock the first division of the Third Corps was attacked, near Auburn, by the cavalry of the enemy. The division was immediately formed, with Graham's brigade in the front line, the Sixty-third Pennsylvania, composed chiefly of conscripts, being in the advance. General Birney, seeing this regiment waver, rode up rapidly and cried out, "Come on, boys; go into them. Charge!" The regiment at once rallied and forced back the enemy. During this short but stubborn encounter the division lost eleven killed and forty-two wounded. Among the wounded were the bugler and two orderlies of the general's escort. After this encounter the division moved on, and encamped with the rest of the corps at Greenwich.

The intelligent correspondent of the *Army and Navy Journal*, writing on October 26, 1863, says that on Thursday, October 22, 1863, General Meade massed his army in the vicinity of Bull Run, eagerly awaiting an attack by the rebels, so that for the third time the Union army tried its fortunes on the same ground. The rebels, however, did not accept the challenge. While the main army was in this position General Birney, with the first division of the Third Corps, was placed in front of Fairfax Station, which was made the temporary depot of supplies, and by the disposition of his troops and the cavalry of Buford and Gregg, provided against any attempt of the enemy to gain our rear. These movements, however, produced no results. The Army of the Potomac, after its fortnight's race up and down Virginia, settled down near Warrenton. This, however, was not regretted by the officers of the Army of the Potomac, who were unanimously persuaded that the line of the Rapidan was a false position. Here the army remained until the first week in November, 1863, when General Meade transferred his front from Cedar Run to the line of the Rappahannock. While this movement was going on the Third Corps moved southward, by way of Kelly's ford, where they had a brisk skirmish. General Birney was temporarily in command of the Third Corps, General French having at the time command of the left column of the army. At Kelly's ford General Birney, by a movement which elicited the admiration of all who witnessed it, made a complete surprise of the enemy, and, though vigorously resisted, effected a crossing with a very small loss. This movement was described by an eye-witness in the following words:—

"During the first week in November, 1863, the Third Corps lay on the right bank of Licking creek, on the Orange and Alexandria Railroad, about four miles west of Warrenton Junction. On the evening of November 6th the order for this movement was received. It placed

General Birney in command of the Third Corps, (General French being assigned to the command of the left grand column of the Army of the Potomac, composed of the Third and Fifth Corps.) His instructions were to move at daylight, the following morning, to Kelly's ford *via* Morrisville, and force the passage of the Rappahannock river.

"By two, P. M., November 7th, the first division was massed, screened from observation, in rear of Mount Holly Church. A few of our cavalry were picketing at this point; the enemy's infantry in force, under Ewell, on the south side of the river, being in plain view; their horses grazing on the low ground, and apparently having no suspicion of an attack, as their pickets were thrown forward to the north side of the river, above Clarence creek. After taking a hasty survey of the ground, and ascertaining where the ford was, General Birney ordered forward the First and Second regiments of United States Sharpshooters, to drive the rebel pickets across the river, De Trobriand's brigade supporting, with orders to dash across, close after the sharpshooters. In the meantime, quickly placing his artillery in position, he opened on the astonished rebels as soon as the sharpshooters got engaged. It was a complete surprise. Pratt's four-and-a-half-inch guns, from the heights near Mount Holly Church, and Randolph's light twelves, at short range, poured in such a fire as utterly confounded them. They sent forward a brigade to support their pickets, but it broke and ran, and our men plunged through the river, capturing between three and four hundred prisoners, and before three o'clock, P. M., we had our first division in position on the south side, and pontoons were being laid for the artillery and the rest of the corps to cross.

"As an example of quick comprehension and rapidity of action, this operation is surpassed by none. No time was lost in needless reconnoitering and giving the enemy a chance to know what we were at. Before he knew there was any thing but cavalry in his front, our guns had opened on him, the infantry was charging, and the thing done, without hardly giving his men time to buckle on their equipments.

"During the night the enemy fell back, and we advanced next day to Brandy Station, driving his rear guard before us. This movement, in conjunction with the crossing at Rappahannock Station by General Sedgwick, compelled Lee to retreat behind the Rapidan, leaving the comfortable winter huts of his army for our men to occupy."

While the Third Corps was thus crossing the Rappahannock at Kelly's ford, the Sixth, under noble John Sedgwick, effected a crossing at Rappahannock Station, with a loss of about three hundred killed and wounded. The Third Corps, after crossing, camped for the night on the south side of the river, and the next morning resumed the advance, followed by the First and Second Corps. About noon they came upon a strong force of cavalry and light artillery of the enemy, which they engaged about two miles east of Brandy Station, and drove them about four miles, the fighting continuing until after dark.

The Third Corps then encamped near Brandy Station, where they remained for nearly ten days, while the damage done to the railroad by the rebel army was being repaired from Rappahannock Station. This gave the men a little rest, and fitted them for the engagement at Mine Run, in which they took an active part. To engage in this movement, the first division of the corps broke camp on the morning of the 26th of November, and crossed the Rapidan the evening of the same day. The next morning the march was resumed at daylight, through a thickly wooded country, of the same nature as that known as the Virginia wilderness. General Prince's division, which led the advance of the corps, came in contact with the enemy about noon, and with Carr's division, became hotly engaged between three and four o'clock, P. M. General Birney's division arrived on the field about four o'clock and immediately relieved that of General Carr, which, composed of inexperienced troops, was being pressed back. The battle raged fiercely until night put an end to the hostilities, when the enemy withdrew, leaving his dead and wounded on the field. This engagement is known by the name of the Battle of Payne's Farm.

In this movement General Warren took a prominent part. After he had made disposition of his forces, he found them inadequate to turn the enemy's right, and called for reinforcements. These were sent him, and two divisions of the Third Corps, under Generals Carr and Prince, reported to him, while General Birney, with his first division, was ordered to support the artillery, thus leaving General French without troops. It was agreed that the attack should be made at eight o'clock on Monday morning, when a vigorous artillery fire was commenced, but General Warren reporting his force still insufficient to insure success, no further operations were attempted, and on Tuesday the army withdrew and repassed the Rapidan by Germania and Culpepper fords, resuming its old front on the Orange and Alexandria Railroad. The critic of the *Army and Navy Journal*, in the number of December 5, 1863, says, "No adequate reason is assigned for this conduct, which is quite incomprehensible. This last campaign is certainly the most fruitless that has yet been undertaken."

The movements resulted principally in a *bon mot*, which at that time was attributed to the commander of the Army of the Potomac, who, it was said, answered a dispatch from General Halleck, requesting information as to the locality and result of the fight. General Meade answered by telegraph, "Mine Run." The authenticity of this joke is doubtful, but its appropriateness was recognized by the army, and for months afterwards the question was asked in camp, "In what two words will General Meade make his report of the last movement?" The answer invariably was, "*Mine Run.*"

WINTER QUARTERS.

AFTER the failure at Mine Run the army went into winter quarters, and no general movements were made until General Grant, in April, 1864, began to direct the movements of the Army of the Potomac. During this period the Government, at last convinced that the rebellion would extend beyond the period for which men had enlisted—for three years—began to induce re-enlistments, with which the army was engaged for several months. During this time General Birney issued to his division the following order:—

HEADQUARTERS, FIRST DIVISION, THIRD CORPS,
January 2, 1864.

[GENERAL ORDERS, NO. 1.]

The Major-general commanding the division appeals to the officers and men, and hopes that all will volunteer to remain until the war for the Union is closed. So far this division has led all others in the army of the United States in re-enlistments, evincing its desire to stand by "*the colors*," and its commander wishes to have the honor of saying that all the regimental organizations led by him during the past campaigns remained unbroken until the last armed rebel has disappeared.

He promises that he will see that the furloughs and bounties promised by the various orders are given, and hopes that every officer and man wearing the "Kearny patch" will at once volunteer for the war.

The division commissary of musters will be ready to muster in all applicants before the 5th instant.

The Major-general commanding the division knows that he has never called on the division without a hearty and cheering response, and is confident of it in this case. This order will be read to each regiment of the command at dress parade this day.

(Signed) D. B. BIRNEY,
Major-general commanding division.

Official:
J. Barclay Fassitt,
Captain and A. A. A. G.

At this period Birney's division consisted of eighteen regiments, of whom fourteen were entitled to re-enlist as veteran regiments, under the terms of the orders from the War Department. Of these fourteen, eleven re-enlisted and went home on furlough as regimental organizations. General Birney, who was constitutionally opposed to boasting of any kind, never lost an opportunity of speaking of this event in his military career. He always claimed that a greater proportion of the men of his division had re-enlisted than in any division of the army. This claim, it is believed, was founded upon fact, and if the reports of the adjutant-general at Washington are ever published, it is thought they will establish this assertion.

During the cessation of active campaigning Birney's division was encamped near the farm of John Minor Botts, of Virginia. The men, as was their custom, had provided for their comfort by supplying their necessities from the adjacent neighborhood. Mr. Botts preferred a claim to the headquarters of the Army of the Potomac against the United States for the depredations which he alleged the Union soldiers had committed upon his premises. This claim, amounting to several thousand dollars, the quartermaster of General Birney's division was directed to pay, provided General Birney would certify to its correctness. This General Birney declined to do, unless Mr. Botts took the oath of allegiance, for he was unwilling to appropriate the money of the supporters of the Union to support their enemies or middlemen. Mr. Botts said that he could not take the oath of allegiance, because the retreat of the Union armies would place his farm within the rebel lines, and such action on his part might subject his property to confiscation. This argument, however, had no effect on General Birney, and he persistently refused to certify to the claims of any one who would not prove his allegiance to the Federal Government by the oath which had been prescribed at Washington. If Mr. Botts has yet been able to prove his claim upon the treasury of the United States, he did so without the official sanction of General Birney.

General Birney's disposition to provide amusement for officers and men of his division was again manifested during this winter. Weekly receptions were organized, which furnished an opportunity for social intercourse among the officers, and a building was constructed in which theatrical representations were given. These became so popular, that before the division moved, they were provided nightly. Besides these amusements, the division and corps had their balls, at which "brave men and fair women chased the glowing hours with flying feet."

These amusements are thus described by the army correspondent of the *New York Herald*, under date of January 23d: "The first army ball of the season is to come off near the headquarters of General Carr, commanding third division of Third Army Corps, on next Monday night. The house is large and commodious, and stands directly beside the railway, about one mile south of Brandy Station, and in sight of the residence of John M. Botts. A ball-room, eighty feet by sixty, is being added, and supper has been ordered for a very large number of guests. The President, Secretary of War, and General Halleck are among the invited guests. A special train will be run to carry the ladies directly to the house, where platforms and walks have been laid to protect them from the mud. The ball is given by the officers of the Third Corps, each brigade of which will be represented. Many of their New York friends, both ladies and gentlemen, are expected to join in the festivities. The arrangements are under the superintendence of Captain Fassitt, of General Birney's staff, and appear to be admirably adapted to success."

Under date of January 27th, the same writer speaks of the ball as follows: "The hop and supper given by the officers of the Third Corps last night were among the most successful affairs of the season. A very large party of ladies and citizens were in attendance, but shoulder-straps and staff-buttons were largely in the ascendant. Among those present were Major-generals French, Birney, Humphreys, and Brigadier-generals Carr, Mott, Ward, and Morris. The room, floor, supper, and management were excellent."

The correspondent of the *New York Tribune* writes the following letter:

"The grand opening ball of the season in the army came off last night, at the headquarters of General Carr, and was largely attended. Among those present were Major-generals French, Birney, Humphreys; Brigadier-generals Ward, Carr, Mott, Morris, and Hon. J. M. Botts and daughters. The music, which was furnished by the band of the third brigade, first division, Third Army Corps, General Torbet's brigade band of Sixth Army Corps, and the band of the Eighty-seventh Pennsylvania volunteers, was of the finest description. The supper consisted of every delicacy obtainable in Washington, and was tastily spread in a long canvass hall, gaily decorated with flowers and evergreens. The dancing-hall was one hundred feet long, and was also elegantly trimmed with evergreens, the national, corps, and brigade colors."

In this way the Army of the Potomac was amused until the early spring of 1864, when a new era dawned upon its career. By a unanimous vote of the nation, the rank of Lieutenant-general was conferred upon General Grant, who, by his brilliant campaign at the West, had proved himself to be the man around whom the country could rally, as in the days of the Revolution the hopes of the nation were centred upon Washington. After he had been made the commander-in-chief of all the armies of the United States, he devoted his energy to the Army of the Potomac, for in the country west of the Alleghanies there was no more work for him to do. Coming eastward, he began to direct the movements of this noble army, which for the first time was to be handled by a man who understood its capability and its mission. On assuming its direction he was asked his opinion of the army, and his reply will live in history. He said, "It is a noble army, in its organization and equipment, but never yet has been taught *to fight its battles through.*"

What criticism could be more complete to any one who remembers Yorktown, Fair Oaks, Antietam, and Gettysburg! No vain boasting prompted this remark: for the man who made it taught the Army of the Potomac to fight its battles thoroughly and effectually, from Rappahannock Station southward, until Richmond was taken and the rebel armies were compelled to surrender, one by one, from Virginia to Texas; thus proving that the Army of the Potomac was the pivot on which the rebellion turned, and, when handled by a general of ability, was able to close the gates of the temple of Janus, and give peace to a country which for years had been desolated by internecine war. How this end was accomplished, and the part which General Birney took in it until his death, will occupy our attention until the close of this sketch.

THE OBLITERATION OF THE THIRD CORPS.

IT was for a long time rumored that changes would be made in the army of the Potomac. Another "reorganization" was to be effected. The order making these changes was dated March 23, 1864, but for weeks before its appearance it was known that the old Third Army Corps was to be officially put out of existence. Against this determination the officers did not protest, nor did they take any pains to ask its postponement or reversal. They, however, felt the blow keenly, and, while they regretted that their conduct and that of their men had not procured for them the consideration of their superior officers, they still felt that they had done their entire duty. By this order the first and second divisions of the Third Corps were transferred to the Second Corps, "reserving their badges and distinctive marks," and were thereafter designated as the third and fourth divisions of the Second Corps. A week after the opening of the campaign the fourth division (which had been the second division of the Third Corps) was consolidated into the third division; so that, by this arrangement, General Birney had under his command all that remained of the old Third Corps. It was a gratification to the soldiers to be again in the same command, although they had been compelled to give up their corps organization and had been reduced to that of a division. The brigades of the division were commanded by Brigadier-generals J. H. H. Ward, Alexander Hayes, and Gershom Mott.

This organization placed General Birney under a new corps commander, Major-general Winfield S. Hancock, whose name stands high upon the roll of honor which has been written of those men who have earned the nation's gratitude by their conduct during the rebellion. Talented, courteous, gallant, big-hearted, and with a bearing which proves that nature intended him for a soldier, he has won a more lasting reputation than any general of our armies who has not been entrusted with an independent command. With his quick eye he soon perceived the merit of his new division general, and during the campaign he never called in vain upon Birney, or his men. Any one who will take the trouble to examine the details of the first campaign of the Army of the Potomac under General Grant, from Brandy Station to Petersburg, will not fail to admit the value of the services rendered by Birney's division. Were the writer to enumerate them in detail, the limits of this sketch would be too extended. General Grant's movements were so rapid, so varied, and so frequent, that a detailed history of the services of any division would make a volume larger than this. The writer will therefore content himself with a rapid enumeration of the movements of General Birney's command.

The Appendix contains no report by General Birney of any of these movements. He had no time to prepare any between the opening of the campaign of 1864 and his death, in October. The absence of these reports is regretted by his superior and subordinate officers; for, as many have said and written to the writer, there are many occurrences of this campaign which no one can explain as well as Birney could have done, and by his death many matters of certainty were resolved into matters of doubt and of speculation.

During this campaign he wrote very few letters, and, as no reports of general officers have yet been published, the only source of information is the correspondence published in the daily papers at the time. These, being hurriedly written, are sometimes inaccurate, as the writers were often compelled to get their information during the excitement of an action. Considering, however, the disadvantages under which they have always labored, it is surprising that so few mistakes have occurred in the letters of army correspondents, and the writer willingly thus expresses his gratitude to them for their industry and fidelity in keeping their readers advised of the movements of our armies. The enterprize of the press, during the rebellion, has been unprecedented; and the people of the United States have, through this spirit of enterprize, been able to read the history of the war as it progressed, a circumstance without parallel in the history of any other nation.

GRANT'S MARCH TOWARDS RICHMOND.

GENERAL GRANT was "ready" to move by the 3d of May, 1864. On that day the army broke camp and, with six days' rations in the haversacks of the men, was put in motion. About midnight the Second Corps was moving towards Ely's ford, over the Rapidan, and on the 4th of May General Birney's division occupied the same ground over which it had fought during the battle of Chancellorsville, just one year previous, and there rested until daylight of Thursday, May 5th.

At daylight the Second Corps was moving in a nearly southerly direction, and had reached Todd's tavern, at the junction of the Brock and Pamunkey roads, when orders were received for an immediate countermarch, to unite with the left of the Fifth Corps, which had met the enemy as early as ten o'clock, A. M., who opposed its further advance with success. This movement was successfully executed, and as soon as General Hancock had formed his line of battle, which extended along the Brock road, with the right a little to the north of the plank road, he gave orders to advance. The enemy was immediately encountered upon entering the woods, which were a thick and tangled growth of small trees and large branching shrubs, preventing the use of artillery, save upon the plank road, where, however, it was not this evening called into requisition. "The contest was exceedingly stubborn and bloody. The corps, however, held its ground," and at dark brought off one of the pieces of artillery, which had been left on the plank road by a portion of Griffin's division of the Fifth Corps, when they were compelled to fall back, early in the afternoon. This was done by a detachment of the Second regiment of Sharpshooters, under direction of Lieutenant-colonel Stoughton. The contest ended about eight o'clock. Among our losses was Brigadier-general Alexander Hayes, commanding the second brigade of Birney's division. He was shot in the head in the first moments of the engagement. He was a graduate of West Point, took part in the Mexican war, and raised the Sixty-third regiment of Pennsylvania volunteers, of which he was colonel. He was known throughout the Army of the Potomac as a fighting general, and much beloved by the men of his command.

At five o'clock, A. M., of Friday, both armies moved to the attack. The Second Corps was very successful, and by ten o'clock had driven the enemy over a mile, when further advance, without assistance, was found to be impracticable. Reinforcements soon arrived from the Ninth Corps, and the battle raged with terrible fierceness until noon, neither side giving or winning ground. About twelve o'clock, while General Birney was talking with General Wadsworth, the firing on our left suddenly increased, and almost at the instant an officer rode up and reported a force advancing on that flank. Ere the report was delivered, it was but too apparent what had been the result of this new movement by the enemy. The first few fugitives flying through the woods were but the swiftest footed, and in five minutes the whole line was rolling back, regiment by regiment, as the solid columns of Longstreet moved along their front. General Wadsworth mounted his horse at the first alarm and rode rapidly towards his division, which was some distance to the right, but had no sooner reached it than he fell mortally wounded.

To stay the tide of retreat was found to be a simple impossibility—not because the men were panic-stricken, but because of the thick woods; and the men poured back to the Brock road, where of their own accord they formed behind the works which they had hastily thrown up the night before. The weight of this attack of Longstreet's corps fell on Birney's division. From this time until a few minutes after four o'clock there was a lull in the storm which had been raging along the left of the line since early daylight. At twenty minutes past four, Longstreet's entire corps was thrown upon the Second Corps front, the third and fourth divisions again sustaining the heaviest of the attack, which was stubborn in the extreme, and lasted for from twenty-five to thirty minutes. At a point where the left of Birney's division joined the right of Mott's, the breastworks, which were built of very dry logs, had, by the carelessness of the men, been permitted to catch fire, so that when the attack was made they were of no advantage to us; and at this point the enemy rushed in, causing great confusion and a falling back of that portion of the line, which, for a few moments, threatened extreme disaster. Fortunately Captain Dow's Sixth Maine battery was posted near, and, although so many of his men were wounded as to disable his pieces, he found recruits in the persons of officers and others who would not be driven back, and materially aided in repelling the enemy, as their dead in his front testified. General Longstreet was wounded in this attack. Lieutenant Calef, an aide of General Birney's, was taken prisoner during this day's fighting. The brigades of Generals Grant, Robinson, Stevenson, and Owen, and the division of General Mott, were all under the command of General Birney during the fighting of this day, and until the 7th, when the corps moved from its position. The fighting of Saturday and Sunday was nothing more serious than skirmishing, and "feeling" the enemy to ascertain his intentions, which were found to be fixed upon retreat.

On the morning of the 7th the corps moved back to Todd's tavern, and on the evening of the 9th two divisions crossed the Po river, with but little opposition, at the point designated for Birney's advance. On the 10th another terrific battle was fought, and the two divisions which had crossed the river Po the night before were compelled to return, at a point lower down, and where the movement was difficult. Birney was the first to recross, and Barlow, of the first division, followed. The enemy followed closely, but the movement was effected in splendid order, with the loss of only one gun, although the artillery fire was very severe. Two regiments of Birney's division, which had advanced across Glady run, were completely surrounded, and fought their way back with considerable loss.

During the progress of these battles the public received information of very few details. Part of the time telegraphic communication between the Army of the Potomac and Washington was interrupted. It was not until May 9th that any thing was heard from General Grant. On May 11th was the first definite information, when he telegraphed to Washington: "We have now entered the sixth day of very heavy fighting. The result to this time is much in our favor. We have taken over five thousand prisoners in battle. I propose to fight it out on this line, if it takes all summer."

On Wednesday, the 11th of May, the fighting was mainly done by the artillery. During the day General Lee sent in a flag of truce, proposing a cessation of hostilities for forty-eight hours, for the purpose of burying his dead. General Grant replied that he had not time to bury his own dead, because he "PROPOSED" to advance immediately. About midnight the Second Corps moved near to Spottsylvania Court House, to displace the enemy's batteries, which had annoyed our army during the day. At dawn on Thursday, sheltered by the dark and a thick fog, the corps advanced quietly and cautiously towards the enemy's works, Barlow's first division and Birney's third division forming the first line. "As they surmounted gradually the rugged and woody space which intervened, the excitement increased, till it broke out in a splendid rush at the rebel intrenchments, which they leaped with loud cheers, dashing into the astonished enemy, and compelling their surrender in mass. It was a gallant charge with the bayonet, hardly a gun being fired. It was a clear surprise, and might have been more fruitful, but for the cheering of some of our men, who could suppress their enthusiasm no longer. As it was, an entire division was surrounded and captured, officers and men,—three thousand prisoners and two generals, Major-general Edward Johnson and Brigadier-general G. H. Stuart. From the position of the lines, the point penetrated seems to have been Ewell's right and A. P. Hill's left, as the captured division was a part of Ewell's (Stonewall Jackson's) corps. This position was strong and one most important to hold, the Second Corps being now a wedge between the enemy's centre and right, and helping to press apart that dangerous structure of works wherein the enemy lay ensconced. So complete was the surprise, that the hostile officers were started from breakfast by the rude intrusion of their unwelcome guests, who, *sans ceremonie*, came to share their meal, like the Commandatore at the table of Don Giovanni. So rapid was the conquest, that in an hour after the charge General Hancock sent the following dispatch to headquarters: 'I have captured from thirty to forty guns. I have finished up Johnson and am now going into Early.'

"The enemy was quickly aroused to the importance of the position he had lost, and about nine o'clock began to charge again and again, with desperate fury, in attempts to repossess the works. Very bloody fighting occurred without intermission for three hours. The rebel columns dashed with unflinching determination against our lines, retiring each time with their huge columns winnowed by cross and enfilading fires of artillery and musketry, now steadily brought to bear. The artillery on neither side was brought into thoroughly effective play; but, although not an artillery battle, it reminded its participants, more nearly than any of the preceding, of Gettysburg and Malvern Hill. Towards noon the enemy, surfeited with slaughter, abandoned for a time his efforts to retake the prize which our men had won so fairly and held so tenaciously; but he successfully disputed any farther advance, and the captured cannon lay covered by the guns of the sharpshooters, neither party being able to carry them away."

This engagement is represented by those who were present as, in many respects, the most trying of any fight between the Rapidan and the James. From the time the enemy's works were taken, until daylight the next morning, the firing on the front of General Birney's division was incessant. His right flank was very much exposed, which was well known to the enemy, who made his most desperate attacks at that point. Over this part of the works there were hand-to-hand struggles, and the dead and wounded rebels lay literally piled one upon another inside their own works. For the entire twenty-four hours the enemy kept up his fire on this point, and regiment relieved regiment, in regular succession, all day and all night, as fast as their ammunition was expended.

The fruits of this assault to Birney's division were eleven battle-flags, and, although the first and third divisions together captured the works and the guns, no number has, so far as is known, been credited to them separately. Each division hauled off the next day those which lay in their front, the whole number being eighteen or twenty.

During the assault General Birney received a severe contusion from a piece of shell, which was his only injury during this campaign. Captain Briscoe, his aide, was the first mounted man in the works, and captured a battle-flag with his own hands. He was severely wounded in the leg.

The fighting continued during Friday and Saturday. Sunday, May 15th, the twelfth day of breaking camp at Culpepper, was the first day of rest the army enjoyed. But this rest was not allowed to all the army, for on Sunday afternoon Birney's division fell back from its position on the right of the line, and in so doing brought on an attack; which demonstrated that the enemy desired to occupy the ground from which we had proposed to withdraw, when the division returned and reoccupied it, after a sharp engagement. During Monday and Tuesday skirmishing and picket firing were kept up day and night, and on Wednesday, the 18th, there was an attack by the first and second divisions of the Second Corps, which produced no result, in which Birney's division took no active part. That night a brigade of the enemy, in reconnoitering our position, attacked General Birney's right and rear, but was quickly repulsed, with the loss of a number of prisoners. At one o'clock, A. M., of the 19th, the corps was again in motion, "by the left flank," and halted on the "Anderson plantation," near the plank road leading to Fredericksburg, by which our supplies were then received.

On Friday, May 20th, the Secretary of War telegraphed to General Dix portions of a telegram from General Grant: "Last evening an effort was made by Ewell's corps to turn our right. They were promptly repulsed by Birney's and Tyler's divisions and some of Warren's troops that were on the extreme right." General Birney was in command of all the troops engaged on Thursday, on our extreme right, including Tyler's division and the detachment from General Warren's corps.

On Friday night was commenced another of General Grant's celebrated flank movements. He determined to make an effort to reach the banks of the North and South Anna, which laid between Lee and Richmond, before Lee could get there; and the race began. About midnight General Torbert's division of cavalry led the advance. It was followed immediately by Hancock's corps, which quietly and cautiously began to steal out from the old battle-ground towards Guineas' station. No sooner had the corps moved than the beating of drums in the enemy's camp showed that he was on the alert, and would contend for the right of way to Richmond.

The Second Corps continued its march, skirmishing and fighting as it moved along, until two, P. M., of Monday, when it arrived at Taylor's (or Chesterfield) bridge, over the North Anna. The day was occupied in skirmishing, reconnoitering, and the work incident to placing troops in position, until six o'clock, when the preparations for assault were completed. "The bridge was commanded at its entrance by a well-built redan, whose extremities were covered by the river and its flanks swept by artillery in works on the opposite bank of the river, as well as by infantry in rifle-pits." The attacking party was composed of the two brigades of Birney's division, commanded at that time by Colonels (now generals) Pierce and Egan, and one regiment of the Excelsior brigade. The dash made by them over the open plain, fully half a mile in width, under front and flank fires, was most gallantly performed, and, as they concentrated around the redan, which was the key-point of the position, those who were mere spectators of the affair minded not the shot and shell which flew in every direction, thought not of seeking cover therefrom, but waited and watched with breathless interest, until our colors were seen on the parapet, when they sent up such cheers as only men can utter in the moment of victory. The bridge was saved. The rebels held the south end during the night, and our pickets held the north end, and foiled all their attempts to destroy it.

After this severe fighting, the march and countermarch continued until Monday, May 30th, when our army was across the Pamunkey. During Monday a severe fight extended along our entire line. Along the left centre, occupied by General Warren, about five o'clock in the afternoon, the enemy made an attack, during which he gained an advantage, and there was danger of General Warren's flank being turned. General Hancock received before dark the order to relieve him by a counter attack, and immediately dashed on the enemy's line, capturing his rifle-pits, which he held all night. This rapid and brilliant movement enabled General Warren to maintain his position, which was then about seven miles from Richmond. About midnight the enemy attempted to dislodge General Hancock from his position, but the movement was unsuccessful, and the enemy retired, leaving a large number of prisoners in our hands.

Early on Tuesday morning another movement began. The Second Corps moved from its position and Birney's division on the right, rushed upon and carried the breastworks on the south side of Tolopotomy creek, after a short but fierce conflict, with a loss of about thirty men. During this attack about thirty prisoners were captured who represented themselves to be from the command of the rebel General Breckinridge. The captured works were abandoned during the night, and on Wednesday, June 1st, Birney's division was marching towards Cold Harbor, where it occupied the left of the line. During Wednesday night the Second Corps performed the movement which had become so familiar to it during the preceding thirty days, and marched from right to left, Birney's division leaving the extreme right of the army and going to its extreme left.

At half-past four o'clock on Friday morning, June 3d, another severe engagement occurred along our entire line. During this day Birney's division was not engaged. It was, for the first time during the campaign, indulged in the luxury of being placed in reserve, but even this did not afford much rest, for during the day it was exposed to a heavy fire of artillery, which the enemy kept up in front of Hancock. In the afternoon the division moved again towards the right of the army and went into position between the Fifth and Eighteenth Corps. Here it remained until the afternoon of the 4th, when it returned to its former position on the left, as support to the first and second divisions of the Second Corps. On the 5th the line was extended still farther to the left, and Birney's division rested at Parker's Mill. This movement occupied until three o'clock, A. M., of the 6th, and here the division rested until the 12th.

From this point General Grant made another change of base. Abandoning the ground for which he had fought for more than forty days, abandoning his line of communications with Washington, and abandoning his base of supplies, he determined to seek new territory, to form new communications, and establish a new base. All this was done successfully, and the army was moved from the Chickahominy to the James river. On Sunday night Hancock's corps moved by Long bridge across the Chickahominy, and thence along the road to Wilcox's wharf on the James, where it arrived before dark on Monday the 12th. The next morning the whole army was transferred to the south bank of the James, without the loss of a wagon or a piece of artillery. Still Grant pushed ahead. He had been compelled to abandon his original intention of moving to the west of Richmond, but ever fertile in resources he came to the east, and during the middle of June occupied the very ground which the Army of the Potomac had occupied two years before. But, in 1864, the Army of the Potomac had learned to fight its battles "*through*," and its position on the south bank of the James was part of a plan which the genius of its commander had determined upon, and even this plan was only a fractional part of the grand combinations which, carried out by Sherman, Thomas, Sheridan, and the different corps commanders, resulted, during the spring of 1865, in the fall of Richmond, the surrender of the rebel armies, and the end of the rebellion.

From May 4th, when the army moved from Culpepper, until June 14th, when the army reached the south bank of the James river, a period of forty-one days, it had been incessantly in motion, and most of the time had been under fire. The intervals of rest, day or night, had been "few and far between." Beside the fatigues of this march and the losses during the almost uninterrupted fighting, the previous movements of the army were almost forgotten, and yet less has been written about this campaign than about any other. The movements were too rapid, the losses too severe, and the sufferings too intense, to enable any newspaper correspondent to follow them or portray them in fitting words. Before the public could be informed of the details of any movement, the attention of the country was engrossed by some new and grander movement, so that it was impossible for any one to trace the exact route of the army during this march, or to obtain at the time a critical view of the rapid movements and masterly combinations which were executed. The march of June, 1863, followed by the battle of Gettysburg; the march of August and September, 1862, followed by the battle of Antietam, with the intermediate campaign, memorable for the defeats at Fredericksburg and Chancellorsville; the disheartening results of Pope's campaign, and the slow march up the Peninsula during the spring and golden summer of 1862, which was prolonged until the malaria of the Chickahominy swamps killed as many men as rebel bullets, and which resulted only in a "change of base" to Harrison's Landing, and produced a nervous anxiety in the army and throughout the country for the safety of the brave and noble men who marched and suffered: have all been mentioned in the foregoing pages, but these all sink into insignificance when compared with the marching and fighting during the forty-one days from Culpepper to the south bank of the James. They were as the explosion of packs of fire-crackers to the continued and severe thunder storm which burst upon the rebellion when Grant began his march. The heavy train, propelled for the first time by the power of steam, moved along with unprecedented rapidity, and, overcoming all impediments in its way, did not stop until the skilful engineer had reached the end of the route.

Established upon the south bank of the James, the army had a resting spell long enough to make change of clothing, unsaddle horses, and recruit exhausted strength. But the rest was not of long duration: it was doomed, like Salathiel, to "march, march, march," until its mission was accomplished.

On Wednesday, the 15th of June, the army was again in motion, and about ten o'clock of that day the Second Corps began to move southward toward Petersburg. During Wednesday night they reached their next fighting point. Before they came up the Eighteenth Corps, under "Baldy" Smith, had captured the outer works of the enemy near Petersburg, which had been constructed for the defence of that city. "During the night Birney's division held portions of the captured earthworks, which the enemy, realizing their importance, in vain attempted to wrest away."

The fighting on Wednesday proved, however, to be only preparatory to the battles of Thursday, Friday and Saturday. General Lee having at last understood the intentions of General Grant, determined to make the intrenchments of Petersburg the commencement of the "last ditch," in which the remains of the rebellion were to be buried. Unaccustomed to such strange strategy, for which no precedent could be found in the books, Lee had scattered his troops, holding them well in hand, so as to be able to concentrate them rapidly, on any given point. When the movement upon Petersburg was developed, the rebel forces were rapidly hurried to the defence of its garrison. Our tired troops, however, could not be marched up in time to pursue the advantage which General Smith had so gallantly gained on Wednesday afternoon. As has been said, Birney's division arrived first and took possession of a portion of the captured intrenchments.

About midnight, while Birney, still mounted and surrounded by his staff, was making disposition of his command, a wagon approached from the direction of the enemy's line. Upon being halted the driver reported that the wagon contained ammunition for "battery number five." "All right," said Birney, "we will take care of it." The next day, the ammunition intended for "battery number five" was sent back to Petersburg, without the wagon and horses, by the artillery of Birney's division. This little episode occurred before Birney had time to establish his picket line, and shows that General Smith's success during the afternoon had completely demoralized the enemy in his front.

Early on Thursday morning General Birney sent Colonel Egan's brigade to a redoubt on the left, which, after a handsome dash, was carried and held. Meanwhile the enemy was sending down troops from Richmond so rapidly, that it became necessary to await the arrival of the Ninth Corps, under General Burnside. The cavalry moved out to the left across the Petersburg and Norfolk Railroad, and occupied the ground for the Ninth Corps. Early in the afternoon the Ninth Corps arrived, after a forced march from Charles' City Court House. The line of battle was immediately formed, with the Eighteenth Corps on the right, the Second in the centre, and the Ninth on the left. Birney's division occupied the right of the centre corps. An assault had been ordered at six o'clock. The attack was promptly made and kept up vigorously for three hours. Birney's division carried the crest in his front and held it firmly. General Barlow, on Birney's left, found the advance more difficult, owing to the concentration of the enemy in his front. His men, however, moved forward under a destructive fire, but the enemy cut off his skirmish line, capturing three hundred men with their officers. After a hard fight of more than three hours' duration, the assault was suspended until morning. During this assault Birney lost about five hundred men.

On Friday, June 17th, General Hancock was unable to maintain the field longer. His old wound, received at Gettysburg, from which he had suffered during the campaign, compelled him to retire. The command of the corps thus devolved upon General Birney, which he retained until the 26th of June, when General Hancock resumed command. During this time the command of the division devolved upon General Mott.

Preparations were made for a daylight attack, and at four, A. M., on Friday, General Burnside ordered Potter's division to take the works in their front. General Potter threw forward General Griffin's brigade, supported by General Curtin's, and after a gallant dash, the position was carried as by a whirlwind; and six guns, sixteen officers, four hundred men and a stand of colors were captured from the enemy. After this success a pause occurred in the assault. By subsequent movements General Burnside, during the afternoon, succeeded in getting within a mile and a half of the city, into which he threw a few shells. The enemy repeatedly attempted to regain the lost intrenchments, but was as often repulsed.

The movements during this day were chiefly confined to the Ninth Corps on the left. The position of the enemy in front of Birney was so strong that he was ordered to withhold an attack. About nine o'clock, however, on Friday evening the enemy rushed down upon the centre, occupied by the Second Corps, but was driven back with severe loss.

During Friday night it was determined to make another assault on Saturday morning at four o'clock. Upon the advance of our skirmishers, preparatory to the assault, it was found that the enemy had abandoned the works in our immediate front for an inner line of defence. A paper was found by some of our skirmishers and given to Lieutenant Shreve, of General Birney's staff, which proved to be an order from the general in command of the enemy's line, making details to construct a new line of defence. To this line the enemy retired, and retained possession of it until the capture of Petersburg, in the spring of 1865. At noon an assault was attempted, under General Gibbon, but without success. In the afternoon a second storming party was organized from Birney's division, then under command of General Mott. "A little before five o'clock General Mott moved out his force in two columns, and in gallant style the two leading brigades burst upon the enemy. They were received with a withering fire from concentrated batteries and musketry, and in spite of the most desperate bravery were forced back with terrible loss. The charge was worthy of the proverbial gallantry of the corps, but it failed of success as the previous charge had also failed."

Sunday, the 19th of June, was comparatively a quiet day. There was skirmishing and cannonading, but no decisive movements. Birney threw a few shells into Petersburg in pursuance of his favorite amusement, to try to "wind up the town clock," but with few perceptible results. It was evident the enemy was strong and secure, and the work of the week had been unsatisfactory.

On Monday, June 20th, new movements were undertaken. Early in the morning all was bustle. The enemy, having recovered from apprehension of the immediate loss of Petersburg, began to operate against the weaker part of our lines. His efforts were counteracted by counter-movements by our army. The Second Corps, under Birney, began to move on Monday night, and on Tuesday morning crossed the Petersburg and Norfolk Railroad and marched in a southerly direction as rapidly as possible, under an intense sun, and in a stifling, blinding dust. The corps pushed on with the same intrepidity which had characterized its previous movements, by the flank, in the face of the enemy. During this day the movements of the remainder of the army were without results. On Wednesday the enemy drove back our advancing columns, and during the day we lost heavily, principally in prisoners. On Thursday, the 23d, our men cut the telegraph on the Danville Railroad, but were driven back in their efforts to capture the road. In Birney's immediate front little of importance occurred on Thursday. During Friday, Saturday and Sunday, the 24th, 25th and 26th of June, nothing was accomplished. The whole army suffered greatly from the heat, the dust was suffocating, and owing to continued drought water was difficult to obtain. On Monday, June 27th, in pursuance of agreement even picket firing ceased, and thus one of the quietest days of the campaign was enjoyed. As often happened during the rebellion, on the cessation of picket firing, the men of the two armies evinced a disposition to fraternize more than the good of the service permitted. This elicited from General Birney an order prohibiting any intermingling, or communication between the opposing lines. The men, therefore, lay quiet all day. Towards evening a refreshing shower of rain cooled the parched air and laid the suffocating dust. During the evening General Hancock resumed command of the corps and General Birney returned to his division.

From this period until July 23d, when General Birney was ordered to the command of the Tenth Army Corps, the division remained quiet, changing position but once, when, on July 12th, they moved, after destroying the works they had erected, to the rear of the Fifth Corps, where they went into reserve. During this time the enemy attempted to transfer the scene of operations from around Petersburg and Richmond to near Washington; but this experiment did not tempt Grant to relinquish his hold. While laying in the intrenchments near Petersburg, General Birney contemplated a short visit home. The fatigues of the campaign had told upon a constitution naturally weak, and impaired by the campaigns of 1862 and 1863. So long as the army was on the march, or under fire, excitement kept him up; but when these stimulants ceased, it was evident that he had over-tasked his energies. He felt himself that he needed rest. On July 21st he wrote: "I am making every exertion to come home and recruit for a week. You will see me in a few days, when I hope that business will permit you to join me in a trip to some quiet place, where I can lay aside shoulder-straps and enjoy a few evenings of quiet talk. I am greatly bored by the want of something to do here. Nothing relieves the monotony of the day but the occasional report of a heavy gun, which for a few moments starts us from our lethargy, but we soon relapse into as perfect quiet as if we were in some grove near Philadelphia."

THE TENTH ARMY CORPS.

THE plans of Birney, however, were entirely broken up by the receipt of an order from General Grant, assigning him to the permanent command of the Tenth Army Corps, which had been for a long time under the command of Major-general Q. A. Gilmore. This corps had taken an active part in the siege of Charleston, and was distinguished for its efficiency. In April it had been moved from Charleston to the Peninsula, and with the Eighteenth Corps, under the command of Major-general Smith, ("Baldy,") composed the Army of the James. General Birney at once took leave of his division in the following order:—

HEADQUARTERS THIRD DIVISION, SECOND CORPS,
July 23, 1865.

[GENERAL ORDER, No. 46.]

In obedience to Special Order No. 64, from Headquarters Armies of the United States, I relinquish command of this division.

In parting with my comrades and companions in arms, after so long and eventful a connection, I may be permitted to say that to me it is a very painful duty. I shall always remember with pride the regiments that I have had the honor to command, and shall feel the deepest interest in their future.

D. B. BIRNEY,
Major-general.

Official:
W. P. SHREVE,
Lieutenant and A. A. A. G.

The *New York Herald* correspondent with the Second Corps, thus speaks of General Birney's departure:—

"There are few attachments stronger than those formed between companions in arms on the battle-field, and hence, though called to assume greater responsibilities and higher honors, it is not without lingering regrets that General Birney bade farewell to the third division, with which he has been so long and so favorably identified. The division has been commanded by him since the death of the lamented Kearny. Its history is intimately and honorably associated with the wonderful campaigns of the army of the Potomac, and General Birney has shown himself worthy of the confidence which has been reposed in him. Those who have had personal knowledge of his operations in the field concur in the opinion that he is an invaluable officer, and his services in this campaign have greatly increased his reputation. He has steadily won his way to the enviable position he now occupies."

On assuming his new command he issued the following order:—

HEADQUARTERS TENTH ARMY CORPS,
IN THE FIELD, NEAR HATCHER'S, *July* 23, 1864.

[GENERAL ORDER, NO. 17.]

In obedience to Special Order No. 64, current series from Headquarters of the United States, the undersigned assumes command of the Tenth Army Corps.

The following named officers are announced as constituting the personal staff: Captain J. C. Briscoe, Fortieth New York volunteers, A. D. C.; Captain Clayton McMichael, Ninth United States infantry, A. D. C.; Captain Charles Noble, One-hundred-and-nineteenth Pennsylvania volunteers, A. D. C.; Captain J. E. Sweet, Twentieth Indiana volunteers, A. A. D. C.

D. B. BIRNEY,
Major-general.

Official:
ED. W. SMITH,
Assistant Adjutant-general.

Birney was soon busily engaged with the details of his new command, which he found to be much scattered; one division, under General Turner, being in the trenches before Petersburg; one brigade holding an intrenched camp on the north bank of the James river, at a point known as Deep Bottom; and the remainder occupying the line between the James and Appomattox rivers. Impressed with the necessity of increased vigilance, and to establish a uniformity which he found to be needed among the officers, he, on July 27th, issued a lengthy order, prescribing the manner of performing picket duty, which is published in full in the Appendix. On July 30th he wrote as follows to a friend: "I am much pleased with my new command. My assignment to it by Grant, in the field, in preference to a dozen others who desired it, nearly all of whom outranked me, was a compliment far greater than if I had been assigned to the corps by the President upon political or personal grounds."

Until Wednesday, the 10th of August, the Tenth Corps remained in the position we have mentioned. Birney was thus deprived of any active participation in the operations of the Army of the Potomac. On the day the mine was sprung, his services were confined to making demonstrations upon the enemy, to keep up the feint which had been ordered along his line, between the two rivers.

Between General Butler, commanding the Army of the James and the department of Virginia and North Carolina, and General Birney, the most agreeable personal relations were soon established. General Butler soon appreciated General Birney's valuable qualities, and gave him his fullest confidence. No one regretted Birney's loss more than Butler, as is proved by his eloquent and touching order, issued when the intelligence of his death reached the army, expressing heartfelt sorrow for the loss of a personal friend and a valuable officer.

THE FIRST MOVEMENT TO DEEP BOTTOM.

FROM the explosion of the mine, on July 30th, the army remained quiet, until near the middle of August, when General Grant determined to invest Richmond on the east with the Army of the James. The movement began on the night of Saturday, August 13th, when Gregg's cavalry division crossed the pontoon bridge over the James to Deep Bottom. This movement resulted in a three days' fight, and the part which Birney performed is thus described in the *Army and Navy Journal*:—

"During the same night (the 13th) the Second Corps, which had been ostentatiously moving down towards Fortress Monroe all day, in transports, was swiftly and secretly returned and disembarked at Deep Bottom. Early on Sunday, the 14th, Foster's brigade, of the Tenth Corps, was pushed forward, while the remainder of our forces were gradually deployed into the required line. The brigade moved out upon Strawberry Plains, and there found the enemy strongly posted in intrenchments, situated on commanding ridges covering the Kingsland road, with a line of rifle pits in front. Considerable skirmishing took place as our advance pressed forward. The enemy gradually fell back to his rifle pits, and at length the Tenth Connecticut and Twenty-fourth

Massachusetts charged the pits, and took them with hardly a struggle, capturing from eighty to one hundred prisoners.

"This success achieved, it now became essential to form all the troops in order of battle, and to push forward as rapidly as possible; for the enemy was hurrying troops over from his right to the region of Malvern Hill. With much exertion and constant skirmishing the manœuvre was made. Gregg's cavalry swept out to the right, clearing the roads of the enemy's pickets and opening the way for the Second Corps. When all was complete, the cavalry covered the right flank, next came the Second Corps, with its left resting upon the right bank of Four Mile creek, and then the Tenth Corps, with its right on the other bank of the creek. These dispositions were made after much skirmishing, and consumed most of the day. General Grant was on the field, with Generals Butler, Hancock, and Birney. Towards evening an effort was made to push the whole line forward. On the left the Tenth Corps moved briskly up and charging the enemy's outer works, in a line of woods, about a mile from the pontoon bridge, succeeded after a sharp engagement, in carrying them, capturing a number of prisoners and four eight-inch howitzers. This brilliant little victory was achieved principally by Foster's brigade."

"On Monday, the 15th, severe skirmishing was kept up all day; but the main effort was to extend our line to the right and secure a stronger position. This was effected by throwing the Tenth Corps across Four Mile creek, to the right of the Second. The cavalry, meanwhile, continued to cover the right flank and skirmished with the enemy.

"On Tuesday a still more determined effort was made to

advance. Gregg's cavalry stretched out on the Charles City road and covered the right flank. Next came Colonel Craig's brigade, of Mott's division of the Second Corps. On their left was the Tenth Corps and, lastly, the remainder of the Second Corps. Early in the morning Birney pushed out his right towards the enemy's intrenchments. The whole country was very thickly wooded, and only a narrow cleared patch here and there was relieved from the dense forest and undergrowth. The difficulties of manœuvring were increased by the intense heat of the day. By noon it had become one of the most sultry and oppressive of the season. The earliest movement was made along the Charles City road, as far as Deep Bottom creek or Deep Run, by the cavalry. At this point it was joined by General Miles's brigade, of Barlow's division of the Second Corps. The column soon found the enemy disputing its further progress, and a sharp fight took place with Chambliss's brigade of Fitzhugh Lee's cavalry. Our forces quickly drove back the enemy to his works, and General Chambliss was killed while rallying his men. The column was then pushed forward on the road to near White's tavern, a point between six and seven miles from Richmond. Here the enemy was found intrenched in a strong position, which some skirmishing proved too strong to be carried. Having ascertained this fact, Miles withdrew his brigade towards the right of the main line under Birney, marching back on the route by which he had advanced in the morning. This retrograde movement gave new confidence to the enemy, and, having now collected a considerable force at White's tavern, he swept down upon Gregg during the afternoon, and drove him back two miles, and across Deep Run.

"Meanwhile still harder fighting was going on in the centre. Our forces, as we have seen, had promptly pushed into the wooded region in their front, between the Central and Charles City roads, near Fussell's mill-pond, on which our right rested. Terry's division of the Tenth Corps was the first to attack, with Foster's brigade in advance, Pond's and Hawley's brigades in support, and Craig's brigade, of the Second Corps, on the right. The country was very much broken, and the men had a hot march through ravine and jungle. At length the enemy's picket line was driven into his works and a brisk artillery fire was opened, under cover of which Birney advanced and captured some slight works, with forty or fifty prisoners. The troops were then reformed, and Pond's brigade charged the main works in handsome style, and, supported by Hawley and some colored troops, carried the intrenchments, after a long struggle, and captured two hundred prisoners and some colors. The fire was very hot, and for an hour the fighting was close and hard, it being at short range, in dense woods. The loss on both sides was very severe, considering the numbers engaged.

"This was the principal contest of the day. As soon as the intrenchments were taken, the troops were set to work to hold them against the enemy. The cavalry had now given away from the right, and the enemy redoubled his attack on the infantry in the centre, in a series of desperate assaults, and at length repossessed the works which had been wrenched from him. In one of these assaults the enemy's General Gherardie was killed. About six P. M. one more effort was made by Birney to retake the works, but it failed. Our losses were roughly estimated at about fifteen hundred, one thousand being set down to the Tenth Corps. The enemy's loss must have approximated to ours, from his having assaulted so desperately in the afternoon. We captured several battle-flags and a large number of prisoners, reckoned at about four hundred. The line at night was substantially as it was in the morning, but during the day our forces had once reached a point about six miles from Richmond."

On Wednesday, the 17th, and during Thursday, the 18th, the Tenth Corps enjoyed comparative quiet. During Thursday night a fierce assault was made by the enemy on the intrenchments occupied by the corps. This was a desperate effort to retake the ground which the enemy had lost, but it was unsuccessful. General Birney telegraphed to General Butler as follows:—

HEADQUARTERS TENTH ARMY CORPS,
August 19, 1864.

The enemy attacked my line in heavy force last night, and was repulsed with great loss. In front of one colored regiment, eighty-two dead bodies are counted. The colored troops behaved handsomely and are in fine spirits. The assault was in column, a division strong, and would have carried the works if they had not been so well defended. The enemy's loss was at least one thousand.

D. B. BIRNEY,
Major-general.

This telegram was repeated by General Butler to General Grant, and by him to the Secretary of War, who, on August

20th, made it a part of his dispatch, nominally to General Dix, but really for the information of the country.

It was during this movement that the soldiers of the Tenth Corps gave to their General (D. B. Birney) the nickname of Deep Bottom Birney, by which he was known during the rest of his career.

In the corps, the battle of Tuesday, 16th, is known as the battle of Fussell's mill, although out of the army it has been termed the battle of Deep Run. For the skill displayed by General Birney, during this movement north of the James, he was recommended by Generals Hancock, Butler, and Grant for the first vacancy in the grade of brigadier-general in the regular army.

The following order was promulgated before the corps recrossed the river:—

HEADQUARTERS TENTH ARMY CORPS,
IN THE FIELD, *August* 19, 1864.

[GENERAL ORDERS, NO. 25.]

The major-general commanding congratulates the Tenth Army Corps on its success. It has on each occasion, when ordered, broken the enemy's strong lines, and has captured during this short campaign four siege guns, protected by the most formidable works, six stands of colors, and many prisoners. It has proved itself worthy of its old Wagner and Sumter renown.

Much fatigue, patience, and heroism may still be demanded of it, but the major-general commanding is confident of the response.

To the colored troops, recently added to us and fighting

with us, the major-general commanding tenders his thanks for their uniform good conduct and soldierly bearing, setting a good example to our veterans, by the entire absence of straggling on the march.

By command of Major-general D. B. Birney.

ED. W. SMITH,
Assistant Adjutant-general.

The movement at Deep Bottom not having produced the desired results, there was again a lull in the storm. Birney returned to his old lines and established his headquarters at "Hatcher's farm" for several days. On Friday, the 26th, the corps moved and took position in the trenches around Petersburg, relieving the Eighteenth Corps, which went north of the Appomattox and occupied the line which the Tenth Corps had vacated.

IN THE TRENCHES.

HE Tenth Corps remained on duty before Petersburg until September the 28th. During this time little occurred to vary the monotony of the soldier's life. The men, however, were not idle. Exchanging the musket for the spade, they threw up earthworks, and among them Fort Stedman, which subsequently became so conspicuous in the annals of the siege. The event of most interest to the men which transpired during this interval was the grand, national salute of shotted guns, which General Grant ordered to be fired along our entire line, when the intelligence of the fall of Atlanta reached the army.

The scene, as witnessed by the corps, is thus described in a private letter written by a member of General Birney's staff, which found its way into the columns of a Massachusetts paper:—

"Last evening, in honor of the victory at Atlanta, we opened all our guns on Petersburg, firing a national salute, or thirty-six rounds from each battery. The firing commenced about eleven o'clock. You cannot imagine either the sight or the sound. The pyrotechnical display would have done honor to the fourth of July, and the noise satisfied the most uproarious of urchins.

"Through the air, describing every variety of curve, some mounting high up and others moving in quick half circles, passing and crossing each other, following one another in rapid succession, or rising from the same point and separating far apart, the bombs were seen, like meteors, as if whole constellations had broken loose and were wildly rushing into chaos. Sometimes they explode high in the air, sometimes near the ground, and one wonders if they fall harmless to the earth, or if they fulfil their mission of destruction; if they go crashing through the roofs and walls of churches, stores, houses, and barns, or are satisfied with knocking a few bricks from the chimneys, or a corner off here and there. All along the horizon you see the quick flash of the explosion of the guns, which looks like the lightning that plays in the clouds at the close of a hot summer's day, and the sound comes up in one continual rumble and roar, which reverberates far away, in the woods and the hollows, to the right and left. Mingling therewith are the insinuating sounds of the percussion shells, from the rifled guns; sounds indescribable by either words, shrieks, or screeches; sounds delectable only when listened to with the consciousness that the guns are not pointed towards or the contents intended to reach you. Our large thirteen-inch mortar is the pet of the line and speaks in thunder tones. It devours nineteen and a half pounds of powder and throws a shell two hundred pounds in weight. Think of such a piece of hardware as a periodical caller. The largest gun which the rebels have opposed to us is planted on the other side of the Appomattox and enfilades a portion of our line. It is said to be of Rodman manufacture, and the shells come sailing quietly along, like comets, but generally bursting in the air and short of their intended mark.

"Doubtless somebody's slumbers were disturbed last night in Petersburg. This is the only general cannonade since we recrossed the James. Occasionally some battery opens when the pickets fire more than usual, or the 'Express' sends over a message, or the General orders the 'town-clock to be wound up,' which by this time must be pretty effectually wound up, unless it has 'run down,' to keep out of harm's way."

Here General Birney's headquarter camp was laid out in the form of a semicircle, the tents shaded by awnings of evergreens, and on each side of the broad avenue a brilliant green lawn was secured by the sowing of oats. To it was awarded the compliment, which Birney, oftener than any other general could appropriate, of being the finest headquarters in the army.

NEW REGIMENTS.

SOON after General Birney was assigned to command the Tenth Corps he turned his attention to increasing its numbers. Early in August he obtained permission from the War Department to raise a regiment of sharpshooters in Pennsylvania. He selected for the command of this regiment Major J. W. Moore, of the Ninety-ninth Pennsylvania volunteers, who had enlisted as a private in a Philadelphia regiment during the three months' campaign, and afterwards entered the service for three years as a second lieutenant. He rose from rank to rank solely by his merits, and when he attracted the attention of his commanding general held the commission of major. Like Birney he was a quiet, unobtrusive man, but resolute and determined, and no inducement or temptation could swerve him from the path of duty. He came to Philadelphia with letters from Birney to the Governor of Pennsylvania, asking that the command of a regiment be given him, and with letters to the writer and other friends of General Birney in Philadelphia, urging them to aid Major Moore in raising the regiment. They at once took hold of the matter with spirit, and, in less than two weeks from his arrival in Philadelphia, Moore went to the front and took his position in General Birney's command as colonel of the Two-hundred-and-third Pennsylvania volunteers. The regiment is still in service, (June, 1865,) but its gallant colonel sleeps in a soldier's grave. His regiment led the attacking party in the assault on Fort Fisher, near Wilmington, North Carolina. Colonel Moore was one of the first to enter the work, and he and Lieutenant-colonel Lyman, of the regiment, fell victims to rebel bullets.

When the regiment left Philadelphia the following notice appeared in the *Philadelphia Inquirer*:—

"THE WAY TO DO IT.—Yesterday morning the Two-hundred-and-third regiment of Pennsylvania volunteers struck tents at Camp Cadwalader, and marched through the city on their way to the front, under orders to report to General Birney, commanding the Tenth Army Corps. They went through without display. No presentation of flags or other ceremony attended their departure. This absence of display has characterized the raising and organization of the entire regiment. On the 15th of August, J. W. Moore, major of the Ninety-ninth Pennsylvania volunteers, commenced recruiting in this city, and subsequently in other parts of the State. He had come up from the front with authority from the War Department to raise a regiment of sharpshooters, to be attached to the Tenth Corps. He went to work earnestly, and in less than thirty days had mustered in about thirteen hundred men—more than was required for his own regiment. The Government were unable to furnish arms and uniforms for the entire regiment, or Colonel Moore would have left the city ten days ago.

"The surplus men will be attached to the Two-hundred-

and-thirteenth regiment, which J. C. Briscoe, major on General Birney's staff, is now raising in the city. Though he has been in town less than ten days, he has already nearly six hundred men. His regiment will be armed and uniformed as sharpshooters, and will be attached to the Tenth Corps.

"The appearance of the Two-hundred-and-third regiment, as they marched through the streets yesterday, was the theme of general remark. More than one-half the men were veterans, and the others were men in the prime of life and able to endure the hardships of the field. Though we have often seen more display on such an occasion, we have never seen a finer body of men, who looked as if they were in earnest, and were not on a holiday excursion.

"Colonel Moore deserves great praise for the energy and tact he has shown in raising the regiment. He has himself come out of the ranks, and is an accomplished soldier. With such men as he has selected, we are sure he will prove himself a competent leader, and the rebels will often get messages from his sharpshooters."

When the great success of Colonel Moore in organizing his regiment was communicated to General Birney, he applied to and obtained from the War Department authority to raise a second regiment of sharpshooters. This authority he transferred to the "Charles O'Malley of the Army of the Potomac," J. C. Briscoe, who was then serving on the staff of General Birney as senior aide. When Birney was assigned to the command of the Tenth Corps, Briscoe had the rank of Captain in the Fortieth New York volunteers. Birney asked his promotion to the rank of Major on the corps staff. This request was complied with, and the promotion made.

Major Briscoe came to Philadelphia armed with letters similar to those which Birney had given to Major Moore. Birney's friends, profiting by the experience which they had gained while raising the Two-hundred-and-third regiment for Major Moore, immediately made a raid upon the purses of their acquaintances, and soon raised three thousand dollars to pay the extraordinary expense which might be incurred in organizing a regiment for Briscoe. The Adjutant-general of Pennsylvania, under the authority of the Governor, designated Briscoe's future regiment as the Two-hundred-and-fourteenth Pennsylvania volunteers. Such had been Moore's success, that when he went to the front with the Two-hundred-and-third Pennsylvania volunteers, he had left in Camp Cadwalader, Philadelphia, three full companies, which had been recruited for his regiment in different portions of the State, before it was known that the regiment was full. These companies Briscoe secured as the nucleus of his regiment, and immediately opened recruiting offices in different parts of the State. At that time there were in Camp Cadwalader five companies of the One-hundred-and-ninety-ninth Pennsylvania volunteers, which was then being organized under the patronage of the Union League of Philadelphia. By his persuasive powers, Briscoe induced the authorities at Harrisburg to permit him to abandon the effort to raise the Two-hundred-and-fourteenth regiment, and to add to the five companies of the One-hundred-and-ninety-ninth the three he had inherited from Colonel Moore. Two more companies were soon obtained from Briscoe's recruiting agents, and thus the regiment was filled within ten days after his arrival in Philadelphia, and Briscoe returned to the front and took his place in the Tenth Corps as Colonel of the One-hundred-and-ninety-ninth Pennsylvania volunteers. His regiment was soon in condition, and shortly after General Birney's death General Butler told the writer that it was one of the finest regiments in his command. Colonel Briscoe kept up its efficiency, although it was out of his power to get the regiment into action until the movement by which General Grant compelled the enemy to evacuate Petersburg. Until that time they were doing picket duty, or similar service, and the assault on Fort Gregg, near Petersburg, was their first serious encounter. Here they did well, and then participated in the pursuit of General Lee. They were engaged in the fight near Appomattox Court House, which was the last engagement which the Army of the Potomac fought. Thus Colonel Briscoe, who, in the skirmish at Big Bethel in 1861, carried the colors of the First New York volunteers as high private in the beginning of the rebellion, led forward his regiment at Appomattox Court House, (in spite of the wound he had received in the assault on Fort Gregg,) and as colonel did his share in giving to the rebellion the stab which caused its death. For his gallantry during this movement he has since been promoted to be a brigadier-general by brevet.

The extraordinary expenses which Briscoe incurred in raising his regiment amounted to less than eight hundred dollars, which left in the hands of the Committee more than twenty-two hundred dollars. During a meeting in

August, 1863, at the house of the Hon. William Millward, one of the Committee, it was decided that the writer should expend a portion of the fund in presenting to Colonel Briscoe a complete outfit. This order was executed, and there still remained in the hands of the treasurer nearly one thousand dollars. The balance was unanimously appropriated to pay for a dinner, which it was proposed should be given to General Birney the first time he returned home, to which all the subscribers to the fund were to be invited. This disposition of the balance was premature, for General Birney came home only to die, and after his death the money, which had been appropriated for festivity, was used to pay for a lot in the cemetery in which his remains were laid, and to defray the expenses of his funeral.

RESOLUTIONS OF COUNCILS.

SUCH had been Birney's success during the campaign of the Army of the Potomac under General Grant, that, for the first time, the authorities of Philadelphia recognized, in a formal manner, the honor he had conferred upon his adopted city by his services during the rebellion. On the 24th day of September, the following resolutions were passed by the Select and Common Councils:—

"*Resolved,* By the Select and Common Councils of the city of Philadelphia, That the thanks of the authorities of the city of Philadelphia are eminently due and are hereby tendered to Major-general David B. Birney, for his brilliant services in the cause of the Union, and his efforts to suppress this unholy rebellion against the authority of the Government and the people of the United States.

"*Resolved,* That the use of Independence Hall be granted to Major-general Birney for the reception of his friends, and in order to afford the citizens of Philadelphia an opportunity of testifying their personal regard for him and their appreciation of his gallantry and patriotism.

"*Resolved*, That the Mayor of the city and Presidents of Councils be requested to carry these resolutions into effect, and that the Clerks of Councils be requested to furnish a copy of the same to General Birney on his arrival in the city."

These resolutions were forwarded to General Birney, but were never acknowledged formally by him. He anticipated coming home, from time to time, and had his health permitted would, on his return, have availed himself of the offer contained in the resolutions. He duly appreciated the compliment intended him, and, though offered late in his career, it was acceptable, for by his success he had long before merited all the honors which it was within the power of the municipal authorities of his adopted city to bestow upon him.

The resolutions were handsomely engrossed and framed, and are now in the possession of his family among many similar testimonials.

NEW MOVEMENTS.

ABOUT the latter part of September it was evident that new movements were contemplated. During the rest which the men of the Armies of the Potomac and the James were enjoying, the principal general officers of both armies were actively engaged in forming new combinations, and laying the plans of renewed efforts to dislodge the enemy from his intrenchments. In these councils Birney, by virtue of his new command, was invited to participate, and he soon made his presence felt by the originality of his suggestions and the comprehensive view which he took of the situation of the two armies. On September 26th, General Grant, accompanied by Generals Butler and Birney, and by Secretary Seward, Hon. Charles A. Dana, Assistant-secretary of War, and Hon. E. B. Washburne, member of Congress from Illinois, went up the James river, in a dispatch boat, as far as Dutch Gap, ostensibly on a pleasure trip, but really on a tour of consultation and observation. During this trip General Grant decided to make the movements which were begun on September 29th.

How well these plans of General Grant were executed will appear hereafter. It is very certain that no one of the Tenth Corps who participated in them, except General

Birney, understood their meaning until they were fully developed. From the nature of the orders given, the staff and general officers of the corps were, of course, aware that a movement was contemplated, but to what point or for what purpose they could not divine. At the time of its commencement there were a number of transports collected at City Point, and rumor said that the Tenth Corps was destined for Wilmington, N. C. This impression was confirmed by the fact that General Graham, who commanded the army flotilla, composing part of the Army of the James, had just returned from a reconnoissance near Wilmington.

Never was a military secret kept with more fidelity. Birney's proverbial taciturnity was exercised to its full extent, and it proved to be not only impervious to the curiosity of the officers of his staff, but even the inquisitiveness of army correspondents could not elicit a hint of what was in contemplation.

SECOND MOVEMENT ON DEEP BOTTOM.

DURING the night of September 28th, the Tenth Corps was moved in light marching order up to Jones' Neck, and thence across the James on muffled pontoon bridges to Deep Bottom. This movement was under the direction of General Butler, whose army consisted of the Tenth Corps under General Birney, the Eighteenth under General Ord, and a division of cavalry under General Kautz. While the Eighteenth Corps, under General Ord, was making the advance, on the Varina road, the Tenth Corps was equally active, and marched from Deep Bottom towards New Market. The latter soon encountered the enemy's pickets, and drove them back to the Kingsland road. At the junction of this road with the New Market road the enemy awaited the coming of our troops. Here strong breastworks had been erected on a commanding position, called New Market Heights, which covered the junction of the two roads. A marshy ground in front, with dwarf trees and a dense undergrowth, rendered the approach to these works very difficult; but Paine's colored division of the Eighteenth Corps, which had reported to General Birney, successfully encountered the natural obstacles of this approach. A murderous fire swept through them at every step, but without firing a shot they marched onward and carried the works at the point of the bayonet. This was the key-point to the enemy's line, and was, therefore, defended with great obstinacy, but Paine's men carried it, in spite of all opposition. He lost nearly two hundred killed, in this gallant struggle, and many more than this number were wounded. Generals Grant, Butler, and Birney were present to witness this conflict, and the next day, when Paine's division rejoined the Eighteenth Corps, General Birney sent them a complimentary letter of thanks for their conduct in the assault upon New Market Heights.

During this time Terry's first division of the Tenth Corps pushed in on the right, driving the enemy from that portion of the heights and retaining the position. Without pausing after these successes, Birney pushed up the road towards Richmond, and soon reached the point of intersection between the New Market and Mill roads. During this time Generals Grant and Birney rode alongside of the troops towards the head of the column. General Grant's presence was instantly known to the soldiers, and acted like magnetism along the whole line. The enthusiasm of the men knew no bounds when they found that their movements were under the eyes of the Lieutenant-general commanding the Armies of the United States. They marched onward and soon carried the works at the intersection of the New Market and Mill roads. This point was covered by earthworks, which were feebly defended, and so rapid was the retreat of the enemy that few prisoners were taken.

The accuracy of General Butler's knowledge of the movements of the enemy was singularly verified after this attack. He had ascertained, and stated before the movement began, what force of the enemy held this point, and of how many men it was composed. After the successful assault a morning report was found in the works, which proved General Butler's statement to be correct, but showed that he had mistaken the strength of the enemy by some twenty men.

After this success, the advance of the Tenth Corps, composed of Foster's second division, easily drove the enemy within six miles of Richmond, at the junction of the Varina and New Market roads. At this point the enemy had erected earthworks, behind which they successfully resisted the further advance of our troops, and it soon became evident that these works on Laurel Hill, as the ground was called, were not then to fall into our possession.

While these movements were going on, the division of cavalry under General Kautz was equally successful. At nine o'clock A. M. General Kautz moved to the right, up the Darbytown or Central road. He met with no opposition until he had nearly reached the tollgate, less than three miles from Richmond. He then reconnoitered the roads on the right, and sent back word that, if he had infantry support, he thought he could go into the city. Immediately Terry's division was sent out to his support. Terry marched across from the New Market to the Central road, and came within view of the spires of Richmond. While he occupied this position, the Fourth Massachusetts cavalry, under Colonel Rand, made a bold reconnoissance and advanced to within two miles of the capitol at Richmond, nearer than any of our troops had been previously during the rebellion. The failure, however, to carry the works at Laurel Hill compelled the return of the infantry under General Terry. The cavalry bivouacked that night on the Fair ground, in the suburbs of Richmond.

This day's movement was gazetted to the country in a dispatch from General Grant to General Halleck, in the following words:—

HEADQUARTERS, CHAPIN'S FARM, 10.45 A. M.,
Thursday, September 29, 1864.

MAJOR-GENERAL HALLECK:

General Ord's corps advanced this morning and carried the very strong fortifications and long line of intrenchments below Chapin's farm, some fifteen pieces of artillery, and from two to three hundred prisoners.

General Ord was wounded, though not dangerously.

General Birney advanced at the same time from Deep Bottom and carried the New Market road and intrenchments, scattering the enemy in every direction, though he captured but few.

He is now marching on towards Richmond.

I left General Birney where the Mill road intersects the New Market and Richmond road.

This whole country is filled with field fortifications thus far.

U. S. GRANT,
Lieutenant-general.

These movements were also described by a correspondent of the *New York Herald*, who, writing under date of September 30th, says:—

"General Butler complimented the gallant commander of

the Tenth Corps, by saying to him, in the presence of his own and General Birney's staff, that he had never known orders more accurately obeyed, nor an offensive movement, depending for its success on the junction of troops moving on converging lines, prosecuted with greater punctuality. Birney was at each of the points laid out for him to attack at the very moment directed in the plan of the general movement. No opposition offered by the enemy, no fatigue suffered by his men, no difficulties in the way of any nature, however formidable, were permitted to check his progress, but at the hour set he was at the junction of the two roads, the point beyond which his movements were contingent upon circumstances, and subject to direction of his superior officers."

On Friday morning, September 30th, the enemy made an unsuccessful attempt to dislodge Birney from the position he had captured the day previous. This movement the *Army and Navy Journal*, in its issue of October 8th, describes in the following words:—

On Thursday evening "Birney withdrew from Laurel Hill to the captured line of works in his rear," and his left formed connection with the right of the Eighteenth Corps at Fort Harrison, or, as it was afterwards named, Fort Burnham. "The result proved the wisdom of these dispositions. No attack was received during the night of Thursday, but on Friday, the 30th, about two o'clock, the enemy made his appearance in heavy force, having been largely reinforced during the night and morning from Petersburg. In front of Stannard's division, of the Eighteenth Corps, (occupying Fort Harrison,) the whole of Hoke's division is said to have been massed, General Lee superintending the attack. His object was to break through the captured intrenchments, and to separate the Eighteenth and Tenth Corps. The attack fell, therefore, mainly on the right of the one and the left of the other. Paine's colored division was getting position, on the left of the colored division which formed the left of the Tenth Corps. On these, about two o'clock, the enemy hurled himself with great violence. He began by a furious cannonade of fifteen or twenty minutes, which was answered by our artillery. Our colored soldiers stood their ground with fidelity, and delivered a withering fire of musketry, while the batteries repaid something of the devastation which had been visited on our ranks the day before. But it was on Stannard's division that the weight of the attack fell. Deploying in three strong lines at the edge of the wood, the enemy charged with great promptitude, under cover of a hot shelling from his iron-clads in the river, and an annoying enfilading fire from the batteries on the bank. A well-directed musketry fire sent him reeling back to the woods before reaching the intrenchments. Again, and still a third time was the charge renewed, but only to be repulsed with great slaughter. Our men had been instructed to depress their pieces, and the musketry fire was at once incessant and murderous. On the breaking of the enemy, General Weitzel succeeded in cutting off and capturing over two hundred prisoners, including officers. Two battle-flags were also captured.

"At evening the rain descended in torrents, and all that night and all day and night of Saturday it continued, putting the roads into wretched condition, rendering the march of troops very difficult. During Saturday several prisoners and refugees were brought in, who were evidently Richmond citizens impressed into the service. The city was said to be in great confusion; business entirely suspended, and nearly every male over fifteen, except invalids, in government service."

On Saturday, October 1st, General Kautz, with his division of cavalry, supported by General Terry, with his division of the Tenth Corps, made another reconnoissance to the right, up the Central and Charles City roads, penetrating to the main line of the defences of Richmond. No body of our troops had been in such close proximity to the city since the opening of the rebellion. Sunday, the 2d, was busily improved in rendering the works behind which our troops lay stronger, by reversing them and placing the abattis on the other side from that it had been while they were occupied by the enemy.

On Monday, Tuesday, and Wednesday, the 3d, 4th, and 5th of October, no movement was undertaken by the Tenth Corps. The enemy in the front kept up a constant picket fire, which was continued with singular ferocity on the 6th. The next day, Friday, the 7th, the battle of Darbytown road was fought, which was an attempt to turn the right flank of the Army of the James, which, had it proved successful, would have compelled its retreat to its intrenched camp at Deep Bottom and the south side of the river. At this time it held a line running nearly north-east and south-west, the left flank resting on the James river near Dutch Gap, and the right of its infantry line extending less than half way to the Central or Darbytown road, from the New

Market road. The cavalry under General Kautz, who reported and was subject to General Birney's orders, protected the right flank, and reconnoitered nearly to the Charles City road. The extreme right was probably five miles distant from Richmond, the left twice that distance.

It was known during Saturday night that a movement was on foot within the enemy's lines, and its nature was readily divined. At early dawn of Friday a brigade of rebel cavalry, with Hoke's and Fields' divisions of infantry, accompanied—as it was afterwards ascertained from prisoners and non-combatants living between the lines—by General Robert E. Lee, commenced moving on the Darbytown and Charles City roads. At six A. M. they burst upon Kautz's cavalry, putting the greater portion of it in utter rout, and sending it streaming back, over the works in which the Tenth Corps was lying, in the wildest disorder, in fact perfectly terror stricken. Kautz had with his cavalry two batteries of artillery—"B" of the First artillery, commanded by Lieutenant Hall, (now colonel of the United States colored troops,) and the Fourth Wisconsin battery. These batteries were left almost without support, although there were some few officers and men who rallied around them and remained until the last. The only road by which this artillery could retreat was a woods road, which had been cut the day before, which was narrow, filled with stumps of trees, and which crossed at one point a swampy piece of ground, which had been but partially bridged. Lieutenant Hall, seeing the flight of the cavalry, counselled the Wisconsin battery to withdraw, while he held the enemy in check as long as possible, so that, even if his own battery were lost, it would be lost in saving another. Hall's men stood to their guns as only disciplined men will stand, although their capture seemed almost certain, all the while sending charge after charge of canister into the masses of troops which, having emerged from the woods, were forming as rapidly as possible on the open field. A confederate officer on the staff of General Fields said to an acquaintance of the writer, whom he met under a flag of truce a fortnight thereafter, "That battery stayed there too long, but it was magnificently served and did us fearful injury." Hall stayed not too long, but only, as he supposed, long enough for the Wisconsin battery to give him a clear road, when he limbered up and left the field. Before he had gone a hundred yards into the woods he found his way blocked by a caisson of the Wisconsin battery overturned in the road, and before it could be displaced the rebels were around him, and, cutting his horses free from his pieces, he left them their dearly-bought trophies.

Meanwhile General Birney, perceiving the intentions of the enemy and comprehending his real designs, was hastily making the necessary preparations to frustrate them. Upon any but the best disciplined troops the panic of the cavalry would have had serious effect, and might have totally unfitted them for resistance. But it was not the case with the veterans of the Tenth Corps, and the stampede was communicated only to a few teamsters and non-combatants, and this was readily quelled by the presence of a few fearless spirits. The road was quickly freed from all impediments, the trains were started for Varina landing, a battery was put in position commanding the approach to our rear by the New Market road, and Terry's division was thrown far round to the right, parallel with the same road, and reinforced by a brigade from Foster's division, under Curtis. This line was formed in the thick woods, for the most part, and but a very small proportion of it was protected by earthworks or rifle pits of any kind. These dispositions were scarcely complete before Fields' division, which had obtained possession of the Central road, advanced to the attack. As he approached the artillery was brought to bear upon his columns, and a disastrous enfilading fire made a momentary confusion in his ranks. In reply, the enemy opened with some ten or twelve pieces, and poured solid shot, shell, and spherical case in one continuous shower, which, although not particularly fatal to our men, who at that point had cover, was the means of disabling so many of the battery horses that, had we retreated, the guns must either have been hauled off by hand or abandoned. Sitting quietly in his saddle, surrounded by his staff and escort, in full view of these rebel artillery men, General Birney watched, at a few minutes after nine o'clock, the attack of Fields' division, dashing over the open space and gaining the woods in front of Terry. "Our infantry remained quiet until the enemy was very close, when all four brigades, rising from their half ambush, poured into him a destructive volley. The chief attack fell upon Abbot's brigade, a part of which was armed with Spencer repeating rifles. This weapon, at such short range, proved very deadly. Shattered though he was by Terry's fire, the enemy still clung obstinately to his attempt, and a fierce musketry battle took place in the woods. Our troops found they had no longer the Richmond militia to contend with, but veterans. After the engagement had been prolonged for half an hour or more, the enemy made a second rush, falling more particularly upon Pond's brigade; but it was equally as unsuccessful as the first, and they commenced thereafter to withdraw, still keeping up the same withering artillery fire."

General Birney at once sent out a force in pursuit, to discover their further intentions and prevent them from establishing themselves, by throwing up works, on the Central road. At this time he sent the following telegram to the major-general commanding the Department:—

HEADQUARTERS TENTH ARMY CORPS,
October 7, 1864, 10.15 A. M.

MAJOR-GENERAL B. F. BUTLER:—

We have repulsed the attack of the enemy on our right flank, with great slaughter. The troops seem to be Fields' and Pickett's divisions. I send you a batch of prisoners. I am extending my right flank. The enemy seem to be intrenching on the Darbytown road.

D. B. BIRNEY,
Major-general.

General Hoke's division, which had moved down the Charles City road, went still farther to our right, his flankers coming in collision with a small force of our men at Signal Hill, a portion of New Market Heights, within musket shot of the works which Birney carried on the 29th of September. So much further, however, did that division have to march than the division of General Fields, that by the time it came into a position to attack, Fields had been thoroughly whipped, and it was deemed prudent not to renew the attack with another division, alone and without reserves. Hence the entire force retreated slowly, and by night such of our cavalry as could be collected were back in the position it occupied that morning.

"Our entire loss was not greater than five hundred, while that of the enemy was estimated at one thousand, which figure it probably reached. Among the latter were about one hundred and fifty prisoners. The Richmond papers claim the capture of over two hundred horses."

This action is also thus described by Thomas M. Cook, Esq., one of the ablest of the corps of correspondents of the *New York Herald*:—

"Hoke's division of rebel infantry, consisting of four brigades, moved out of Richmond at an early hour last evening on York river turnpike. Fields' division, of equal strength with Hoke's, moved out from the rebel line of works immediately beyond the right of our infantry line and advanced down the Central road.

"Kautz's men were put to confusion and broke in the wildest disorder. At the same time the announcement was received of Hoke's advance, which increased the panic and caused a disgraceful stampede. Men, horses, wagons, etc., started for the rear at a fearful pace.

"The artillery alone maintained its position, courageously fighting against the fearful odds opposed to it. The guns were served very rapidly and handled efficiently; but the rebels advanced steadily upon them until within forty feet, when the artillerists mounted their horses, cut traces, and started after the cavalry. A single regiment of mounted men, Colonel Sumner's New York mounted rifles, remained upon the field, until the artillery withdrew.

"During the early morning General Birney was busily engaged forming his troops to receive the onset of the rebels. During the previous day and throughout the night he had been suffering from a malarious fever, and was so seriously ill as to have placed himself in care of a physician, the medical director of his corps; but when the alarm was sounded to battle he was up and in his saddle, despite the remonstrances of his medical adviser, and throughout the day remained with his troops, though during the afternoon he was compelled to leave his saddle and accept a more comfortable means of locomotion in an ambulance.

"Terry's division was assigned the post of honor for the day, it being formed on a line at right angles with our main line, stretching along parallel with the New Market road, about five hundred yards north of that thoroughfare. The right of this line was in deep woods and partially strengthened with rude and hastily constructed rifle-pits. The left stretched across an open field and occupied strong works that had been constructed previous to this affair. In these works Lieutenant-colonel Jackson, Chief of Artillery, had placed four batteries of six guns each. From this position a clear view could be had of the fields over which the rebels must pass to reach the woods, in which the right of the line was posted, which fields were literally swept by these guns.

"The formation of the line gave the third brigade, Colonel H. M. Plaisted, of the Eleventh Maine, commanding, the right; the second brigade, Colonel Joseph C. Abbott, of the Seventh New Hampshire, commanding, the centre; and, the first brigade, Colonel F. B. Pond, of the Sixty-second Ohio, commanding, the left.

"The rebels in their previous reconnoissances had discovered, as they supposed, the right of our infantry line, and the cavalry being stampeded, they now pressed on in what seemed to them the shortest route to pass our right and strike in our rear. The position held by the second and third brigades they supposed to be unoccupied, and so it was until fifteen minutes before the attack came; in this course, therefore, they headed.

"At ten o'clock they commenced their movement, and at the same moment our formidable array of artillery opened upon them, enfilading them more and more perfectly as they advanced, and doing great execution. They brought out two batteries into a little point of woods opposite the position of our guns and attempted to silence our deadly fire; but Colonel Jackson met this attempt by planting a couple of rifle batteries in the rear of the main line, which, firing over the others, did good execution upon the rebel batteries, causing one of them to limber up and get out of the way in a hurry, its horses being so badly used up that it became necessary to drag the pieces away by hand. In the meantime the fire upon the advancing rebel line of battle was not slackened, nor was its execution less fearful. But still the rebels pressed on, and were soon in the woods, beyond range of our artillery.

"The main attack fell upon the second, or central brigade, the brigades on either flank being lightly engaged.

The second is about half armed with Spencer's repeating carbines, and had a strong skirmish line, composed wholly of men with this weapon, thrown well out to the front. These lay concealed behind a thicket of underbrush until the enemy was in close range; then suddenly rising they poured volley after volley with great steadiness into the rebel lines, causing a momentary halt. But again the line advanced, and our skirmishers, having exhausted their carbines, steadily gave way to the rear, and uncovered the main line of battle. Here were more carbineers, and more men who understood using this terribly destructive weapon.

"The action now became intensely hot. The woods were filled with a continuous roar of musketry, and the savage work of butchery was going on with marked rapidity. Our men displayed a steadiness and coolness seldom equalled and never surpassed.

"The rebels were obstinate and determined; but, finding that they could not drive our men from their position, finally gave way and retired in confusion. The battle had lasted about half an hour, but during that short space of time over one thousand of the rebels left their bones to enrich the sacred soil.

"Our own losses in killed, wounded, and missing, were a trifle over a hundred. It was the cheapest victory ever won on a battle-field.

"The rout of the enemy was complete; so much so that their officers were utterly unable to rally them for a second charge, thus admitting the day to be ours. They went back, leaving many of their dead and a number of their wounded in our hands.

"The result of the attack on our part was the loss to the infantry of about one hundred men in killed and wounded, mostly of Abbott's brigade. The rebels suffered very heavily. The ground is yet strewn with their dead, while numbers of bodies are known to have been taken back by them, and some were buried on the field. Besides this we captured about two hundred and fifty prisoners.

"Among their slain was Brigadier-general Gregg, com manding a brigade of Fields' division. His body was taken back by the rebels. We have rumors of another general officer being killed, but it is by no means certain. They lost a number of field officers, from colonels down, leaving some of the bodies on the field.

"The field in which our artillery was posted was hot beyond all description. Nothing could live on it uncovered by the breastworks. The enemy's two batteries in front of the guns of Fort Gilmer, firing over the woods, and some batteries farther down their line, all poured their shot and shell in that direction.

"Our batteries were terrible sufferers. Their horses were killed without stint, and the losses of men with them by no means small. Battery E, of the Third United States artillery, lost three men killed and nine wounded, and fourteen horses killed. Battery D, of the First United States, lost one killed and four wounded, and ten horses killed. The Fifth New Jersey battery lost six horses. Battery C, of the Third Rhode Island, report four men wounded and five horses killed. Such heavy losses to artillery are seldom known, and attest the vigorous character of the enemy's attack.

"The rout of the cavalry was a disgraceful affair, and came near costing us the entire position on this side of the river. It fell upon this corps at a moment when our men needed to be fortified with all their steadiness, coolness and courage. It sent our trains stampeding to the rear, and disorganized all the non-fighting force. General Kautz lost ten pieces of artillery, a very large number of horses, and a great many men, all which will give the enemy an opportunity to claim a victory and show the trophies and plunder. Yet, whatever they may claim, an attacking party was never more handsomely repulsed and sent back, than were they when they struck Birney's infantry. Not an inch did any of our men budge during any part of the fight, but, on the contrary, gained ground, and in the evening advanced and took up the position that had been so shamefully abandoned by the cavalry.

"The enemy, it seems, did not stop until the walls of Richmond sheltered one of his divisions, and the works along James river the other. It will doubtless be long ere he attempts again to turn our flank, but if he attempts it he will make his calculations of success on the concentration of overwhelming numbers to pour upon us.

"I regret to say that this evening General Birney is worse. The excitement and fatigue of the day on his previously exhausted system is now telling. Still he will not apply for a leave while there is a prospect of a battle, but, at any personal risk, and disregarding the remonstrances and appeals of his friends and the advice of his physicians, will share with his troops all their dangers and glories."

SICKNESS AND DEATH.

HE responsibilities of the command of the new corps, and the exertion it demanded from the new general, proved to be more than he could endure. During the quiet of the 4th, 5th, and 6th of October, exhausted nature had refused to do more, and for these days he was unable to leave his tent, being under the care of the medical director of the corps. Yet in spite of the exhaustion produced by the combined action of disease and medicine, Birney did not fail to respond to the demand made upon his energies on Friday, October 7th. When the intelligence of the movement of the enemy reached him, early that morning, his strong will, controlling his physical infirmities, enabled him to rise from the cot in his tent and again mount his favorite horse Eclipse. During this day he was in the saddle until noon, when he was no longer able to sit his horse. He was then placed in an ambulance until near dusk, when, after the repulse of the enemy, he was driven to his headquarters, which he left only to return home, under the imperative command of General Butler, who, on Monday, October 9th, visited him and ordered him home without delay.

Turning over the command of the corps to General Terry on Sunday evening, he left the scene of conflict on Monday morning, the 10th, on the Greyhound, the dispatch boat of General Butler, which was placed at his disposal. The boat reached Baltimore during Monday night. On Tuesday morning he telegraphed to the writer at Philadelphia, who, by the courtesy of S. M. Felton, Esq., then President of the Philadelphia, Wilmington, and Baltimore Railroad Company, (whose interests Birney had so faithfully protected during the early days of the rebellion, when he was lieutenant-colonel of the Twenty-third regiment of Pennsylvania volunteers,) provided for him a special train to Philadelphia. He reached Philadelphia about two P. M., on Tuesday, the 11th of October, attended by three of his staff, Captains Graves, Noble, and Ford. This day happened to be election day in Pennsylvania. The contest was a spirited one, and its result was doubtful. On that day was to be decided whether Governor Curtin should be continued in office three years longer, or should surrender to the candidate of the Democratic party. General Birney was determined to do all in his power to decide this question, and, though unable to leave or enter his carriage without assistance, insisted upon going to the polls before going home. His vote was challenged, by one of the minions of the Copperhead ward-committee, attending at the polls for the purpose of throwing out the ballots of loyal men, on technical grounds. The challenge, however, proved unavailing, and the officers of the election gladly received Birney's vote for his friend Governor Curtin and the entire Republican ticket, State, county, city, and ward. So great was Birney's suffering that, during the challenge at the polls, he was unable to give the number of his house, which he had owned and lived in for several years.

The writer saw him, within half an hour after the scene at the polls, in bed, in his dwelling-house, No. 1920 Race street. He was then suffering from the effects of disease, and his mind was dark and cloudy. His first salutation was, "Well, I voted, and have done all in my power to defeat these infernal copperheads, who have done more to prolong this rebellion than the rebels. Don't fail to do your duty to-day to your country. Vote as I have, or don't vote at all."

"Don't let any doctor come near me. I am not sick; I only want rest. In a few days I will be all right. Can't you arrange a trip to the country, where I can be unobserved and we can have a good time, without any fuss or ceremony."

The writer pacified him as well as he could, and in a few minutes the interview was interrupted by the entrance of Dr. Gerhard, who had for a long time been General Birney's family physician. He saw that the condition of his patient was critical, and lost no time in ordering the prescriptions which his skill and experience suggested. No pains were spared by Birney's family and friends to effect his restoration. On Thursday, after his return home, he seemed to rally, and until Tuesday morning, October 18th, strong hopes were entertained of his recovery. At the instance of the writer, Dr. John Neill, whose skill in such cases had become almost proverbial, was called in to assist Dr. Gerhard, and both physicians held out to the family and friends their confident expectation of their patient's recovery.

During the latter part of the week, Birney's friends in

Philadelphia were admitted to his sick-room, and they all believed and hoped that, after a few days of quiet, he would be able to return to his command. Plans for the future were discussed, in which all united, and a campaign was laid out, from which all anticipated much pleasure. But all these castles in the air were soon dissolved, and the plans were thwarted by the death of the man for whose comfort they had been devised. On Tuesday morning, October 18th, General Birney's symptoms were of the most alarming character. He was attacked by a violent hemorrhage of the bowels, which his physicians were unable to check, and it soon became manifest to them that the end was near at hand. But they concealed their apprehensions from the family and friends, who, until an hour previous to his death, believed that the skill of the physicians would conquer the disease. During Tuesday General Birney was delirious, and a few incoherent expressions he uttered showed that his mind, in its wanderings, was bent upon military movements. Few of his sentences could be understood. About noon he rose in his bed and said: "Boys, the road through the woods will soon be completed; we must move on it cautiously, and make an attack on the flank." Later in the day he called to his body-servant and said: "John, tell the staff to get ready. I'm going now." About an hour before he died he straightened himself up and, with a significant gesture, said: "Keep your eyes on that flag, boys!" He then fell back, and never spoke afterwards words which could be understood.

About eight o'clock in the evening a number of his friends had collected in the parlor, having come to ascertain his condition. They knew that the night before he was improving, and were not prepared for the change that had taken place during the day. While they were assembling, the writer was summoned to the scene up-stairs, where he saw his friend in the agonies of death, surrounded by his wife and little children, who by this dispensation were deprived of their noble and generous-hearted protector.

In a few moments his spirit had fled; "the silver cord was loosed, the golden bowl was broken," and David B. Birney had yielded up his spirit as a sacrifice upon the altar of his country. It was not his lot to die on the field, pierced by a rebel bullet. He had passed through the ordeal of war for three years and a half without receiving a severe wound, and had almost begun to believe that he bore a charmed life, and would live to see the day when his country, reunited, partially by his own efforts, would emerge from the furnace of the rebellion strong, prosperous, and happy. But he counted in vain. Though he had penetrated almost within rifle-shot of the capitol at Richmond, it was not his privilege to march into the doomed city, at the head of his column. He saw the result of his fidelity to his country, and that of those brave men who had fought under him, only from the spirit land. By his last words he proved that, though compelled to lay by his sword, his heart was still in the cause for which he had made so many sacrifices. Never doubting that the old flag would again wave in its splendor from the St. Lawrence to the Gulf of Mexico, and from the Atlantic to the Pacific, on his death-bed he, in his delirium, exhorted his men to keep their eyes upon it. Let all obey his injunction, and, keeping our eyes on the flag, resolve that it shall never be trailed in the dust, so long as we have strength to keep it flying over every foot of territory of the United States of America.

General Birney's death created a profound sensation in the city of Philadelphia, in the army, and throughout the country.

On Wednesday, October 19th, the press of Philadelphia announced the sad event in the following language, which is quoted to show the estimation in which he was held in his adopted city. The editor of the *North American and United States Gazette* wrote as follows during the night of Birney's death:—

"DEATH OF GENERAL DAVID B. BIRNEY.—We regret to announce the death, last evening, at his residence in this city, of malarious fever, of the intrepid Major-general David B. Birney, the veteran commander of the Tenth Army Corps of the United States. His career in this war was one fraught with honor to himself and his country, and there will be a voice of sincere mourning for him wherever there is a patriotic heart in this republic. He was the son of the celebrated James G. Birney, the well-known candidate of the Liberty party for the Presidency of the United States. His father was originally a Southern planter and a large slaveholder, but, becoming convinced of the wrongfulness of slavery, he freed his slaves, and removed to a Northern State. * * * * * * * * *

"The volunteer officers of this war have produced no

nobler specimen of the soldier than Major-general David B. Birney. His name is identified with nearly every battle in which the Army of the Potomac has been engaged. His modesty long caused him to be overslaughed in the command of a corps, which he had fairly won, but at length he reached his true position, and commanded the Tenth Army Corps in all the late operations on the James river. He passed through a thousand perils from bullet and shell to fall a victim at last to the malaria which has swept away so many of our gallant men. In him Philadelphia loses a son of whom she has reason to feel proud. He leaves a widow and family."

On October 20th, the editor of the *Philadelphia Inquirer* wrote as follows:—

"IN MEMORY OF MAJOR-GENERAL DAVID BELL BIRNEY.—On Tuesday night last, October 18th, Major-general Birney, commanding the Tenth Corps of the Army of the United States, died in this city, of a malarious fever, with which he was attacked during his recent active and arduous service in front of Richmond. This mournful event was briefly mentioned in these columns yesterday, but the high character of General Birney, and the circumstance that he was an honored citizen of Philadelphia, make it fitting that we should pay some further tribute to his memory, that his patriotic services shall be placed on record in the journals of the day, and that his soldierly virtues may be held up as examples to his compatriots of the army. * * * * *

"In July last General Birney was promoted to the command of the Tenth Corps, and on the 13th of August he commenced the movements to the north of the James which, followed up by his skillful operations of the 29th of September last, carried our lines up the New Market road to within signt of Richmond. Here he added the victory of 'New Market Heights' to his already proud cluster of honorable fields; and here, too, he was seized with that fatal fever which has deprived his country of his services forevermore. But he kept the field, and when his lines on the Central road were attacked on the 7th of October, he left his sick bed to repulse the rebels who had scattered the cavalry of Kautz. General Butler, in reporting this battle, says: 'The enemy then swept down the intrenchments towards Birney, who waited their assault, and repulsed it with heavy loss to the enemy.' And again—'Birney took the offensive, and has reached and occupies the intrenchments which the enemy took from Kautz.'

"This, less than two weeks ago, was General Birney's last battle. Even while it was raging the hand of death was upon him, and he was brought home only to lay down the life he had devoted to his country.

"In person General Birney was a strikingly handsome man. He was tall, straight and lithe, and of the pure Saxon complexion. His face was remarkably intellectual. His manners were kind and courteous, and his voice was gentle as a woman's. Having entered the service as a lieutenant-colonel, he dies the commander of a *corps d'armee*, at the age of thirty-nine, esteemed as a man by all who knew him, and honored by his country as one of her best and noblest soldiers."

The *Evening Telegraph*, edited by a friend of General Birney, who was in his house at the time of his death, made the following announcement on October 19th:—

"MAJOR-GENERAL DAVID BELL BIRNEY.—When the news spread through our city this morning, announcing the death of General Birney, it caused universal sorrow, and cast a gloom over the entire community. It is but a few days since we recorded in our columns his return home from the army, on account of serious illness contracted in camp. At the time it was not considered dangerous, and no one anticipated a fatal termination. But since the hour he arrived in Philadelphia he gradually became weaker and sank away, until last night, when his noble spirit took its flight, and his martial form grew cold in death.

"General Birney was a Southerner by birth, having been born in Alabama. His father was the celebrated James G. Birney, a man noted for his love of liberty and those principles of freedom in defence of which his gallant son has now laid down his life.

"When the tocsin of war was sounded throughout the nation, General Birney left a prosperous business and gave himself to the cause of his country. Having long been connected with our citizen soldiery, he was promptly chosen Lieutenant-colonel of the Twenty-third Pennsylvania volunteers, and served through the three months' campaign. Returning, he reorganized the regiment and went to the field as its commander. Here he won the warmest praises of his superior officers, and being strongly recommended, was appointed brigadier-general of volunteers early in 1862. As commander of a brigade, and of a division, he distinguished himself in almost every battle fought by the Army of the Potomac; and the President, appreciating his gallantry and great services, in May, 1863, sent him the commission of a major-general. The public remember well how nobly and bravely General Birney bore himself in the terrible battles from the Wilderness to Petersburg. His last meeting with the enemy was on the south bank of the James early in this month, when he defeated the rebels, and sent them flying into Richmond before the impetuous advance of the Tenth Corps, of which he but a short time previous had been appointed commander.

"General Birney's death will be heavily felt in the army, where he was a great favorite with both officers and men. No nobler spirit has led our heroic legions to battle in this war for the Union than David Bell Birney. There will be many an eye suffused with tears among his brave veterans when the sad word reaches them, 'Birney is dead!'

"Our sympathies, and those of our people, are with them and with his bereaved family and friends. The nation has lost in him one of its most illustrious sons, and Freedom one of her most trusty champions."

The *Evening Bulletin*, which had always followed General Birney's career with a jealous care for his reputation, contained the following editorial the day after his death:—

"DEATH OF MAJOR-GENERAL BIRNEY.—We recently announced that Major-general David B. Birney, commanding the Tenth Corps in the Army of the Potomac, had arrived in this city, suffering from disease contracted while in service before Petersburg. We have now to state the melancholy fact that he died last evening, at his residence on Race street. He was about thirty-nine years of age, and had been in the service ever since the opening of the war. He commanded the Twenty-third Pennsylvania volunteers, and from that position he was called to the wielding of a brigade. On the 23d of July he was chosen by General Grant to lead the Tenth Corps, having brilliantly distinguished himself during the whole of General Grant's splendid campaign from the Rapidan to the south side of the James river. His career is now cut short before the grand object of that campaign is attained, but his record is a noble one, in which every Philadelphian takes honorable pride.

"General Birney was born in Alabama. His father, James G. Birney, was a planter in that State, who manumitted his slaves and came to the North, and afterwards was the abolition candidate for the presidency. General Birney was engaged in practising law in this city up to the opening of the war, and only relinquished active civic business at the stern call of patriotism. His memory will be forever honored in connection with the rest of the noble host who have laid down their lives for freedom and the Union."

The press of New York united with the press of Philadelphia in lamenting the death of a man who had earned a national reputation. The *New York Herald*, of October 20th, contained the following:—

"MAJOR-GENERAL DAVID BELL BIRNEY.—The country is again called upon to mourn the death of another of its distinguished heroes. Major-general D. B. Birney died at his residence, 1920 Race street, Philadelphia, on the evening of the 19th instant, of fever contracted in the arduous campaign against Richmond.

"David Bell Birney was born in Huntsville, Alabama, on the 29th day of May, 1825. He was the son of the Hon. James G. Birney, at one time the anti-slavery candidate for the Presidency, and a gentleman of prominence in the liberal party of his State. When quite young the subject of the present sketch removed with his father to Cincinnati, Ohio. He originally studied law, but instead of entering immediately into practice engaged in mercantile pursuits. For several years he remained in the West, and in 1848 made his home in Philadelphia, Pennsylvania, where he resumed the practice of his profession. After the first call for troops, upon the outbreak of the present war, Mr. Birney busily engaged in the recruitment of the Twenty-third regiment of Pennsylvania volunteers for three months, and was commissioned lieutenant-colonel. * * *

"As a companion and friend he was ever affable, polite and sociable. A strict disciplinarian, he was yet accessible to the humblest private in his command, who could approach him with an assurance of a patient hearing and a just determination of his suit. He was generous as he was brave, and, with firm Christian principles, always approved himself an honest and a noble man.

"In the present campaign against Richmond it was his misfortune to find his encampment among the malarious marshes of the famous Chickahominy. Here, after driving the rebels into the very gates of the rebel capital, achieving a series of victories that had promised not only to make his name famous in history, but to give him a more extended field of usefulness in the immediate present, he contracted the fatal disease that caused his death. The malaria had affected him so seriously as to demand medical assistance, and a course of treatment had been commenced that promised, with a few days of quiet and repose, a full restoration to health, when, on the morning of the 7th instant, the rebels made their desperate attempt to turn our right flank. Contrary to the advice of his physicians, and despite the earnest remonstrances of his friends, Birney mounted his horse at daylight, and, amid an unsurpassed storm of bullets and shell, from which he was miraculously delivered unhurt, he directed every movement of his gallant command. But the exertion, added to the weakening effect of his medicine, was too much for him. At midday he was compelled to call an ambulance, and, reclining in such a conveyance, he continued in the field until night. The prostration that followed baffled the skill of the best physicians. On the following day he reluctantly consented to apply for a leave of absence from the field, provided the medical director would give him a certificate of disability that would not appear to be based upon a childish complaint. On the morning of the 9th instant he left for his home in Philadelphia, promising to return within ten days. The passage home increased his malady, and on arriving in Philadelphia he had barely sufficient strength left to alight from his carriage at the polls of the ward in which he resided, and deposit his ballot for the Union candidates. Such was his last public act. From that day he sunk gradually but steadily, despite all the careful nursing of an affectionate wife, the comforts of home, and the skill and unremitting attentions of his family physicians, and finally quietly expired late in the evening of the 18th.

"It is expected that his funeral will be attended from his late residence in Philadelphia to-morrow, though the precise hour has not yet been named."

The first number of the *New York Ledger*, published after the death of General Birney, contained the following article by "Fanny Fern," who, shortly before his death, had paid General Birney a visit at his headquarters:—

"THE LATE GENERAL BIRNEY.—General Birney *dead!* It seems but yesterday that I spent that lovely autumn day at his encampment, and rode with him to the lines to see the shells thrown into Petersburg. But yesterday I dined with him, and laughed and chatted merrily while the band played outside, and sat afterwards at the door of his tent in more serious mood, hearing from his own lips incidents of the war. But yesterday that he there put in my hands a photograph album, and with beaming eyes pointed to the pictures of his wife and children, and spoke gaily of a visit from the former during the winter. Looking at those sweet faces even then I shuddered and said softly to myself—*perhaps!* But as I listened to the merry laugh of his eldest boy, who was darting hither and thither, into one tent and out another, with his face so full of sunshine, it was impossible not to catch some of it. I see General Birney now, as we rode away, standing in the glow of that gorgeous sunset, with his hat raised, and the smile upon lips now so cold! I hear the sweet music of the band upon the green. I see the groups of convalescent soldiers just come back from the hospitals standing about their general, who was so kind to them and so thoughtful of them. Alas! the longer I live the more I fear to utter that little word 'Good-bye.' That bridge between this world and the next which one may never again cross. But of that desolate home in Philadelphia who shall speak? Those sweet pictured faces come before me with the smiles faded out and the eyes misty with tears. The boy's ringing 'papa,' as he bounded from his side that glorious bright day, makes my heart ache to remember. God send our country its equivalent for the costly lives laid down in its defence, and comfort the broken hearts which are learning, the land over, the stammering lesson, 'Thy will be done.'

"'My men got homesick last winter,' said General Birney to me, 'so we got up a ball for them. There were many of the officers' wives there, and the bustle of preparation and decoration amused and cheered the poor fellows.' 'But these awful Virginia roads,' said I, with sides still aching from the bumps I had lately received; 'these awful Virginia roads!' 'Oh!' said he, 'we lighted fires, all along, but notwithstanding there were shrill cries of distress from some of the pitfalls! However, all went very merrily, and I congratulate myself that I made my men happy for a while at least.' For the same reason he had beautified the encampment where we found him. All the tents were ranged in the form of a circle, his own opposite the entrance. Each tent was perfectly covered with green boughs, which hung over it like a green curtain, leaving only room to enter. The ground in the midst was graded off in the most careful manner, and recently sown with oats, that late in the season it might look green and pleasant; while a nicely gravelled path led through it from the general's tent to the entrance gate-posts, where was planted a flag-staff, surmounted by one of the enemy's shells. Nothing could exceed the neatness and beauty of the whole arrangement. But more beautiful still was the motive which prompted it all—'to make things look home-like for the men.' No wonder 'the men' fight well under such officers. I felt constantly, while with General Birney, how it could be that, in his sympathetic, magnetic atmosphere, those immediately connected with him could say, as they did, to me, 'We would any of us gladly die for him.'

"How different from those generals to whom 'their men' are but so many machines or automatons, wound up to work out their will; who never think that *they, too,* have homes and wives, and children, of whom they think, in the dreary days and nights, till the homesick longing to look upon them seems to dwarf every other thought.

"Oh, it is a great thing for a successful general to keep his heart warm in his breast, electrically responsive to the joys and sorrows and needs of those subordinate to him. Woman as *I* am, I know I could fight, undaunted, a thousand battles, if I lived so long, with such a general as that."

The *Army and Navy Journal*, of October 22d, noticed the death of General Birney in the following article:—

"MAJOR-GENERAL D. B. BIRNEY, the commander of the

Tenth Army Corps, died at his residence in Philadelphia, on the 18th inst. He had but a few days previously come up from the army, his health seriously impaired by the effects of a malarious climate, and it was hoped that rest and a more salubrious air would restore him to health and duty. But death came speedily. * * * * * * * *

"Of General Birney's record during this last campaign, it is not necessary to speak other than generally. His name, as his position, has been a conspicuous one, and he has on all fields won reputation as an industrious, efficient officer, ambitious of distinction in his profession, and willing to sacrifice health and ease in the cause of the country."

THE FUNERAL.

HE Councils of Philadelphia, immediately after General Birney's death, passed unanimously a joint resolution, tendering to the family the use of Independence Hall, so that the remains might lie in state. But, while grateful for this offer, it was declined, because the family intended that the funeral should be conducted in the most simple manner. It was determined that the remains should be removed directly from the house to Woodlands Cemetery without display or ceremony, and Friday, October 21st, at two o'clock, P. M., was the time selected. It was found, however, impossible to make the funeral a private one. The numerous organizations, civil and military, of which General Birney had been a member, wished to participate in doing honor to his memory, and General Cadwalader, who was in command at Philadelphia, desired to do all in his power to pay proper military honors to the memory of his deceased friend. Yielding to these requests, prompted as they were by feelings which do honor to human nature, General Birney's family and immediate friends consented to a funeral, which proved to be one of the most solemn and impressive ever witnessed in Philadelphia.

Before the time fixed the writer was in attendance at the house, and by one o'clock, P. M., an hour before the time announced for the ceremonies, the crowd was so great that he was compelled to send to the nearest police-station for policemen to preserve order and keep the street clear. They soon arrived and did their duty efficiently. Observing in the crowd a number of soldiers wearing the "red diamond," many of whom were on crutches, and all of whom were evidently inmates of hospitals, the writer approached them and ascertained that they had obtained leaves of absence for the day, from the various hospitals around Philadelphia, to attend the funeral; but, being unable to march in the procession, they had come to the house before the time fixed for the ceremonies, hoping to be able to see the remains of their general. They were at once admitted, and such a scene as transpired in that parlor the writer had never witnessed before and hopes he may never again. These soldiers, wearing the "red patch," disfigured and maimed for life, surrounded the coffin and wept like children. Their grief was sincere, and its manifestation far exceeded the testimonials of respect which were shown to the deceased later in the afternoon. Quietly and sorrowfully this band of men, who all bore permanent marks of their encounters with the enemy, left the house to give place to the funeral ceremonies.

These ceremonies began an hour later than the time announced by the press. This delay was occasioned by the desire of the family to await the arrival of a brother and several of the staff of the deceased general, who it was known had left Washington in the early train of that morning. Owing to its detention they did not arrive until three o'clock, P. M., when the ceremonies commenced. After an impressive address by the Rev. Henry A. Boardman, D. D., the procession moved along the route prescribed, on which thousands had congregated. At Thirty-ninth and Market streets the procession halted, and the coffin was borne by soldiers thence, to the grave in Woodlands Cemetery. As they passed under the canopy of trees, whose autumn leaves were blazing in the setting sun, the scene was indelibly impressed upon the memory of all who witnessed it. At the grave all the civic and military honors due the rank of the deceased were observed in due form. His masonic brethren paid their last tribute of respect, and, after the carriages had left the cemetery, the firing party performed their duty, solemnly and impressively. This accomplished, they returned to the gates of the cemetery to rejoin the military escort, while the writer remained at the grave until the grave-diggers had thrown in the fresh earth. When the firing party reached the gates the bands of the military escort, forgetting the funeral dirges they had played during the afternoon, broke with one consent into the inspiring air of "Rally Round the Flag, Boys," and in this they were joined by the voices of the soldiers, numbering about two thousand men. As the wind bore these strains over the new-made grave, after that autumn sunset, the effect was sublime, and never to be forgotten by those who were present.

The funeral services were thus noticed in the *Evening Telegraph* of October 21st:

"OBSEQUIES OF MAJOR-GENERAL D. B. BIRNEY.—The city yesterday had quite a mournful appearance. All the flags were at half-mast, and the shutters of many of the houses in the neighborhood of General Birney's residence, and along the line of procession, were closed in honor of the funeral of Major-general Birney.

"At two o'clock, according to notice, the house was opened, and a great rush of citizens and soldiers followed. All were anxious to see the body of the General. Arrangements were made by which the great stream of people was kept in motion, and the crowd admitted at the front door were permitted to retire through the back.

"The body of the General was dressed in full major-general's uniform. On his breast was a cross of japonicas, and at his feet a wreath of the same flowers. The coffin was covered with a black cloth, and mounted with silver. On a silver plate on the lid was the following inscription:

DAVID BELL BIRNEY,
Major-general United States Volunteers,
Born May 29, 1825.
Died October 18, 1864.

"The officers under General Birney, his staff, and some private soldiers then took a last, lingering look at all that remained of their loved General. The wife and family of the deceased then took leave of the cherished husband and tender parent.

"After quiet had been restored, and the door closed, Rev. H. A. Boardman, D. D., of whose church the deceased was a member, read a number of appropriate selections from the Scriptures, and delivered the following address:

"There is scarcely any word in the human language so significant of evil as the brief monosyllable, war. It embraces almost every form of natural evil, and almost every type of moral evil. In its ghastly train are poverty, famine, pestilence, sickness, wounds, death, widowhood and orphanage, the black pall and the grave. Mingled with these forms of natural evil are infidelity, atheism, profaneness, licentiousness, and rupture of social and civil ties. The war in which we are engaged has a bad preeminence over all the wars recorded in history. It is a war against wise and beneficent institutions, begun amidst general and unexampled prosperity, amongst brethren having a common ancestry and a common heritage, bound together by the strongest civil, commercial, historical, and religious ties that ever bound a people. It is also amongst Christians worshipping the same God; more sacred and indissoluble ties never bound together any people.

"Here in this house to-day we are in a position to see the criminality of war. This whole city gives itself up today to mourning. The aged and the young, the soldier and the citizen, come here to-day to testify their respect for his character, gratitude for his services, and sympathy with this stricken household, and the righteousness of the struggle in which our country is engaged. It is right that it is so. It is meet that we should attest our sympathy on this mournful occasion with this afflicted family, and with the noble army who have gone to bless the land. I have said that sorrow attends war. The occasion before us is a mournful evidence thereof. There are tens of thousands of like scenes all over the land. What village is there that has not its Rachels weeping for their children, and will not be comforted because they are not? In secluded homes, in quiet villages, as well as in princely houses of magnificent cities, may be seen the terrible effects of this accursed rebellion. I feel that this is not the time nor the place to go into a review of General Birney's life and services. When three and a half years ago that fatal battery was opened upon Fort Sumter, he, with thousands of others, heard it as a call upon him. He forsook his business pursuits, and all his domestic ties, and gave himself up to the service of our country. He has withheld himself from no exposure, and has shunned no dangers. He has laid all that was dear to him upon the altar of his country. He has denied himself the coveted enjoyments of his home, and has only visited it at long intervals, and then only for brief periods at a time. He gave himself entirely up to the service of our country. It will appreciate the offering. A man of indomitable energy, sagacity to read men and things, with a just ambition, it befell him to take a prominent part in this fatal war. He participated in the battles of the Peninsula, Fair Oaks, Seven Pines, Malvern Hill, on the bloody heights of Fredericksburg, in the impenetrable wilderness of Chancellorsville, and on the well-fought field of Gettysburg—wherever there was danger he was there: before Petersburg, south of it, north of it, until that battle, under his direction, a few months ago, in which he led his men within the intrenchments of Richmond. Only two weeks ago to-day he left a sick bed against the remonstrance of his physician, was in the saddle for ten hours, turned a defeat into a glorious victory, and returned to his tent and laid himself down—shall I say to die? God, in His high mercy over this afflicted family, was pleased so to order that he came home to die. The last week of his life was spent here in the affectionate care of his family, under the guidance of the most skillful physicians. Neither affection nor skill could save him. He died from disease contracted in the swamps of Virginia. Therefore it was, nothing could arrest that fatal malady, and he must succumb to the conqueror that conquers all. He fell asleep enjoying the solace that above all things solaces every man, be he peasant or prince — the solaces of religion and peace with God. God ordered his last moments to be those of comparative ease and quiet. While his disease was delirious, he was fighting his battles over again, and calling his men to fix their eyes upon the flag. Do you wonder that these young men who have been with him in all his hard-fought battles are here to-day? His record is without a stain. His services were greatly appreciated and honorably rewarded. The crowning honor of his military career was probably fatal to him. He ought to have returned to his home before disease had already set in, but, with a whole corps depending upon him, he felt that it was his duty to be with them.

"I need not dwell on these things; you knew him as your townsman; it does not surprise you that our city has come up here to do him honor. All that public sympathy can do—all that the precious consolation of the gospel of Christ can do, is done, and will be done to temper this bitter cup. God's way is in the sea. Here is a man who has passed through thirty, yes, nearly forty great battles, yet an ever-unseen hand guards him from every peril. Shells flying around him fall without injuring him; thousands fall at his side, and ten thousand at his right hand, yet he comes home to die. Let me say that it behooves us all to stand with our loins girded and our lamps trimmed, knowing that there is a Conqueror who conquers all, and the feeblest of us may gloriously triumph over the last enemy, trusting in that God who is mighty over all things.

"You, gentlemen, soldiers, who interpose your breasts between rebellion and ruin and us, let me here in the presence of these remains—in the presence of that manly face and that mute voice which has so often rung out on the battle-field—let me counsel you to make your peace with God through the blood of the Lamb. To-day we should learn another lesson also. We ought to learn to cherish more fondly the beneficent institutions God has given us. Here is something of what their maintenance has cost us. The precious lives—this shedding of blood. May God so order our affairs that this fatal struggle may be brought to a righteous, honorable, and lasting end." * * *

The day after the funeral the following editorial appeared in the *Press*, from the pen of its editor, Hon. John W. Forney:—

"THE BURIAL OF A SOLDIER OF FREEDOM.—When, at the beginning of the war for the preservation of the American Government, David Bell Birney volunteered his services, he had no doubts, either as to the justice or as to the sequel of the great controversy into which our country had been precipitated; and when his sword was accepted his heart went with it. The career of this incomparable soldier, who died in consequence of health impaired in the service of his country before he had reached the age of forty, is a signal illustration of the truth that he who enters into a great fight with a sincere and religious belief in the morale of that fight, is sure to be remembered—sure to be honored, living, and to be mourned, dead. Many have gone into this struggle for the preservation of the Government without first considering and weighing the principles involved in that struggle, and, while perilling their lives, have allowed themselves rather to look upon their sacrifices as a cold duty. Such as these, however, have themselves only to blame if their deeds are not indelibly impressed upon the popular heart and forever cherished in the popular memory. Major-general Birney was not only a soldier of freedom, but a soldier of conscience. He fought for his country, not simply because he had the allegiance which we all owe to it, but he fought for it because he loved it, and because, above the mere matter of duty and obedience, he entertained the higher principle, intense and passionate attachment to the great idea that this war can never close until the entire institution of human slavery is extirpated.

"There was something in the character of this young

general peculiarly fascinating. The writer of this article does not remember ever having met him, although it was our fortune, on more than one occasion, to assist his friends, and to stand between him and unjust antagonism. But no man could have been supported as Birney was supported if he had not been a chivalric, an unselfish, and fearless patriot. It is related that one of the last acts of his life was to vote the Unconditional Union ticket in the Tenth Ward of this city, on the 11th of October, just as he was returning home, utterly debilitated, from the Army of the James.

"There is in this single act a text and a teaching far more eloquent than poetry or prose, and he, doubtless impressed with the belief that the seeds of death were gnawing at his heart, felt that in the enjoyment of this last and most precious privilege of human freedom he was proving, by his contribution to the civil power of his Government, the sincerity of his devotion in the tented field. His remains were yesterday followed to the cemetery in which they are now entombed by such a cortege of soldiers and citizens as will long be remembered. The highest dignitaries of the State came forth to honor him. The Governor of Pennsylvania showed by his presence how earnestly he appreciated his great qualities, and in the long line that accompanied the hearse to that mausoleum which shall hereafter be a shrine for patriotic citizens to worship at, came General Sickles—the superior of General Birney in more than one bloody battle—testifying by his presence with his mutilated body, his sense of the high and soldierly ability that distinguished the lamented deceased, and how profoundly he mourned the loss of a brother-soldier.

"There is something in the life and death of such a man as Birney singularly calculated to awaken the sensibilities of the dullest. It rekindles the fire of the men who are in the army, and lights a spark of patriotism in the bosoms of those who are not in the army. *The soldiers most successful in this great struggle for freedom are those who have believed in the justice of our cause.* The only defeated men have been those who have hesitated about the issues involved in it. Had General McClellan grasped the *baton* of command in the profound consciousness that he was not fighting as a mere martinet—that he was not called to obey the orders of certain military chieftains, but that the destinies of a free people had been intrusted to his charge, and that he was warring against slavery in the belief that slavery had begun the war against the Union—he would not now be the candidate of a party that denounces this contest for American freedom as a failure, and he would not now be a sort of potentate of peace, and the only hope of those who expect to defeat and to destroy our country. Hooker, Sherman, Grant, Farragut, Sheridan, Sickles, and all the winning men, whether on the land or sea, in this struggle, have a religious faith, not simply in the justice of our cause, but in its victorious sequel. We repeat that no man has finally failed, on the land or the sea, who has really believed that the right is with us, and that God is with the right. There is not a disgraced general or a defeated commodore to-day who does not fall back upon copperhead philosophy, and upon so-called Democratic arguments, for the purpose of attacking the Government that has retired him. Let us then honor the actions of those who live in the belief that our cause is just, and let us cherish the memory of those who, like Birney, have fought, bled, and died in the consciousness that their country was never more worthy of their sacrifices than when, in order to save ourselves from death, she took up arms against human slavery."

The following description of the funeral appeared in the *New York Herald* of October 23d, from the pen of T. M. Cook, Esq., one of the army correspondents of that paper, who had been with General Birney in the camp and the field :—

"The funeral of the late Major-general David B. Birney was attended with distinguished honors and solemnities, from his late residence in Philadelphia, on the afternoon of Friday.

"The day will be long remembered by every dweller in Philadelphia, as well as by all temporary sojourners in that goodly city, because of the very general air of sadness and mourning that pervaded the entire community. In every street, from public buildings, hotels, private residences, and all other conspicuous places, the American flag, draped in mourning, and set at half-mast, was displayed from sunrise to sunset, while throughout the day the sullen booming of minute-guns betokened the national character of the grief that centered in that locality.

"The funeral services were appointed to be held at the late residence of the distinguished dead at two o'clock, P. M. The Select and Common Councils of the city, in general meeting, on the previous evening, in adopting resolutions of condolence with the immediate family of the deceased, had proposed to make the funeral a public affair, the expenses to be borne by the city; and in contemplation of such an affair had set apart the famous and historical Independence Hall for the ceremony. But the repugnance of the immediate family to such a display, and their desire to bury their own dead with simple and unostentatious Christian ceremonies, led to the rejection of the empty honors proposed by the city authorities, and the funeral was appointed, as stated, to be held at the family residence. The distinguished rank and position occupied by the General at the time of his death, however, forbade an entire compliance with the wishes of his bereaved relatives. Custom and the regulations of the service, no less than the universal desire of the public, demanded a burial in accordance with the rank of the deceased, and the universal bereavement of the community would be satisfied with nothing less. Therefore it was arranged for a private ceremony at the house, after which the body should be attended to the grave with all the pomp and show the popular will demanded.

"As early as noon hundreds of people began wending their way towards the former residence of the deceased, and by half-past twelve o'clock the streets in that vicinity were thronged with dense masses of men, women, and children. Conspicuous in the multitude were large numbers of soldiers, convalescents from the various hospitals in and about the city, disabled soldiers, (armless and legless,) soldiers on temporary furlough, private soldiers as well as officers, members of Birney's old command, as well as many from all other departments of the army. The throng evidenced, by its promiscuous character, the universality of the grief the sudden death of this brave and gallant officer had awakened.

"At one o'clock, in obedience to the repeated demands of this throng, the doors of the house were thrown open to admit the multitude to a last gaze at the dead. Arrangements were perfected to admit the people by the front door and allow them to pass out at a side entrance. The body, lying in its plain coffin, was exposed upon a centre-table in a large drawing-room. The pictures and ornaments of this room were tastefully draped with the American colors and the colors of the various corps with which the General had served—the Third, Second, and Tenth.

"The coffin was plain mahogany, covered with black cloth, having upon the lid a silver plate with the following inscription:

DAVID BELL BIRNEY,

Major-general United States Volunteers,

Born May 29, 1825.

Died October 18, 1864.

"The body was dressed in the full uniform of a major-general, with the corps badge and the decoration of the Third Corps Union, of which he was Vice-President, fastened upon his left breast. A cross of most exquisite white japonicas rested upon his breast, and a wreath of the same beautiful flowers lay nearer his feet. The face, which bore evidence of the wasting character of the disease that had conquered him, was still life-like and natural, and betokened the quiet and peaceful manner in which the spirit had taken its flight. Several sets of side-arms and equipments, gifts of friendship and admiration, were grouped upon a side table.

"Brigadier-general William Birney, a brother of the deceased, and Chaplain S. S. Jennison, brother-in-law, were to arrive from the army at half-past one o'clock P. M., to attend the funeral. A delay in the arrival of the train detained them until half-past two, until which hour the services were delayed, and the doors of the house remained open to admit the public. During all this time there was no diminution of the crowd that poured in, requiring the utmost efforts of the police to regulate it and keep it in motion. Probably during this hour and a half not less than five thousand people passed through the house, many shedding tears as they passed beside the remains of the beloved dead. Finally, when all was ready for the commencement of the services, it became necessary to close the doors in the face of an equally great multitude who were begging for admission.

"The services at the house were simple, solemn, and impressive. They were conducted by Rev. Henry A. Boardman, D. D., of the Presbyterian church, of which the family are members. They were introduced by reading selections from the psalm commencing "Lord, make me to know my end," etc. After this were read some passages from St. Paul's Epistle, commencing "Wherefore, seeing we also are compassed about with so great a cloud of witnesses," etc. Dr. Boardman then delivered a short address to the company assembled, followed by a touching and impressive prayer, which, with the benediction, closed the exercises.

"The family then drew near the coffin, and improved the last opportunity of looking upon the face of the loved one. It was a sad and heart-rending spectacle as the bereaved widow, followed by the orphaned children, drew near the shrine of their heart's devotion. The lamentations, and sobs, and cries of the deeply-stricken family, appealed, in no ordinary manner, to the sympathies of all beholders.

"While these touching and impressive scenes were transpiring within the house, Brigadier-general Ellet was engaged without in forming the escort and arranging the funeral cortege. This was no easy matter, considering the dense mass of people that thronged the streets and choked up, for several blocks in either direction, every avenue of approach. But after persevering efforts the military line was formed, the troops facing the house, in readiness to salute the body as it was brought out.

"The procession was appointed to move at three o'clock; but it was precisely four as the remains were brought out of the door. This delay was occasioned in a great measure by the difficulty of forming the escort in the midst of so vast a crowd of spectators. The coffin was borne to the hearse by soldiers of the old Twenty-third regiment of Pennsylvania volunteers, formerly commanded by Birney. It was followed by the pall-bearers as follows:—Major-general Cadwalader, Major-general Sickles, Commodore Engle, United States Navy, Brigadier-general Gwyn, and Colonel Peter Sides.

"As the body appeared the escort presented arms, the muffled drums beat a solemn roll, and a battery detailed for the purpose commenced firing minute-guns, which were continued until the burial was completed.

"The hearse was drawn by four black horses, and was surrounded by a detail of the City Troop (of which organization Birney was a member) as a guard of honor.

"The escort immediately moved down the street and halted to give place to carriages for the mourners and friends, and to form the civic part of the procession. When fully formed the following was the organization of the cortege:

"Detachment of police, under command of the Chief of Police.

"Band.

"Brigadier-general Ellet, commanding escort, and staff.

"One-hundred-and-eighty-seventh regiment Pennsylvania infantry, with detachments from two militia regiments.

"First Troop Philadelphia city cavalry, S. J. Randall, M. C., commander.

"Detachment of United States marines, with drum corps.

"Carriages containing the officiating and other city clergymen.

"Pall-bearers in carriages.

"Band.

"Hearse, with guard of honor.

"The General's body-servant, leading the General's favorite horse 'Eclipse,' presented to him by General Sickles—the horse fully caparisoned.

"Carriage containing the widow, Wm. Jennison, Esq.,

her father, Brigadier-general William Birney, and Mrs. J. G. Birney, mother of the deceased.

"Carriage with Captain Graves, of the General's personal staff, and the children—Agatha, Frank, Willie, and Belle. (Two children, David B., Jr., three years old, and Kearny, an infant, did not go to the grave.)

"Mr. and Miss Jennison, and Chaplain S. S. Jennison, brothers and sister of Mrs. Birney, and Mrs. William Birney.

"Officers and soldiers of the Twenty-third regiment of Pennsylvania volunteers in citizen's dress, the regiment having served its full period of enlistment.

"Captains Noble and Ford, of the General's staff, and Captains Fassitt and Moore, recently of the same connection.

"Other staff officers formerly serving with Birney, and the staff of Major-general Sickles.

"The Governor of Pennsylvania and staff.

"The Mayor of Philadelphia.

"Numerous carriages, with intimate friends of the family.

"Band.

"Franklin Lodge, No. 132, A. Y. M., (of which Birney was a member,) and deputations from other masonic orders, on foot.

"Officers of the army who have served under Birney—on foot, under direction of Colonel Collis.

"A large deputation of other officers and soldiers of the army.

"Union League of Philadelphia, on foot.

"The National Union Club of Philadelphia, on foot.

"Members of the bar of Philadelphia, and citizens generally.

"The procession was one of the most lengthy and imposing that has ever been seen in Philadelphia. When fairly organized and moving it could be measured only by miles. The entire city seemed to have turned out, either as participants in or spectators of the solemn pageant. The line of march from the residence to the cemetery covered a distance of about three miles, and along the entire route the streets were so densely packed with people that it was frequently with great difficulty the cortege forced its way through. The slow, measured time of the solemn dirges played by the several bands also contributed to increase the time consumed in reaching the cemetery, and it was finally dark as the body was lowered into its last resting-place.

"The brief religious exercises at the grave were conducted by Rev. Dr. Ducachet, of the Protestant Episcopal Church. The coffin, wrapped in an American flag, was rested over the grave, the mourning friends surrounding it, while files of soldiers were just visible, through the faint twilight, in the background. The clergyman, when all was ready, in a clear tone recited one or two passages of the Episcopal burial service, commencing, 'We commit his body to the grave, earth to earth, ashes to ashes, dust to dust,' etc., and closed with the benediction.

"The body was then lowered into the grave. It was, indeed, a mournful scene. The shades of night were gathering so rapidly as already to render objects but dimly visible. The harsh grating of the coffin as it descended into the ground, the audible groans and sobs of the stricken widow, the plaintive cries of the bereaved children, the sympathetic sobs of the attending multitude—all conspired to give impressiveness and deep solemnity to the event.

"And then the mourners moved away, having deposited their loved one, in their wished-for unostentatious manner in his last resting-place; and when they had withdrawn beyond hearing, the more pompous and showy ceremonies of a masonic burial were carried out, succeeded by a military salute becoming the rank of the dead. Thus the sensitive shrinking of the family from a grand, empty show, was respected both at the house and at the grave, and the public desire for an opportunity to render homage to the dead gratified, while the formal grandeur of a military pageantry was not necessarily omitted.

"And thus terminates, in the very full of its usefulness, the brief career of Major-general Birney. In recording this imperfect sketch of the sad event, the writer cannot refrain remarking upon a most singular coincidence it affords. On the 28th of September, not a month since, in a communication to the *Herald*, from the Tenth Corps, mention was made of the fact that the hospitalities of the city of Philadelphia had been tendered to General Birney, and that so soon as he could be spared from the field it was his intention to meet his fellow-citizens, on which occasion his former superior officer, General Sickles, and Governor Curtin, with other dignitaries, would be present. He has indeed been from the field, and his fellow-citizens have gathered about him, testifying by their presence their appreciation of his worth as a citizen, and his gallantry and bravery and ability as a general. In the assemblage, too, were Major-general Sickles and Governor Curtin. How singularly exact the appointment was kept, but how mournfully different from what had been anticipated were the circumstances of the meeting! Thus is brought out in startling characters the great truth, that man proposes, but God disposes."

ORDERS ISSUED IN THE ARMY.

ON the death of General Birney being made known to his old comrades in arms, they sorrowfully did all in their power to honor his memory. The following order was issued by General Butler, commanding the Army of the James:—

HEADQUARTERS DEPARTMENT VIRGINIA AND NORTH CAROLINA,
ARMY OF THE JAMES. IN THE FIELD, *Oct.* 21, 1864.

[GENERAL ORDER, NO. 135.]

SOLDIERS OF THE ARMY OF THE JAMES:—

With deep grief from the heart the sad words must be pronounced—Major-general David B. Birney is dead.

But yesterday he was with us—leading you to victory. If the choice of the manner of death had been his, it would have been to have died on the field of battle as your cheers rang in his ear. But the All-wise "determineth all things well."

General Birney died at his home in Philadelphia, on Tuesday last, of disease contracted in the field in the line of his duty.

Surrounded by all that makes life desirable—a happy

home—endeared family relations—leaving affluence and ease, as a volunteer, at the call of his country—he came into the service in April, 1861. Almost every battle-field whereon the Army of the Potomac has fought has witnessed his valor. Rising rapidly in his profession, no more deserved appointment has been made by the President than General Birney's assignment to the command of the Tenth Army Corps. The respect and love of the soldiers of his own corps has been shown by the manner they followed him.

THE PATRIOT—THE HERO—THE SOLDIER. By no death has the country sustained a greater loss.

Although not bred to arms, he has shown every soldierly quality, and illustrated that profession of his love and choice.

It is not the purpose of this order—nor will the woe of the heart of the officer giving it now permit him—to write General Birney's eulogy.

Yet even amid the din of arms, and upon the eve of battle, it is fit that we, his comrades, should pause a moment to draw from the example of his life the lesson it teaches.

To him the word DUTY, with all its obligations and incentives, was the spur of action. He had no enemies save the enemies of his country—a friend, a brother to us all: it remains to us to see to it, by treading the path of duty as he has done, that the great object for which he has struggled with us and laid down his life shall not fail, and his death be profitless.

Soldiers of the Tenth Army Corps! Your particular grief at the loss of your brave commander has the sympathy of every soldier in the army. It will be yours to show your respect to his memory by serving your country in the future, as with you Birney has served it in the past.

By command of Major-general Butler.

ED. W. SMITH,
Assistant Adjutant-general.

General Couch, commanding the Department of the Susquehanna, ordered that all flags within the department be displayed at half-mast during the day of the funeral.

General A. H. Terry, temporarily commanding the Tenth Army Corps in the absence of General Birney, issued the following order:

HEADQUARTERS TENTH ARMY CORPS,
IN THE FIELD, VA., *October* 25, 1865.

[GENERAL ORDERS, NO. 43.]

As a token of respect for the memory of the late commander of this corps, Major-general David Bell Birney, the colors of the regiments, of the batteries, and of the several headquarters, will wear the usual badge of mourning for the period of thirty days from November 1st.

By command of Brevet Major-general A. H. Terry.

WM. P. SHREVE,
Lieutenant and A. A. A. G.

The day after General Birney's death, General De Tro briand, who was temporarily in command of General Birney's old division, issued the following order:

HEADQUARTERS THIRD DIVISION
SECOND ARMY CORPS, *October* 19, 1864.

[GENERAL ORDERS, NO. 64.]

It is with profound regret that the Brigadier-general commanding has to convey to this command the sad news of the death of Major-general D. B. Birney, after a brief illness, in Philadelphia. Nowhere such a lamentable loss will be more deeply felt than in this division, the glorious records of which are so much identified with the gallant services of the worthy successor of Kearny and Hooker.

He died before the end of the struggle in which he took such a noble and conspicuous part, but his devotion to the country, his fidelity to duty, his gallantry in action, and his brilliant efforts for the triumph of the Union, will remain among us as an example to follow, while his personal qualities will endear his memory among all those who served with him or under him.

By order of Brigadier-general De Trobrian.

S. P. FINKELMIER,
Assistant Adjutant-general.

Colonel J. W. Moore, of the Two-hundred-and-third Pennsylvania volunteers, conveyed to his men the sad news of the death of their General in the following language:

HEADQUARTERS TWO-HUNDRED-AND-THIRD REGIMENT
PENNSYLVANIA VOLUNTEERS, (BIRNEY'S SHARPSHOOTERS,)
BEFORE RICHMOND, *October* 23, 1864.

[GENERAL ORDERS, NO. 7.]

Since it has pleased the Divine Ruler of the Universe to take from us our able and gallant commander, Major general D. B. Birney, who gave up his life in defence of his country and its laws, it is fitting that some token of respect should be paid to his memory.

From the outbreak of the rebellion until the time of his death, he was ever among the foremost in the conflict, and has borne aloft the standard of freedom so faithfully and unflinchingly as to awaken in the minds of his countrymen the liveliest emotions of respect and admiration. And although we may cherish in our *hearts* the remembrance of his past deeds and virtues, yet, while our friends in the North are showing, by various symbols of mourning, that they have appreciated his value, and now feel his loss, it especially behooves us, who were under his immediate command, to present to the world some *outward sign* to prove that we too lament his untimely death. It is therefore ordered that crape shall be worn upon the sword-hilt by the commissioned officers of this regiment, and that the colors shall be draped in mourning for the space of thirty days from this date.

By order of Colonel J. W. Moore,

JOHN A. LESLIE,
Adjutant.

PROCEEDINGS OF CIVIL ORGANIZATIONS.

THE Councils of Philadelphia, at their first meeting after General Birney's death, passed the following resolutions:

"*Whereas*, It has pleased Almighty God to remove by death from our midst Major-general David B. Birney, at a time when our citizens were seeking an opportunity to do honor to his worth and bravery; when his many deeds of valor had commended him to our highest considerations of warmest sympathy; when, with Hancock, and Meade, and Grant, and a long list of worthies, he had gained for himself undying honors, and ranked himself a brave, bold, and courageous officer; when, after slow advances, flank movements, dashing charges, and severe battles, the 'Army of the Potomac,' under fearless and able generals, had driven the Confederates within the rebel capital, and when Richmond was almost within the grasp of the Union forces. And

"*Whereas*, It is but due to the memory of the deceased that our citizens should honor him with a public burial; therefore,

"*Resolved, by the Select and Common Councils of the City of Philadelphia*, That the use of Independence Hall be tendered to the family of the late Major-general David B. Birney, for the purposes of a public funeral.

"*Resolved*, That we deeply deplore the loss of a brave general, a courageous soldier, a distinguished civilian: his many deeds of valor, his many sacrifices, his bold and fearless example, will be held in grateful esteem by us, his fellow-citizens. And while we regret his departure from among us at a time when his courage, his efficient services, his best energies, together with those of his honored associates of the 'Army of the Potomac,' were about to be crowned with success, and victory was about to be proclaimed in the occupation and possession of the rebel capital, we humbly submit to the decree of Heaven in this sore and afflictive dispensation.

"*Resolved*, That we tender to the family of the deceased our heartfelt sympathy and condolence, and hereby testify our sincere appreciation of his worth and merit, his valor and courage, his many sacrifices and services in defence of our firesides and homes, our flag and our country.

"*Resolved*, That a committee of five members from each branch of Councils be appointed, together with the President of each chamber and the Mayor of the City, to make arrangements for a public funeral of the deceased from Independence Hall, if agreeable to the wishes of his family. And that a copy of these resolutions be engrossed and presented to his consort, in grateful appreciation of the distinguished courage, bravery, and devotion that marked her husband's promotion, from the lieutenant-colonel to a major-general of volunteers in the United States army."

The annual report of the Board of Trade of Philadelphia, of which General Birney was a member, written during the week of his death by its President, Wm. C. Ludwig, Esq., who had for years been a firm friend of General Birney, contains the following tribute to his memory:

"Another of our members who departed this life during the past year is Major-general David B. Birney, a gentleman whom we all respected for his private virtues and his eminent abilities. Sacrificing a lucrative business, and the comforts and happiness of home and friends, he determined, when the standard of rebellion was first raised, to devote his whole life and all his energies to the cause of his beloved country; and the record he has left behind him shows how faithfully he discharged his sacred duty. From the time he first entered the service he braved every danger, and was engaged in most of the important battles of the war. The proud reputation which he has justly won by his unflinching bravery and his skill and efficiency as a commander in the army that is heroically struggling to subdue this unrighteous rebellion, merits from us a tribute to the memory of an honest citizen, a gallant soldier, and a pure, chivalric, self-sacrificing patriot."

At the first meeting of the First Troop of Philadelphia City Cavalry, which acted as the guard of honor at the funeral, a committee was appointed to draft resolutions, expressing the sense of the company. The following extract is made from the minutes of the meeting:

"The Committee, appointed to present resolutions expressing the sense of the members on the death of the late Major-general Birney, made the following report, which was unanimously received and adopted:

"*Whereas,* It has pleased an inscrutable Providence to remove by death (whilst in the service of his country) our late fellow-member, Major-general David B. Birney, therefore,

"*Resolved,* That the members of this Troop unite with the loyal citizens of our whole country in mourning the loss of so true a gentleman and so gallant a soldier; one whose career of distinguished honor and usefulness will ever be cherished in the affections of the people, and whose name will be written high upon the roll of those noble martyrs and heroes who have fallen in the grand struggle now going on for the preservation of our country's honor and nationality.

"*Resolved,* That, whilst sorrowing over the death of our late associate, whose life promised so much for his friends and country, we nevertheless recognize and bow before the mysterious will of an all-wise, all-merciful God, 'Whose way is in the sea, and Whose path is in the great waters,' yet 'Who doeth all things well.'

"*Resolved,* That the usual badge of mourning be worn by the members for thirty days.

"*Resolved,* That a copy of these resolutions be transmitted to the family of the deceased, and that they be published in the daily papers."

The following report of the proceedings of a meeting of the officers of the Custom House in Philadelphia appeared in the daily papers of the city:

"TRIBUTE OF RESPECT TO THE MEMORY OF MAJOR-GENERAL BIRNEY.—The clerks and others connected with the Philadelphia Custom House held a meeting yesterday, after business hours, to pay a mark of respect to the illustrious dead. Mr. Charles Pryor was called to the chair, and Mr. Benjamin Huckel was appointed Secretary. Messrs. S. Snyder Leidy, B. Huckel, Thomas J. Smith, Thomas W. Martin, and Dr. Griffin were appointed a Committee on Resolutions. They reported the resolutions adopted on similar occasions. Messrs. T. W. Martin, William J. Canby, and Abraham Myers were appointed to make the necessary arrangements to attend the funeral of General Birney."

The action taken by officers who had served under General Birney was reported by the press, as follows:

"A meeting of the officers who have served under Major-general David Bell Birney was held at the Continental Hotel, on Thursday, October 20, 1864, at half-past seven o'clock, P. M.

"On motion, Colonel C. H. T. Collis was called to the chair, and Captain Thomas J. Diehl appointed Secretary.

"On motion of General Gwyn, a committee of five was appointed to prepare resolutions expressive of the object of this meeting.

"On motion it was resolved, that the officers who have served under General Birney shall attend his funeral in full dress-uniform, and shall assemble at the house of Captain J. M. Davis, No. 2021 Arch street, at one o'clock, on Friday, the 21st instant.

"On motion of General Gwyn,

"*Resolved,* That we hereby extend an invitation to all officers in the service, now in the city, to attend with us the funeral of General Birney, and assemble at the house of Captain Davis for that purpose.

"On motion, a committee of two were appointed to wait upon Colonel John F. Glenn, and extend the same invitation to the officers of the Twenty-third regiment Pennsylvania volunteers.

"The Committee on Resolutions reported the following, which were unanimously adopted:

"*Whereas,* We have heard with sorrow the death of our late commander, Major-general David Bell Birney, whose worth we learned to know and appreciate from our associations of the camp and field:

"*Resolved,* That in the death of General Birney the army has lost an able and gallant soldier, the nation a true and enthusiastic patriot, who devoted his whole energy to the accomplishment of the cause in which he was engaged.

"*Resolved,* That as representatives of the thousands who have been marshaled to battle under his able leadership, we feel it our duty to place upon record our high admiration of the bright page which he has made in the history of the Republic.

"*Resolved,* That we will attend the funeral of General Birney in a body, and wear the usual badge of mourning for thirty days.

"*Resolved,* That a copy of these resolutions be transmitted to the family of General Birney."

A TESTIMONIAL FUND.

THE city of Philadelphia, during the rebellion, nobly performed its entire duty. In proportion to its population it has sent as many regiments to the field as any city in the Union. Many citizens who remained at home have, by their influence and their purses, done all in their power to aid the officers of the Government in their efforts to put down the rebellion, and have thus rendered services far more valuable than if they had shouldered their muskets and gone to the field. One man, and he not a wealthy one, has been instrumental in furnishing to the Government six regiments of infantry and a company of cavalry, at a private expenditure of more than twenty thousand dollars, of which he furnished more than half from his own purse.

A few liberal-hearted men of Philadelphia have been instrumental in raising a fund of twenty thousand dollars, which was presented to Brigadier-general R. H. Anderson; in purchasing and presenting to Major-general Meade a furnished dwelling, at an expense of more than twenty thousand dollars; and in paying a similar compliment to Lieutenant-general Grant, at an expenditure of more than fifty thousand dollars. Besides these instances of liberality, many funds have been raised by individual efforts to promote the organization of regiments and to provide for the support of the families of officers and soldiers who had suffered in the cause of the Union. Among the men who did their full duty in this respect were Jay Cooke, the untiring agent for the sale of the Government loans; Clarence H. Clark, the President of the First National Bank of Philadelphia; George H. Stuart, the President of the Christian Commission; A. J. Drexel, the senior member of the well-known house of Drexel & Co.; David Faust, the President of the Union National Bank of Philadelphia, and George Bullock, the most active member of the firm of Benjamin Bullock & Sons. No one ever applied in vain to any of these men for influence or money. They were always ready to respond to such calls, and it is to such men throughout the country that the Federal Government owes its success.

Knowing the liberality of the citizens of Philadelphia, the writer determined, after the death of General Birney, to inaugurate a movement to raise for his family a fund of at least thirty thousand dollars. Governor Curtin, with that liberality of heart for which he is proverbial, in a political address, which, during the campaign in which he was engaged, he delivered on the evening of the funeral at the Academy of Music in Philadelphia, made use of the following language:—

"To-day, I, with others, followed to the grave a soldier of the Republic, late a citizen of Philadelphia. I knew him well; indeed I had the honor of giving him his first commission. I was connected with every promotion he received from the National Government, and followed him with pleasure as he became more distinguished, from battle to battle, and became dearer and dearer to truly loyal men everywhere. Philadelphia did herself honor to-day when she honored the remains of General David B. Birney. He had braved the dangers of battle forty times, yet his life was spared, that he might return to die in the midst of his loving family. Ever remembering the old flag under which he had so often fought, he exclaimed with his last breath, and as his life went out, 'Boys! keep your eyes on that flag.' And so the noble Birney fills a soldier's grave. And he has left a wife and children behind him. I have frequently committed to the people of Pennsylvania the care of the soldier's wife and children, and now we have a law of our Commonwealth by which we assist to nurture the destitute orphans of our brave martyred heroes. While I ask not for charity, I trust, in justice, that the people of Philadelphia will not forget the six little children of General Birney."

Acting on this hint a meeting of the friends of General Birney was called at the Continental Hotel on Monday evening, October 25th, "to take measures to raise a testimonial fund to his memory." George Bullock, Esq., was called to the Chair, and J. Barclay Fassitt, Esq., appointed Secretary.

The following letter was read from Major-general Sickles, who had come to Philadelphia to attend the funeral of General Birney:—

"CONTINENTAL HOTEL, PHILADELPHIA,
October 24, 1864.

"GENTLEMEN:—

"It would give me the utmost satisfaction to attend the meeting of the associates and friends of the late Major-general Birney, to be held this evening in Philadelphia, and I regret being compelled to return to New York to-day, so that I cannot be present.

"The services of that distinguished officer deserve the signal recognition of his countrymen, and especially do they merit honor at the hands of his fellow-citizens of Pennsylvania.

"I beg to be made acquainted with the arrangements you may agree upon, and I am sure there are many besides myself in the city of New York who will desire to participate in the proposed testimonial to the memory of the gallant and accomplished Birney.

"With high regard, gentlemen,

"I am your most obedient servant,

"D. SICKLES,

"Major-general U. S. A.

"Messrs. DAVIS, TOBIAS, BULLOCK and WINEBRENNER."

The following resolutions were then submitted and unanimously adopted, after appropriate remarks by Messrs. C. B. Barclay, O. W. Davis, J. B. Harding, J. W. Everman, and B. H. Moore:—

Resolved, That in acknowledgment of the valuable services rendered his country since April 19, 1861, by the late David B. Birney, and the sacrifices he has made in the cause of the Union, it is our duty, as it will be our pleasure, to use our means and influence to provide and set apart for the benefit of his family a fund which, added to his estate, will yield an income at least equal to the pay he received, so that they will suffer no pecuniary loss by his death.

Resolved, That we hereby invite officers and soldiers who were his companions in arms, or who have at any time been under his command, the members of the associations with which he was connected, and all who desire to do honor to the memory of a brave soldier, a kind friend, a true patriot, and an accomplished gentleman, to unite with us in the effort we hereby inaugurate.

Resolved, That the chairman of this meeting appoint a committee of fourteen members, who shall have authority to take such measures as they may deem expedient to procure subscriptions to the fund we intend raising, and to dispose of them in such manner as in their opinion will do honor to the memory of our late friend, David B. Birney, and promote the comfort of his family.

The chair then appointed the following committee:—O. W. Davis, George Bullock, A. J. Drexel, C. H. Clark, Joseph F. Tobias, D. S. Winebrenner, William Millward, A. D. Jessup, J. W. Everman, Henry C. Howell, C. B. Barclay, B. H. Moore.

After the adjournment of the meeting the committee was organized by the appointment of O. W. Davis as Chairman, and J. B. Fassitt as Secretary. Caleb Cope, Esq., was appointed Treasurer.

The committee continued their exertions during the fall of 1864 and the spring of 1865, until they believed further effort would be unavailing. The widow of General Birney acknowledged the receipt of this fund in the following note to the contributors:—

"PHILADELPHIA, *April* 22, 1865.

"TO THE CONTRIBUTORS TO THE
BIRNEY TESTIMONIAL FUND:—

"GENTLEMEN:—

"It is with an overflowing heart that, for myself and my children, I thank you for your munificent donation for our benefit. If any thing could palliate the affliction which has been visited upon us, it is the evidences which have been afforded me of the grateful remembrance of the services of my husband, by his friends and fellow-citizens of Philadelphia, and his country.

"The fund you have so generously contributed I and my little ones accept with gratitude, and receive it as a substantial tribute to the memory of one who, from the earliest days of the rebellion, devoted all his energies to the defence of right, in a struggle which he long foresaw would be terrible, and which, from his childhood, he had been taught to look for in his own day and generation. His country he placed first in his affections, and sacrificed all for its good. I am deeply grateful to you for this tribute to his memory.

"Yours, very respectfully,
"M. ANTOINETTE BIRNEY."

The fund thus raised amounted to nearly thirty thousand dollars, and has been appropriately invested for the benefit of the family, by the trustees appointed by the committee to receive subscriptions.

THE END.

HE writer thus ends his sketch of the life of his friend. It has been prepared hurriedly during such hours as could be spared from constant business engagements. His sole purpose has been to do honor to the memory of a friend, and to put on record the history of a life which is worthy of the imitation of all who are willing to sacrifice personal interests for the good of their country.

When the history of the rebellion is written, Birney's name will always occupy a subordinate position, but only because he was never assigned to an independent command, where his fine executive abilities, his quick perception, and his power of concentration could have been called forth. He will not take rank with Grant, Sherman, Sheridan, or Thomas, but among the corps commanders of the armies his name will always be prominent. What he did was always well done, and he executed the orders of his superiors with energy and intelligence, never permitting any consideration of personal comfort or interest to interfere with the discharge of his duty. In camp, on the march, or during action, he conscientiously and fearlessly filled every requirement of the service. Though the duties he assumed at the commencement of the rebellion were at variance with the whole current of his life, he soon fitted himself for their fulfillment, and discharged them faithfully and creditably. He had never sought position or preferment, nor did he, after entering the army, resort to any of the conventional modes of obtaining reputation; but steadfastly and earnestly he pursued the career which duty pointed out.

Had his life been spared a few months longer, he would have witnessed the fall of Richmond, the surrender of all the rebel armies, and the end of the rebellion; and this to him would have been ample compensation for all the privation he had undergone. Returning his commission to the Government, he would have returned to civil life, to repair his shattered fortune and to occupy the position to which his superior business talents justly entitled him. But this privilege was denied him, and after three years and a half, the most of which was spent in an active campaign life, he was called away, just as the dawn of his country's splendor was about to burst forth. All this he felt during his rational moments upon his death-bed, and he lamented the fate which, denying that he should not die by the hand of an enemy, still decreed that he should not behold the restoration of the Union, and the success of the experiment, which, in 1776, our forefathers inaugurated to prove to the world that man is capable of self-government.

APPENDIX.

APPENDIX.

KEARNY'S REPORT OF WILLIAMSBURG.

HEADQUARTERS THIRD DIVISION, HEINTZELMAN'S CORPS,
WILLIAMSBURG, *May* 6, 1862.

CAPTAIN:—

I have the honor to report that, on receiving orders on the 5th inst., at nine A. M., the division took up its line of march, and shortly after came upon the crowded columns before us.

At ten and three-quarters A. M. an order was received from General Sumner to pass all others, and to proceed to the support of General Hooker, already engaged.

With difficulty, and much loss of time, my division at length made its way through the masses of troops and trains that encumbered the deep, muddy, single defile, until, at the Brick Church, my route was to the left, the direct road to Williamsburg. At half-past one, P. M., within three and one-half miles of the battle-field, I halted my column to rest for the first time, and to get the lengthened files in hand before committing them to action. Captain Moses, of the General's staff, with great energy assisted me in this effort. Almost immediately, however, on orders from General Heintzelman, our "knapsacks were piled," and the head of the column resumed its march, taking the "double-quick" where-ever the mud-holes left a footing.

Arrived at one mile from the engagement, you in person brought me an order for detaching three regiments, one from Berry's, the leading brigade, and two from Birney's, the second, to support Emory's horse, to the left of the position.

Approaching nearer the field, word was brought by an aide-de-camp that Hooker's cartridges were expended; and with increased rapidity we entered under fire. Having quickly consulted with General Hooker, and received General Heintzelman's orders as to the point of onset, I at once deployed Berry's brigade to the left of the Williamsburg road, and Birney's on the right of it, taking to cover the movement and to support the remaining battery, that had ceased to fire, two companies of Poe's regiment.

As our troops came into action, the brave men remaining of Hooker's division were passed, and our regiments promptly commenced an unremitting, well-directed fire. However, from the lengthening of the files, the gap occasioned by the withdrawal from the column of three regiments, and the silence of the battery, I soon was left no alternative than to lead forward to the charge the two companies of the Second Michigan volunteers, to bear back the enemy's skirmishers, now crowding on our pieces. This duty was performed by officers and men with superior intrepidity, and enabled Major Wainwright, of Hooker's division, to collect his artillerists, and to re-open fire from several pieces. A new support was then collected from the Fifth New Jersey, which, terribly decimated previously, again came forward with alacrity.

The affair was now fully and successfully engaged along our whole line, and the regiments kept steadily gaining ground. But the heavy strewn timber of the abattis defied all direct approach. Introducing, therefore, fresh marksmen from Poe's regiment, I ordered Colonel Hobart Ward, with the Thirty-eighth New York volunteers, to charge down the road, and take the "rifle-pits" (in the centre of the abattis) by their flank. This duty Colonel Ward performed with great gallantry, his martial demeanor imparting all confidence in the attack. Still the wave of impulsion, though nearly successful, did not quite prevail; but, with bravery, every point thus gained was fully sustained. The left wing of Colonel Riley's regiment, the Fortieth New York volunteers, was next sent for, and, the colonel being valiantly engaged in front, came up brilliantly, conducted by Captain Mindil, chief of General Birney's staff. These charged up to the open space, and silenced some light artillery; and, gaining the enemy's rear, caused him to relinquish his cover. The victory was ours. About this period, General Jameson brought up the rear brigade and the detached regiments, having previously reported them in the midst of a severe fire. A second line was established, and two columns of regiments made disposable for further moves. But darkness, with the still drizzly rain, now closed; and the regiments bivouacked on the field they had won.

The reconnoissances during the night, and the early patrols of the morning, revealed the enemy retiring; and General Heintzelman in person ordered into the enemy's works (which our pickets of the One-hundred-and-fifth Pennsylvania, under Lieutenant Gilbert, were entering with General Jameson) the Fourth Maine regiment, to erect thereon its standard and take possession in full force.

I have to mark out for the high commendation of the General-in-chief, Generals Jameson, Birney, and Berry, whose soldierly judgment was only equalled by their distinguished courage. I refer you to their reports to do justice to the names of the gallant officers and men under their immediate command. Having confined myself principally to the centre, the key of the position, I report as having conspicuously distinguished themselves, imparting victory all around, Colonels Poe, of the Second Michigan, and Hobart Ward, of the Thirty-eighth New York volunteers.

Never in any action was the influence of the staff more perceptible. All were most efficient and defiant of danger. I especially notice Captain Smith, Assistant Adjutant-general of General Berry, and predict for him a career of usefulness and glory.

My own staff were truly my means of vision in this battle in the woods. I have to deplore the loss of my chief of staff, Captain Wilson, who was killed while putting in execution my desire for a general onset, at the period of the last charge, falling within the enemy's lines. Also of Lieutenant Barnard, late of West Point, at the end of the engagement, after having previously lost a horse. Captain Wm. E. Sturges, my aide, was brave, active, and judicious. Lieutenant Moore, another of my aides, renewed in this field his previous distinction gained abroad. My volunteer aide, Mr. Watts Depuyster, bore himself handsomely in this his first action.

Our batteries were on the field, but were not required; Major Wainwright (Hooker's division) having, by much personal effort, resumed the fire of several pieces. But Captain Thompson, U. S. A., the chief of my division artillery, in the midst of a heavy fire, gave me the benefit of his experience.

I have, sir, the honor to be,
Very respectfully,
Your obdt. servt.,
P. KEARNY,
Brigadier-general commanding Division.

CAPTAIN CHAUNCEY MCKEEVER,
Assistant Adjutant-general, Heintzelman's Corps.

SUPPLEMENTAL REPORT.

HEADQUARTERS THIRD DIVISION, HEINTZELMAN'S CORPS,
CAMP BERRY, BARHAMSVILLE, VA., *May* 10, 1862.

SIR:—

The events which crowded on us after the battle of the 5th—its stormy night, the care of the wounded, the attentions to the slain, the collection of the trophies, the moves of the next day—having prevented my report embracing the distinguished acts of individuals not serving in my presence, induced me to request that the superior authority of the corps commander would be employed to use as my own the separate reports of my brigade commanders, who so ably sustained my efforts by their gallantry, and who so amply fulfilled the high prestige which they had won as colonels of noble regiments.

The lists of the generals of brigades comprise the names of the following officers and regiments:

The right of my line consisted of two regiments of the second brigade, General Birney, viz.: the Thirty-eighth New York volunteers, Colonel Hobart Ward, and the Fortieth New York volunteers, Colonel Riley, the other two regiments of this brigade having, a mile back from the field, been detached to join General Emory. The Thirty-eighth New York was the regiment that, sent for by me, charged down the road and took the pits and abattis in flank. Colonel Ward has already been noticed as one of the "bravest of the brave." He reports that Lieutenant-colonel Strong certainly deserves mention for his gallantry. It would be unjust to mention any one line officer before another where all behaved so well. This regiment lost one hundred and twenty-eight men on the 21st of July, 1861, at Bull Run. This day there were nine officers killed and wounded out of nineteen, in this regiment, who went into action.

The Fortieth New York, under Colonel Riley, performed noble and efficient services. Colonel Riley, with great spirit, held the right wing with half his regiment, after the Thirty-eighth and half the Fortieth had been withdrawn to act under my personal direction. The part of the Fortieth acting on the road, against the central pits and abattis, charged down the road, into the plain, beyond the enemy's flank, and drove off by their fire two pieces of artillery, brought expressly against them. Fortune favored them.

The battle on the left of the line was a series of assaults by the enemy, and repulses and onsets by ourselves, the fresh reinforcements of the enemy continually tending to outflank us. General Berry was on the alert, and, by good arrangements and personal example, influenced the ardor of all around him. His regiments fought most desperately. Their losses attest it. It was one of them, Colonel Poe's Second Michigan, more directly under my control, which maintained the key-point of our position. Two of its companies led off with the first success of the day, whilst covering the artillery. Colonel Poe has already won a reputation in Western Virginia. He was a distinguished officer of the U. S. Army before taking command of this regiment. I especially notice him for advancement: his talents, his bravery, his past services, merit it.

Colonel Hayman, (Captain Seventh U. S. Infantry,) commanding the Thirty-seventh New York volunteers, on the extreme left, was charged with guarding against the enemy's turning our flank. His duty required vigilance and pertinacity.

Colonel Terry, commanding the Fifth Michigan volunteers, was principally engaged in carrying rifle-pits in the woods. His loss is the highest on the list of killed and wounded.

In closing this supplemental report of the location and merits of regiments and individuals, it is proper to include, although not attached to my command, General Grover, who, with an untiring courage, whilst most of his men, having been relieved by our arrival, were taking the needed respite after their long hours of severe fighting, still brought up into line along side of us several hundred volunteers, who followed his example, encouraging them to the fight.

This report would also be incomplete did I fail to mention the meritorious services of our medical corps. They were everywhere aiding the wounded and establishing ambulances. One of them, Dr. J. H. Baxter, medical inspector of field ambulances, of Acting Surgeon-general Tripler's staff, assisted me greatly during the action by carrying orders.

With the trust that the division has done its duty and fulfilled your expectations,

I have the honor to be,

Very respectfully,

Your obedient servant,

P. KEARNY,

Brigadier-general commanding Division.

CAPT. C. McKEEVER,

Assistant Adjutant-general, Heintzelman's Corps.

BIRNEY'S REPORT OF WILLIAMSBURG.

HEADQUARTERS BIRNEY'S BRIGADE, KEARNY'S DIVISION,
CAMP NEAR WILLIAMSBURG, VA., *May* 6, 1862.

SIR:—

I have the honor to report that, after a wearisome march of six hours on yesterday, through deep mud and a drenching rain, my brigade being heavily burdened with knapsacks, haversacks and shelter-tents, I received an order from General Kearny to relieve the troops under my command from all encumbrances and move forward to the scene of action, some three miles distant, as rapidly as possible. Leaving under guard all knapsacks, etc., the brigade, although jaded and wearied, moved forward as rapidly as the roads would permit.

On nearing the front, by order of General Heintzelman through Captain McKeever, I detached the Third and Fourth Maine regiments and proceeded with the Thirty-eighth and right wing of the Fortieth New York regiments, to the right of the road, and relieved, opportunely, fragments of regiments that had been in the fight. They marched steadily to the front and drove the enemy, after a furious contest, from the woods, who fell back over the fallen timber and opened a destructive fire from rifle-pits. They were supported by their batteries, which poured a well-aimed and destructive fire into our ranks. The Thirty-eighth and right wing of the Fortieth New York behaved nobly and maintained their position during the contest. The Thirty-eighth New York regiment, under Colonel Ward, were ordered to charge down the main road in advance of the Michigan regiments, and piercing the enemy's centre, to carry the rifle-pits by the flank; and the left wing of Colonel Riley's regiment, Fortieth New York, were ordered, in like manner, to follow the Thirty-eighth New York to take the enemy in the rear. I sent, with this wing, Captain Mindil of my staff, and under General Kearny's presence he led them to the dangerous position assigned them. Captain Gesner of the left wing and Captain Mindil behaved well under the terrible fire that greeted them, and led the brave officers and men under them gallantly and worthily. Night coming on put an end to the pursuit, and, amidst the darkness and rain, we waited the morning. During the night the Third and Fourth Maine, that had been, previous to the contest, detached by order of General Heintzelman, reported to me for duty in front; and, by order of General Kearny, I moved them to the front to relieve the Thirty-eighth and Fortieth New York regiments. I pushed them on to the enemy's works, found them deserted and troops to the left of us in possession.

My brigade has lost several gallant officers and many brave men in this contest. Where so much gallantry was displayed it is difficult to select those most deserving of notice. To Colonel Ward, Captains Mindil and Gesner, fell the good fortune to lead the most important charges, and they were well supported by the gallant officers and men under them. Colonel Riley maintained well his position, and executed the orders with coolness and efficiency. The loss of the rebels in front of my regiments was terrible. Those that remained on the ground, some forty, were decently buried. The Thirty-eighth New York regiment, or "Scott Life Guard," preserved well the high reputation it gained for gallantry at Bull Run; and although in that engagement and this it has lost fifteen officers and one-third of its members, it is still ready to devote the balance to support our flag. I ask that Congress will, by special resolution, authorize this regiment to place upon its colors "Bull Run" and "Williamsburg," and the Fortieth New York or "Mozart" regiment "Williamsburg." I trust that the general commanding division, seeing how well two of my regiments carried out his orders, will never hesitate to rely upon my brigade. Lieutenant-colonel Strong, Thirty-eighth New York regiment, deserves special mention for his gallant conduct. His wound, although disabling him, I am happy to report is not mortal, and he will be soon returned to his regiment.

Very respectfully, your obdt. servant,

D. B. BIRNEY,

Brigadier-general commanding Brigade.

CAPT. W. E. STURGES,

A. A. A. G., Kearny's Division.

KEARNY'S REPORT OF FAIR OAKS.

HEADQUARTERS THIRD DIVISION, HEINTZELMAN'S CORPS,
INTRENCHED CAMP NEAR SAVAGE'S, *June* 2, 1862.

SIR:—

On the 31st ultimo, at three P. M., I received an order to send a brigade of my division by the railroad to support Keyes' corps, said to be severely engaged.

Birney's brigade was designated, and, getting most promptly under arms, advanced accordingly.

Captain Hunt, aide-de-camp to General Heintzelman, arriving from the field, made me aware of the discomfiture of most of Casey's entire division. The retiring wagons and a dense stream of disorganized fugitives arrived nearly simultaneously. As a precaution, I ordered some picked Michigan marksmen and a regiment to proceed and occupy the dense woods bordering on the left of our position, to take in flank any pursuers. I, however, soon received General Heintzelman's directions to order forward, by the Williamsburg road, the remaining brigade and to retrieve the position the enemy had driven us from. I put myself at the head of the advanced regiment and set forward without delay. I also sent written orders for Jameson's brigade, camped at our *tete-de-pont*, near Bottom's bridge, (three miles in rear,) to come up without delay. This order met with General Heintzelman's approval. On arriving at the field of battle we found certain zigzag rifle-pits, sheltering crowds of men, and the enemy firing from abattis and timber in their front. General Casey remarked to me, on coming up, "If you will regain our late camp, the day will still be ours." I had but the Third Michigan up, but they moved forward with alacrity, dashing into the felled timber and commencing a desperate but determined contest, heedless of the shell and ball which rained upon them. This regiment, the only one of Berry's brigade not engaged at Williamsburg, at the price of a severe loss, has nearly outvied all competitors. Its work this day was complete. This regiment lost ten officers and one hundred and fifty-six men. One company, of fifty picked marksmen, lost its captain killed, its lieutenant wounded and twenty-six men. I take pleasure in particularizing Colonel S. G. Champlin wounded, Lieutenant-colonel A. A. Stevens, Major Pierce, and Captains J. C. Smith, E. S. Pierce, and Lieutenant G. E. Judd.

The next regiment that came up, the Fifth Michigan, again won laurels as fresh as those due them for Williamsburg. Its loss then was one hundred and forty-four. Its loss this day was six officers and one hundred and fifty-three men; its noble officers did their duty. I directed General Berry with this regiment to turn the slashing and gain the open ground on the enemy's right flank, which was perfectly accomplished. The Thirty-seventh New York was arranged in column to support the attack. Its services, in the sequel, proved invaluable.

In the meanwhile my remaining brigade, the One-hundred-and-fifth and Sixty-third Pennsylvanians, came up under General Jameson, the other two regiments having been directed, one to Birney and one to Peck. It is believed that they did well, and most probably urgent reasons existed, but I respectfully submit that it is to the disadvantage of a constituted command to take men from their habitual leaders; and not to be anticipated that a brave though weak division can accomplish the same results, with its regiments thus allotted out to those whom they neither know nor have fought under; at the same time that it diminishes the full, legitimate sphere of the commander of the division. Of these regiments, the One-hundred-and-fifth was placed in the slashings, now vacated by the oblique advance of the

Third Michigan, whilst eight companies of the Sixty-third Pennsylvanians, led by Lieutenant-colonel Morgan, and most spiritedly headed by General Jameson, aided by his daring chief of staff, Captain Potter, were pushed through the abattis, (the portions never until now occupied by us,) and nobly repelled a strong body of the enemy, who, though in a strong line and coming up rapidly and in order, just failed to reach to support this position in time, but who, nothing daunted, and with a courage worthy a united cause, halted in battle array and poured in a constant, heavy roll of musketry fire. The One-hundred-and-fifth Pennsylvania lost eleven officers and two hundred and forty-five men. The Sixty-third Pennsylvania lost eight officers and one hundred and forty men.

This was, perhaps, near six o'clock, when our centre and right, defended by troops of the other divisions, with all their willingness could no longer resist the enemy's right central, flank attacks, pushed on with determined discipline and with the impulsion of numerous concentrated masses. Once broken our troops fled incontinently, and a dense body of the enemy pursuing rapidly, yet in order, occupied the Williamsburg road, the entire open ground, and penetrating deep into the woods on either side, soon interposed between my division and my line of retreat. It was on this occasion that, seeing myself cut off, and relying on the high discipline and determined valor of the Thirty-seventh New York volunteers, I faced them to the rear against the enemy and held the ground, although so critically placed, and, despite the masses that gathered on and had passed us, checked the enemy in his intent of cutting us off from the White Oak Swamp. This enabled the advanced regiments, averted by orders and this contest in their rear, to return from their hitherto victorious career, and to retire by a remaining wood-path known to our scouts, (the saw-mill road,) until they once more arrived at and remanned the impregnable position we had left at noon, at our fortified division camp. The loss of the Thirty-seventh New York is severe, viz.: seven officers and eighty men. At Williamsburg its loss was ninety-five; it there formed our extreme left; Colonel Hayman, its colonel, has ever been most distinguished; he revived, this day, his reputation gained in Mexico. Adjutant James Henry, Captain James O'Beirne and Lieutenants W. C. Green and P. J. Smith, were particularly distinguished for courage and activity.

The detached brigade under Birney had been ordered to support by the railroad side—not to attack. It accomplished this successfully; for I understand that it enabled General Couch, who had been cut off with a brigade, to form the junction with the army. The Fifty-seventh Pennsylvania volunteers (Jameson's brigade) having been on fatigue, were ordered to report to General Birney, and was seriously engaged. Its loss was five officers and ninety-seven men. This brigade on the following day, having been kept out in advance of the division camps, performed, under Colonel J. H. Hobart Ward, a brilliant charge. The loss of the brigade has been seven officers and one hundred and eighty-three men.

The Second Michigan volunteers, Colonel Poe, and two companies of the Sixty-third Pennsylvania volunteers, having been on distant pickets, were late to join in the battle, but arrived most opportunely to resist the advanced pursuers of the enemy near our intrenched camp, and aided in giving me time to organize its defence. Its loss was two officers and fifty-three men.

The Eighty-seventh New York volunteers were detached with General Peck. I refer you to him for favorable notice. Its loss was six officers and seventy-five men.

It is, perhaps, within the limits of my report, to mention General Peck, who was distinguished and wounded in Mexico. On the discomfiture of the right and centre he rallied near the saw-mill several hundred of the fugitives, and was coming with them from there again to the field, when I directed him to anticipate the enemy and man the retrenched camp. In doing this, I particularize a noble regiment, the First Long Island Legion, under Colonel Adams.

I have again to dwell on the exemplary conduct of the brilliant officers of the staff. Captain Potter, General Jameson's Assistant Adjutant-general, who had already attracted notice at Williamsburg, was here as conspicuously gallant, as extremely useful. I have to regret, in the loss of Captain Smith, Assistant Adjutant-general of General Berry's staff, the premature fate of one whose gallantry at Williamsburg made me anticipate a career which he fulfilled again in this action. My acting aide, Lieutenant Mallon, rendered me great services, and was wounded. My aide, Captain Sturges, was left with General Birney; Captain Moore was sent after my artillery, and was, as usual, active.

I have again to regret that the unequalled batteries, Thompson's, (Second U. S. Artillery,) Randolph's, and Beam's, were not employed, from there being other batteries substituted.

In finishing this report I trust you will bring to the attention of the General-in-chief that, masters of the lost camp and victorious and in full career, the fate of the centre decided our own, and that the regiments were suddenly stopped by orders dispatched to them, and by hearing the fire of their support, the Thirty-seventh New York, in rear of their entire line; but, undismayed and in good order, they effected their retreat.

I have also to call to your attention that the loss of my regiments, only five thousand fighting men all told, have again, within a very short period, paid the penalty of daring and success, by the marked and severe loss of near one thousand three hundred men. I have again to bring to notice for conspicuous good conduct, Generals Jameson, Berry and Birney; the latter acted in an independent command; the two former led in person the advance of their men.

Among numerous prisoners was Colonel Bratton, of Sixth South Carolina volunteers, taken by Colonel Walker, Fourth Maine.

The losses of the enemy were even vastly severer than our own, and in places the slain were piled in confused masses.

I add, in conclusion, that the enemy's success of the afternoon did not prevent me, that very night, from pushing forward Major Dillman and two hundred Michigan marksmen to the saw-mill, (one mile in advance,) whence he boldly threw out reconnoissances in the vicinity and to the left of the late battle-ground.

Very respectfully, your ob't servant,

P. KEARNY,

Brigadier-general commanding Division.

CAPT. CHAUNCEY MCKEEVER,

Assistant Adjutant-general, Heintzelman's Corps.

BIRNEY'S REPORT OF FAIR OAKS.

HEADQUARTERS BIRNEY'S BRIGADE, FIRST DIVISION, THIRD CORPS,
HARRISON'S LANDING, *July* 8, 1862.

SIR:—

I have the honor to report for the information of the general commanding the division, the part taken by this brigade in the battle of Seven Pines, on the 31st of May, 1862. My brigade was composed of the Thirty-eighth and Fortieth New York regiments, and the Third and Fourth Maine regiments.

The Thirty-eighth had been detailed on the 30th of May for picket duty, and were being relieved when the firing on the 31st of May commenced, so that there were only about one hundred men of this regiment in the action. Two companies of the Fortieth New York had been detailed as guards over commissary stores; my brigade was thus reduced to about thirteen hundred strong.

At three o'clock, P. M., I received an order from General Kearny to move the brigade up the railroad and report by a staff officer to General Keyes. Ten minutes after three o'clock, P. M., my column was in motion, led by the Fourth Maine volunteers, followed in order by the Fortieth New York, Third Maine, and the remnant of the Thirty-eighth New York. Before I had reached the railroad, at fifteen minutes past three o'clock, General Kearny rode up and ordered me to return to the Williamsburg and Richmond road and man the line of rifle-pits thrown up, called, by him, the second line. Upon reaching this point, he himself stationed the Fortieth New York in the rifle-pits, and detached a large number as sharpshooters in and around the house used as a hospital. He ordered the Fourth Maine to the right of the Fortieth in the woods.

At this time one of my aides informed me that General Kearny had sent his Acting Assistant Adjutant-general, Captain Sturges, with the Third Maine and Thirty-eighth New York up the railroad. I asked General Kearny whether he had given this order; he replied that he had, but ordered me to gallop over to the railroad and stop them, and to form one in column of companies on the railroad and to deploy the portion of the Thirty-eighth in the field as skirmishers on the right flank, so as to cover that flank. He ordered me to obey no order to move from that position unless the order came through him. He stated that the disordered troops, now pouring through our lines, could not be rallied; that the enemy had Casey's camp and first line of works, and the only hope of successfully stopping his progress was the second line. He ordered me to take position on the railroad, and sent Captain Sturges, his Acting Assistant Adjutant-general, to remain with me. I made the disposition of the Third Maine and Thirty-eighth New York as ordered, and then made efforts to rally the fugitives from the front. I succeeded in rallying and attaching to the Thirty-eighth New York some hundred men of the Twenty-third regiment Pennsylvania volunteers, formerly commanded by myself; one company of this regiment, under Captain Adolph Cavada, had been on picket duty on the railroad, where my line crossed, and willingly joined my command. I was under many obligations to Captains Gwyn, Cavada and Lieutenant J. B. Fassitt, of the Twenty-third regiment Pennsylvania volunteers, for their active assistance in my efforts to reform the fugitives.

At five o'clock, P. M., Lieutenant Hunt, of General Heintzelman's staff, rode up and ordered me to advance up the railroad to the support of Keyes' corps. I at once moved, with the Third Maine leading, and sent my aides, Major J. F. Tobias and Captain Mindil, to withdraw the Fortieth New York and Fourth Maine from the position in which they were posted by General Kearny, and to order them to follow. As I moved, Colonel Campbell, of the Fifty-seventh regiment Pennsylvania volunteers, reported to me that he had been ordered to proceed up the railroad. I assumed command of his regiment and assigned him position in my column.

After advancing a mile up the railroad the firing became heavy upon my left, and I ascertained, by inquiry, that the men engaged were part of Couch's division, Keyes' corps, which I had been ordered to support. At this point the enemy opened a scattering musketry fire from a woods that ran to the railroad in front, and I at once deployed my column into line of battle. Finding that the firing on the left was getting more to the rear, I led into the woods the Fifty seventh regiment Pennsylvania volunteers and Fortieth New York, and succeeded, after a sharp contest, in driving back the enemy from his attempt to turn the right flank of our troops. The loss of the Fifty-seventh was very heavy—its gallant colonel falling, severely wounded, the major killed, and the list of the casualties very large.

Captain Brady, of the Pennsylvania artillery, now rode up to me and said, that he came from General Couch, who sent word that his command had been cut off, but he had found a road by which to extricate his artillery, through the swamp, and if I could hold the railroad and prevent the enemy from cutting him off, he could extricate himself.

I sent word to him that I had been sent to his support, and would and could hold the railroad. At this time, (about six o'clock,) Captain Suydam, of General Keyes' staff, rode up to me and told me that General Heintzelman ordered me to advance still farther up the railroad. I asked him if General Heintzelman knew where I was, and that my command was going, then, into action between the railroad and Williamsburg road. He replied, that Generals Keyes and Heintzelman were some two miles in the rear, and he knew nothing beyond the order. I at once made disposition to move forward, throwing out skirmishers and withdrawing the Fortieth New York volunteers. The Fifty-seventh Pennsylvania volunteers were thrown into too much confusion in the woods to withdraw.

My skirmishers in front were constantly engaged, and in advancing we captured some two hundred prisoners. When my lines reached the woods near Fair Oaks Station, an oblique artillery fire from my right across my front commenced. To advance would have subjected me to this fire, and supposing that it was General Sumner, who had crossed and was advancing, I sent successively three aides to report to him my position, instructions and to ask orders.

The orders from him were to connect with General French, commanding his left, and advance *pari passu.* He also sent the Seventh Massachusetts, Colonel Russell, to report to me, in order to strengthen my command, as the position held by me was important.

At this time Captain Hassler rode up to me from General Kearny, and ordered me to return at once to the position assigned by him to me at three o'clock. Before obeying this order I sent my aide, Captain Linnard, to him, to advise him of my connection with General Sumner's command, and to state that if I withdrew there would be a gap of half a mile between his right and Sumner's left, with the enemy in force in its front ready to move through in the morning.

He repeated the order for me to return. I placed out a strong guard, under Major Pitcher, of the Fourth Maine, and, preceding my column, went to General Kearny's tent and explained to him the position of my brigade and the importance of the position. He concurred with me and ordered me to remain. I did so, and at ten o'clock, P. M., had my connection perfect with General French. The railroad embankment afforded natural rifle-pits, and I posted my brigade behind it and bivouacked for the night, throwing out strong pickets. The enemy was in force in our front and made no attempt at concealment, but built fires, talked aloud, and was evidently preparing for another attack, which was made the next morning. I anticipated it during the night, and, though a heavy rain was falling, my command was under arms and prepared for the enemy.

At daylight, while making preparations for the attack, an order reached me from General Kearny, requiring me to turn over the brigade to the officer next in rank and report to him. I did so, at once, and found General Kearny. He said he had received an order from General Heintzelman to place me under arrest. I asked him the cause. He said he did not know, but he would not act on the order until I could go to General Heintzelman with a message that he (General Kearny) assumed all the responsibility for my actions of the previous day. I went at once and requested, through Lieutenant Hunt, an interview with General Heintzelman. I was told, in reply, that any communication must be in writing. I left General Heintzelman's headquarters, and did not resume command of the brigade until after the finding of the court-martial, convened to try the charges against me, had been approved by General McClellan.

My brigade, however, under Colonel Ward, to whom I surrendered the command, did valuable service on June 1st, and, being protected partially by the embankment behind which I had placed it, suffered comparatively little loss. Of the details of their subsequent action I am unable to speak.

It is, of course, a matter of congratulation that my conduct met the approval of the general commanding the division, and that in his report of what transpired he does ample justice to my command.

I am your obedient servant,

D. B. BIRNEY,

Brigadier-general commanding Brigade.

CAPT. W. C. STURGES,

A. A. Adjutant-general, Kearny's Division.

ORDER OF COURT-MARTIAL.

HEADQUARTERS ARMY OF THE POTOMAC,
CAMP LINCOLN, VA., *June* 19, 1862.

[GENERAL ORDER, NO. 135.]

I. Before a General Court-martial, of which Brigadier-general Andrew Porter, volunteer service, is President, convened at Savage's Station, Va., by virtue of Special Orders, No. 180, Headquarters Army of the Potomac, of June 14, 1862, was arraigned and tried Brigadier-general D. B. Birney, U. S. Volunteer Service, on the following charges and specifications:

CHARGE FIRST.—"*Disobedience of orders.*" Specification. In this, that he, the said Brigadier-general D. B. Birney, U. S. Volunteer Service, having been ordered by proper authority to advance his brigade on the Richmond and York River Railroad, towards the enemy, to the support of General Keyes' corps, did fail and neglect to obey said order, although repeatedly ordered to do so. This at or near the bivouac near Savage's house, on the railroad from Richmond to York river, on or about the 31st of May, 1862.

CHARGE SECOND.—"*Conduct prejudicial to good order and military discipline.*" Specification. In this, that the said Brigadier-general D. B. Birney, U. S. Volunteer Service, having been ordered to advance his brigade on the Richmond and York River Railroad, and engage the enemy, did neglect and fail to obey said order, and did halt his troops on the railroad, about a mile from the place where the battle was raging. This at or near the bivouac near Savage's house, on the railroad from Richmond to York river, on or about the 31st of May, 1862.

PLEA.—"*Not guilty.*" After mature deliberation on the testimony adduced, the Court finds the accused, Brigadier-general D. B. Birney, U. S. Volunteer Service, as follows:

Of the specification of the first charge: "Not guilty." Of the first charge: "Not guilty." Of the specification of the second charge: "Not guilty." Of the second charge: "Not guilty."

And, therefore, the Court does honorably acquit the said Brigadier-general D. B. Birney, U. S. Volunteer Service, of the said charges and specifications.

II. The proceedings of the General Court-martial in the foregoing case are confirmed. Brigadier-general D. B. Birney, U. S. Volunteer Service, is accordingly released from arrest, and will resume his sword and the command of his brigade.

III. The General Court-martial, of which Brigadier-general A. Porter is President, is dissolved.

By command of Major-general McClellan.

S. WILLIAMS,
Assistant Adjutant-general.

COMMENTS OF THE PRESS UPON THE COURT-MARTIAL.

SAVAGE'S STATION, *June* 18, 1862.

As will be seen by the following orders, the recent court-martial instituted in the case of Brigadier-general D. B. Birney, for alleged misconduct at the recent battle of Fair Oaks, has honorably exonerated him of the charges, and he has resumed command of his brigade. As we have previously stated, we had the most entire confidence in the ability of the General to disprove the charges upon which he was arrested, and the finale of the matter shows how correct we were in our opinion.

BRIGADIER-GENERAL D. B. BIRNEY:

The commanding general has approved the proceedings of the court-martial acquitting you, and has ordered General Heintzelman to release you from arrest, and restore you to the command of your brigade.

By command,

S. WILLIAMS,

Assistant Adjutant-general.

HEADQUARTERS THIRD DIVISION, THIRD CORPS,
CAMP NEAR SEVEN PINES, VA., *June* 19, 1862.

[GENERAL ORDERS, No. 21.]

BRIGADIER-GENERAL D. B. BIRNEY:

Having been returned to duty with all credit, you will re-assume command of the second brigade.

P. KEARNY,

Brigadier-general commanding Division.

On the back of this order was the following in General Kearny's handwriting:

GENERAL BIRNEY:—It gives me great pleasure to put in force the within directions.

The court-martial sat at Savage's house on Monday last at ten o'clock.

General Heintzelman was the first witness called. He stated that he knew nothing personally of the matter; he did not know what brigade was ordered to go up the railroad; that the orders that he sent were through aides; he was surprised that he had been called as a witness.

Lieutenant Hunt, aide to General Heintzelman, next testified. He was ordered by General Heintzelman, at a quarter before five o'clock, on Saturday, to find General Birney, who was on the railroad, and order him to proceed up the railroad to the front; that he found General Birney, at about ten minutes after five, on the railroad, and ordered him to do so; that General Birney immediately ordered his brigade forward, and that as he left he saw them moving up the road.

Next witness called was Lieutenant Norton, aide to General Heintzelman. Testified that he had been sent with orders, but, meeting Hunt, did not carry them. Did not see General Birney.

General Kearny testified that about three o'clock on Saturday he received an order from General Heintzelman to send a brigade up the railroad to report to General Keyes; that he ordered General Birney to execute this order; that, after giving this order, he proceeded up the Williamsburg road, and, witnessing a panic among the troops retreating, he ordered the brigade of General Birney to be placed in the rifle-pits, and to remain on his (Kearny's) right; that he sent Captain Sturges, his aid, to General Birney to see that his order was executed; that this brigade was detached afterwards, by order of General Heintzelman, from his command and sent up the railroad; that he knew nothing personally of the distance that General Birney went up the railroad, or the time that he received the order; he never knew such an order was given; that he was ordered up the Williamsburg turnpike; that his two brigades being driven back, and forced by detour by the saw-mill to get back to the position that he had held before being ordered to the front, he sent an order to General Birney, at about half-past six o'clock, to fall back and form a connection with his right on the railroad, connecting General Birney's right with the left of Sumner's corps; that this order was promptly executed. He also stated that the position taken by General Birney was an admirable one; and the security afforded by the excavations of the railroad saved, on the next morning, great loss of life, enabling the brigade to repulse the enemy. General Birney, he said, was distinguished for his prompt obedience of all orders, and that at Williamsburg he had mentioned him for his conduct in that engagement.

Captain Sturges, Assistant Adjutant-general to General Kearny, testified that at three o'clock on Saturday an order was sent by General Kearny to General Birney to move his brigade up the railroad to the support of General Keyes; that ten minutes afterwards the order was countermanded by General Kearny, and General Birney was ordered to take a position behind the rifle-pits; that at five o'clock he received an order, through Lieutenant Hunt, from General Heintzelman, to proceed up the railroad to the support of General Keyes' corps; that General Birney immediately moved up the railroad at "double-quick;" that he went with him a mile, and then returned to General Kearny; that then he saw no more of him (General Birney).

Captain Hassler next testified. (This gentleman is an aide-de-camp to General Jameson.) He was sent by General Jameson with the Fifty-seventh regiment Pennsylvania volunteers up the railroad to General Birney; General Birney took command of the regiment, and, when he marched up the railroad, placed it in action in support of the First Long Island regiment, one of Couch's division, which was being outflanked by the enemy; that they drove the enemy before them with the bayonet, with the loss of one colonel wounded and a major killed; that he returned at this time to General Jameson, who was with General Birney, and reported the fact to General Kearny; General Kearny sent him back to General Birney with instructions to move his brigade immediately back to the place whence he had been ordered by Lieutenant Hunt, and to hold that position, connected with his (Kearny's) right. That he found General Birney, with his brigade, near Fair Oaks, and gave the order to him; that General Birney said to him: "Are you sure that your order is right? I have received a great many contradictory orders to-day, and it should have been in writing;" that General Birney sent back with him Lieutenant Linnard, his aide, to see General Kearny, and state that he had made the connection with General Sedgwick on his right, and was ordered up the railroad by General Heintzelman, and ask whether, under these circumstances, he still wished his order obeyed; that the enemy was still strong on his left and rear. That he then returned.

Colonel Ward, Thirty-eighth New York, next sworn. At three o'clock he had been placed on the right of Birney's brigade, and deployed his regiment, as skirmishers, in the woods; that at five o'clock he received from Birney an order to move up the railroad, which he did immediately after the Third Maine. After proceeding three-quarters of a mile, heavy firing being heard on the left, he received a command from Birney to "double-quick" to the brigade camp into line of battle in the front field, and the two regiments, the Fifty-seventh Pennsylvania and the Fortieth New York, were sent up the road on the left, and put in action; that the point was continually harassed by the sharpshooters of the enemy; that after remaining in this field twenty minutes, he was ordered again to move forward; that the brigade was then moved up to within a quarter of a mile of Fair Oaks, when Captain Hassler rode up with orders from General Kearny to return immediately with the brigade. General Birney, hesitating, halted the brigade, and then sent back an aide to find out whether General Kearny knew that General Heintzelman had ordered him forward; that upon the return of the aide, General Birney retired to the spot held by him from three to five o'clock; that Birney left the brigade here, and rode to General Kearny's to get further instructions; that upon his return he put the brigade in motion again, and occupied the advanced post held by him in the afternoon, and formed a connection upon the right with Sumner's corps, by a line of pickets; that he, Ward, took command of the brigade after Birney had been relieved, and attacked the enemy with the same disposition of troops.

Captain Mitchell, of Birney's staff, also testified to the principal facts as above.—*Army Correspondence of Philadelphia Inquirer.*

The following communication appeared in the *Philadelphia Inquirer:*

EDITOR PHILADELPHIA INQUIRER:

The reported arrest of this officer on the battle-field, and the statement made by the reporter of the *New York Herald*, that had his brigade obeyed the order of General Heintzelman at the battle of Fair Oaks many valuable lives would have been saved, have brought upon General Birney unjust and undeserved censure. His immediate friends, confident of his bravery and energy, have never doubted that when the smoke of the battle-field passed away he would be fully exonerated from all blame. Had he been charged with some rash act, his friends could have believed it possible; for by nature he is impulsive; and they could believe that he had undertaken some rapid movement, resulting in disaster; but no one who knows the man would, without conclusive evidence, believe that he was ever too slow.

As the reasons of his arrest are to be the subject of inquiry by a military tribunal, it would be injudicious to anticipate the evidence which will be offered; but it is only just to General Birney that some explanation be made in response to the unfair accusations, which have no other foundation than the statement of a reporter, prepared the day of the battle, and before he could possibly have had time to ascertain the part performed by the brigade under the command of General Birney. Precedents are not wanting to show that the first reports damaging to the character of an officer are seldom verified. The charge against General Smith, of drunkenness, before Yorktown, had no other foundation than that his horse stumbled and fell. It was immediately announced that he was drunk on the battle-field, and, but for fortunate circumstances, his brigade would have been cut to pieces. Based upon newspaper authority, the statement was made on the floor of Congress; but in less than ten days the truth was known, and General Smith was vindicated in the estimation of those who had charged him unjustly. Other generals have been charged with inefficiency, cowardice and treason; and have, for a time, rested under the most unjust imputations; but reparation has invariably followed investigation.

General Birney cannot claim exemption from the chances of war; and if, while attempting to execute the conflicting orders given during the panic which ensued upon the unepxected rout of General Casey's division, on Saturday, May 31st, it appeared to General Heintzelman that General Birney had disobeyed orders, it becomes him as a good soldier to remain quiet under the charge until the time for explanation shall arrive.

There is no man from our city who has made greater sacrifices to do his duty to his country than General Birney. He abandoned a large and lucrative business, and threw his whole energies into his new career. His promotion from lieutenant-colonel to brigadier-general, during the first eight months of the war, was solely the result of the opinion of his competency, based upon his conduct; for he had no friends at court, nor had he ever been engaged in political life.

The reports which were prepared on Sunday, and published in two of the New York papers, on Tuesday and Wednesday, were evidently prepared without inquiry. General Birney, with his brigade, did halt; but it was in pursuance of orders. He was "not within a mile of the enemy," but within the reach of the bayonet; and those now living, who were in his brigade on Saturday afternoon, do not say that there was any omission of duty, or any failure to perform any service which the position of the brigade permitted.

The imputation upon General Birney, which the reports referred to imply, do not cast a shadow upon him alone, but on the officers and men under his command. The services they rendered were valuable and important. Human flesh and blood could not have done more; and the number of killed and wounded from their ranks attest that the contest in which they were engaged was not bloodless. For their sake, as well as that of their general, this statement has been prepared; and it is hoped that it may, in some measure, disabuse the impression which the public mind may have formed from the unfounded allegations rendered current by the hastily-prepared reports of the battle.

KEARNY'S REPORT OF CHARLES CITY CROSS ROADS.

HEADQUARTERS THIRD DIVISION, THIRD ARMY CORPS,
July 6, 1862.

CAPTAIN:—

I have the honor to report as follows on the moves and battles of last week:

On the 28th of June, at midnight, I received orders to prepare to retire from Fair Oaks. This was executed at six A. M., regularly and without annoyance, the enemy appearing with distrust, as we left without pressure. My division then took up its position in the very strong fortified camp near Savage's. In the afternoon we received orders again to retire across the White Oak Swamp. This I executed by the back (or mill) road. Some artillery and my Twentieth Indiana marksmen held this place for several hours after the retreat commenced, and manned the works on the right of the road, for the purpose of preventing the enemy from hurrying us.

Colonel Brown, Twentieth Indiana, greatly distinguished himself. His regiment lost some killed and wounded, as the enemy shelled the works towards the last, and parties of his advance and our rear guard became engaged.

Fearing lest the roads to the White Oak Swamp bridge and Brackett's ford might be unduly clogged with troops, I proposed crossing at Jordan's ford, three miles below my camp. I had reconnoitered it in the morning, and found that the enemy was in force on the Central road, but not on the Charles City road, and did not then seem to be on the lookout. General Robinson was to cover my retreat, and was cautioned against the enemy's troops arriving from across the Williamsburg road. General Birney with his brigade was to lead the march; General Berry to follow.

It was found, after crossing the double arm of the swamp at Jordan's, that our moves had been expected; and it being problematical whether the relative position of the lines of retreat justified a full engagement, after a successful engagement of the advanced pickets, and, on learning that the road to Brackett's ford was then free, I withdrew the troops and proceeded by that ford; General Berry's brigade, however, finding Fisher's ford unobstructed, passed by that route. This same night by ten P. M., the whole division was encamped on and near the Charles City road, at a point subsequently (during the battle) occupied by General Slocum.

In the morning, June 30th, I drew up in a very strong position on the Charles City road. Subsequently, I was assigned to guard the New Market road and the country thence to the Charles City road, a space of near two and a half miles. In taking up my line of battle, General Robinson, with the first brigade, was posted on the left; his left on the New Market road supporting Thompson's battery. General Birney divided the distance with him to the Charles City road, and General Berry was in reserve. General Slocum was to the right of my line of battle; General McCall to its left.

The enemy's attack commenced on General McCall, at about two P. M. At about three P. M., it seemed to be fully developed; but as I rode over to visit it, it did not seem to me to be unduly threatening, further than from the shape of his line; its left being greatly refused, it had disadvantages for myself, although advantageous for those to whom the enemy must present his flank in making an attack upon them. At four P. M., the attack commenced on my line with determination and vigor, and in such masses as I had never witnessed. Thompson's battery, directed with great skill, literally swept the slightly falling, open space with the completest execution, and, mowing the enemy down by ranks, would bring the survivors to a momentary halt; but, almost instantly after, increased masses came up and the wave bore on. These masses coming up at a rapid run, covering the entire breadth of the open ground,—some two hundred paces,—would alone be checked in their career by gaps of the fallen. Yet no retreat; but again a fresh mass would carry the approaching line still nearer. If there was one man in this attack there must have been ten thousand, and their loss by artillery, although borne with such fortitude, must have been unusual. It was by thousands, the irrepressibility of numbers, they persisted. The artillery, destructive as it was, ceased to be a calculation.

It was then that Colonel Hayes, with the Sixty-third Pennsylvania and half the Thirty-seventh New York volunteers, moved forward to the line of the guns. I have here to call to the attention of my superior chiefs this most heroic action on the part of Colonel Hayes and his regiment. The Sixty-third has won for Pennsylvania the laurels of fame. That which canister failed in effecting, was now accomplished by the determined charge and rapid volleys of this foot. The enemy at the muzzles of our guns, for the first time sulkily retired fighting, and ground having been gained, the Sixty-third was ordered to "lie low," while the battery once more re-opened its ceaseless work of destruction.

This battle saw renewed three onsets, as above, with similar vicissitudes, when, finally, the enemy betokened his efforts as passed, by converting his charges into an ordinary line fight of musketry, embracing the whole front of the brigade; for by this time he was enabled to do so, from Thompson's pieces having been withdrawn, after expending their canister and becoming tired of the futility of round shot. It may have been at that time about seven and a half P. M. Full daylight remained, and anticipating that the enemy, foiled in the attempt to carry the New Market road and adjacent open ground, would next hazard an attack towards the Charles City road, or intermediate woods, my attention was called there. I therefore left every thing progressing steadily on the left, and visited the entire line to the right. Notwithstanding that the line was long, and that no reserves, excepting the weak Third Michigan, existed, the cheerful manner and solid look of Birney's brigade gave assurance of their readiness to be measured with the foe; and they met my warning of the coming storm with loud cheers of exultation.

Half an hour or forty minutes may have been thus passed. I then returned to the extreme left of my line. Arriving there, I found that Colonel Hayes had been relieved by Colonel Barlow, with the Sixty-first New York,—the head of General Caldwell's brigade, sent to me from Sumner's corps, and which had reported to General Robinson.

Almost in the commencement of the action, within the first half hour, as I had plainly foreseen and warned my superior, General Heintzelman, and General Humphreys' engineer, who most kindly had gone over the line with me, every man was engaged, or in position, or in close support. The Eighty-seventh New York volunteers had been ordered by General Heintzelman to Brackett's ford, and the First New York was diverted from me by a misapprehension of Colonel Dyckman. This fact I announced to General Heintzelman, without asking reinforcements, since I did not conceive them necessary; nor would they have been, but for the diverting of my First New York volunteers, a very strong regiment, to General McCall.

The Sixty-first New York volunteers, under its most intrepid leader, Colonel Barlow, vied with the brave regiment he had relieved, and, charging the enemy, bore off as a trophy one of his colors. It had subsequently taken up its position to the left of the One-hundred-and-fifth Pennsylvania, and been subsequently retired, but none appointed to take its place, that breastwork being left unoccupied.

It was at this juncture that I arrived from my right. Finding McCall's position abandoned, although not occupied by the enemy, I placed in it the First New Jersey brigade, General Taylor. I then knew it to be in true hands. I observed that, while the enemy was amusing my entire front with an ordinary musket fire, strong parties of rebel skirmishers, in the gloom of the evening, rendered dense by the murky fog and the smoke, were feeling their way slowly and distrustfully to the unoccupied parapet. Galloping back to find the nearest troops, I met General Caldwell, who, under General McCall's supervision, was putting two or more of his regiments into line, to the right of the road, a quarter of a mile in rear of the breastworks, to move up in order. Circumstances denied this delay; and, accordingly, I directed General Caldwell to lead a wing of a regiment at double-quick up the road, to open on these rebel skirmishers. This was done promptly; but from their being foreigners, not with a full comprehension, and embarrassed by the darkness, they fired at the rebels, but in the direction of others of my own line; and thus, after the enemy was swept off the arena, it left for some little time our troops firing at each other. To increase this confusion, the residue of the brigade, who had not filed into the woods and formed on the road, opened on us all who were in front. It is my impression that General McCall must have been killed by this fire.

The errors of cross-firing having at last subsided, the Fifth Michigan gallantly crossed the parapets and pursued the retiring enemy. The Eighty-first Pennsylvania then, nobly responding to my orders, gallantly led by Lieutenant-colonel Connor and Captain Miles of General Caldwell's staff, dashed over the parapets, pursued, charged, and by a few vigorous volleys finished the battle at nine and a half o'clock at night. I remained much longer on the field, and then reported to General Heintzelman at his quarters.

In concluding my report of this battle, one of the most desperate of the war,—the one most fatal if lost,—I am proud to give my thanks, and to include in the glory of my own division, the First New Jersey brigade, General Taylor, which held McCall's deserted ground, and General Caldwell, whose personal gallantry and the bravery of whose regiments not only entitle them to share in the credit of our victory but also ever after engender full sympathies between the two corps.

In this engagement, the coolness and judicious arrangements of General Birney influenced his whole command to feel invincible in a very weak position. General Berry, as usual, was active. The fearful losses his noble regiments have sustained, reducing them to scarce two hundred to a regiment, oblige me to preserve such heroes for the decisive moments. Still, they will not be repressed; and the Fifth Michigan, under Major Fairbanks, was the first to pursue the enemy. I regret for ourselves that he, almost the last of our nobly distinguished at Williamsburg and Fair Oaks, and the forced advance of June 25th, is dangerously wounded. I have to state that this division has been extremely used. This has prematurely reduced to nothing regiments of the highest mark. I have reserved General Robinson for the last. To him, this day, is due above all others in the division, the honors of the battle. The attack was on his wing. Everywhere present, by personal supervision and noble example, he secured us the honors of victory. As to the action of my artillery, (Battery G, Second U. S.,) it has never been equalled for rapidity and precision of fire and coolness amidst great loss of men and of horses. The gallantry of its commander, Captain Thompson, identifies him with its distinction.

Our losses have been severe; and when it is remembered that this occurs to mere skeletons of regiments, there is but one observation to be made: that previous military history presents no parallel.

Very respectfully,

Your obedient servant,

P. KEARNY,

Brigadier general commanding Division.

CAPTAIN McKEEVER,

A. A. G. Third Army Corps.

KEARNY'S REPORT OF MALVERN HILL.

HEADQUARTERS THIRD DIVISION THIRD ARMY CORPS,
July 6, 1862.

CAPTAIN:—

I have the honor to report that, at the close of the battle on the New Market road, our men remained in position until midnight, when orders were brought from General Heintzelman to effect a retreat, as General Franklin had already abandoned his position.

This movement was effected quietly and rapidly by the troops, but at some sacrifice, from the want of transportation; and by daylight we were in a newer and stronger position.

It was toward noon when the battle was renewed at Malvern Hill. In this battle all our regiments were on the alert and under artillery fire, and all lost more or less from the enemy's shelling. None but our artillery and skirmishers were immediately engaged. Captain Thompson managed his battery with the full genius of that arm, whilst Captain Randolph, with his Parrot guns, punished all who attacked him, silencing several times batteries that were sweeping our front, or covering their columns of attack on General Couch, to our left.

The Fourth Maine particularly distinguished itself by its coolness in holding the ravine in our front, and daringly engaged the skirmishers of the enemy's attacking columns. Their loss was considerable.

The brigades of Generals Robinson and Berry were principally in reserve, but were constantly sent forward in support, as the tide of battle swerved to and fro on our left. The first line was held by General Birney with coolness and firmness, and his regiments, even under fire, erected for themselves well-arranged rifle-pits. Had the next day witnessed renewal of the battle, success was sure.

Our loss has been nine hundred and fifty-one in the several engagements. It was at midnight that we were again called upon to move in retreat; and, tired as we were and all our commands, it was again executed with much regularity, and we arrived by ten A. M. at Harrison's Landing.

I am, very respectfully,

Your obedient servant,

P. KEARNY,

Brigadier-general commanding Division.

CAPTAIN C. McKEEVER,

A. A. G. Third Corps.

KEARNY'S REPORT OF SECOND BULL RUN.

HEADQUARTERS FIRST DIVISION THIRD ARMY CORPS,
CENTREVILLE, VA., *August* 31, 1862.

COLONEL:—

I report the part taken by my division in the battles of the two previous days. On the 29th, on my arrival, I was assigned to the holding of the right wing, my left on the Leesburg road. I posted Colonel Poe, with Berry's brigade in the first line; General Robinson's first brigade on his right, partly in line and partly in support; and kept Birney's most disciplined regiments reserved and ready for emergencies. Towards noon I was obliged to occupy a quarter of a mile additional on left of said road, from Schurz's troops being taken elsewhere.

During the first hours of combat, General Birney, on tried regiments in the centre falling back, of his own accord rapidly pushed across to give them a hand to raise themselves to a renewed fight.

In early afternoon, General Pope's order, per General Roberts, was, to send a pretty strong force diagonally to the front, to relieve the centre in the woods from pressure. Accordingly, I detached for that purpose, General Robinson with his brigade, the Sixty-third Pennsylvania volunteers, Colonel Hayes; the One-hundred-and-fifth Pennsylvania, Captain Craig; the Twentieth Indiana, Colonel Brown; and, additionally, the Third Michigan, under Colonel Champlin. General Robinson drove forward for several hundred yards; but the centre of the main battle being shortly after driven back and out of the woods, my detachment, thus exposed so considerably, in front of all others, was obliged to cease advancing, and confine itself to holding its own. At five o'clock, thinking—though at the risk of exposing my fighting line to be enfiladed—that I might drive the enemy by an unexpected attack through the woods, I brought up in addition the most of Birney's regiments—the Fourth Maine, Colonel Walker and Lieutenant-colonel Carver; the Fortieth New York, Colonel Egan; First New York, Major Burt; and One-hundred-and-first New York, Lieutenant-colonel Gesner—and changed front to the left, to sweep with a rush the first line of the enemy. This was most successful. The enemy rolled up on his right; it presaged a victory for us; still our force was too light. The enemy brought up rapidly heavy reserves, so that our further progress was impeded. General Stevens came up gallantly in action to support us, but did not have the numbers.

On the morning of the 30th, General Ricketts, with two brigades, relieved me of my extra charge of the left of the road, and I again concentrated my command. We took no part in the fighting of the morning, although we lost men by an enfilading fire of the enemy's batteries. A sudden and unaccountable evacuation of the field, by the left and centre, occurring about five P. M., on orders from General Pope, I massed my troops at a point indicated; but soon re-occupied with Birney's brigade, supported by Robinson's, a very advanced block of woods. The key-point of this new line rested on the brown house, towards the creek. This was held by regiments of other brigades. Soon, however, themselves attacked, they ceded ground, and retired without warning us. I maintained my position until ten, P. M., when, in connection with Generals Reno and Gibbons—assigned to the rear guard—I retired my brigades.

My command arrived at Centreville in good order at two A. M. this morning, and encamped in front of the Centreville forts. My loss in killed and wounded is over seven hundred and fifty—about one in three; in some regiments engaged a great deal severer: in the Third Michigan one hundred and forty out of two hundred and sixty. None were taken prisoner, except my engineer officer, Lieutenant Briscoe, who returned to the house supposed to be held by the troops alluded to.

It makes me proud to dwell on the renewed efforts of my generals of brigades, Birney and Robinson. My regiments all did well; and the remiss in camp seemed brightest in the field. Besides my old, tried regiments, which have been previously noted in former actions and maintained their prestige, I have to mark the One-hundred-and-first New York and Fifty-seventh Pennsylvania volunteers, as equalling all their comrades have done before. Their commanders, Lieutenant-colonel Gesner and Major Birney, have imparted to them the stamp of their own high character. The Sixty-third Pennsylvania and Fortieth New York volunteers, under the brave Colonel Egan, suffered most. The gallant Hayes is badly wounded. The loss of officers is great. That of Colonel Brown can hardly be replaced. Brave, skillful, a disciplinarian, full of energy, and a charming gentleman, his Twentieth Indiana must miss him sadly. In him the country loses one who promised to fill worthily a high trust. The Third Michigan, ever faithful to their name, under Colonel Champlin and Major Pierce, lost one hundred and forty out of two hundred and sixty combatants. Colonel Champlin is again disabled. The staunch Fourth Maine, under Walker and Carver, true men of a rare type, drove on through the stream of battle irresistibly. The One-hundred-and-fifth Pennsylvania volunteers were not wanting. They are Pennsylvania's mountain men; again have they been fearfully decimated. The desperate charges of these regiments sustain the past history of this division. Randolph's battery of light twelves was worked with boldness and address. Though narrowly watched by three long-reaching, enfilading batteries of the enemy, it constantly silenced one of theirs in its front, and ricocheted its shot and shell into the reinforcements moving from the enemy's heights down into the woods.

On the 27th, with two sections and Robinson's first brigade, Captain Randolph had powerfully contributed to the success of General Hooker at Bristow Station.

Captain Graham's First U. S. Artillery, put at General Siegel's disposition, as repeatedly drove the enemy back into the woods as the giving away of the infantry left his front unobstructed. His practice was beautifully correct, and proved irresistible. On the 31st, Captain Graham, not being required on the right, was sent to the extreme left, and rendered important services with General Reno, firing until late at night.

Lieutenant ———, a German officer of distinction, put at my disposal by General Siegel, with two long-range Parrot guns, covered our right flank and drove off an enemy's battery and regiments. I name these officers as ornaments to their branch of the service.

I must refer to General Hooker to render justice to the part taken by my first brigade, under General Robinson, and Randolph's battery, in the affair of the 27th at Bristow Station.

Again I am called on to mention the efficiency of my staff. Captain Mindil, often cited, brave and intelligent, was the only military aide present to assist me, but Surgeon Pancoast, medical director of the division, not only insured the promptness of his department, but with heroism and aptitude carried for me my orders.

Very respectfully,

Your obedient servant,

P. KEARNY,

Major-general commanding Division.

LIEUTENANT-COLONEL C. MCKEEVER,

Chief of Staff Third Army Corps.

BIRNEY'S REPORT OF CHANTILLY.

HEADQUARTERS FIRST DIVISION, THIRD CORPS,
FORT LYON, VA., *September* 4, 1862.

COLONEL:—

I have the honor to report the part taken by this division in the battle at Chantilly, between Centreville and Fairfax Court House, on Monday, September 1st.

The division reached Chantilly at about five o'clock, P.M., under orders from General Heintzelman to support General Reno, and found him actually engaged with the enemy. Under orders from General Kearny I reported my brigade to General Reno, and by him was ordered to the front. On reaching that point, I found the division of General Stevens retiring in some disorder before the enemy; the officers in command of regiments stating that their ammunition had been exhausted. I immediately ordered forward the Fourth Maine volunteers, which gallantly advanced, and was soon in active conflict, and successively took forward the One-hundred-and-first New York, Third Maine, Fortieth New York, and First New York regiments. These held the enemy, and sustained unflinchingly the most murderous fire.

At this juncture, General Kearny reached the hill, with Randolph's battery, and, placing it in position, aided my brigade by a well-directed fire. I then pointed out to the General a gap on my right, caused by the retreat of Stevens' division, and asked for Berry's brigade to fill it. He rode forward to examine the ground, and, dashing past our lines into those of the enemy, fell a victim to his gallant daring.

I sent forward the Thirty-eighth New York and Fifty-seventh Pennsylvania to complete our victory. They advanced gallantly; and when night closed, my brigade was in full possession of the battle-field on which it was engaged.

General Kearny not returning, and supposing that he had been taken prisoner, I assumed the command of the division; and, ordering forward Robinson's and Berry's brigades, relieved my tired regiments and held the battle-ground until three o'clock A. M., at which time the division followed the corps of General Reno to Fairfax Court House.

During the night we removed our wounded. Our loss has been heavy.

I was ably supported by the commanding officers of my regiments, all of whom sustained the high character accorded by our late, lamented commander in his report of Friday's engagement. Lieutenants Lee and Phillips, of my staff, deserve especial mention for their untiring efforts in carrying my orders to all parts of the field. I have mentioned these, in previous reports, for gallantry. Robinson's brigade had been placed upon the left of my brigade by General Kearny, to support Graham's battery. It was not, unfortunately, called upon to engage the enemy, but assisted greatly, with Berry's brigade, during the night, in holding the field in face of a vastly superior force of the enemy. I was much indebted to General Robinson and to Colonel Poe, commanding Berry's brigade, for their prompt assistance and the gallant bearing of their tried commands

I am, very respectfully,

Your obedient servant,

D. B. BIRNEY,

Brigadier-general commanding Division

LIEUTENANT-COLONEL McKEEVER,

Assistant Adjutant-general, Third Army Corps.

BIRNEY'S REPORT OF FREDERICKSBURG.

HEADQUARTERS FIRST DIVISION, THIRD CORPS,
CAMP PITCHER, *December* 17, 1862.

CAPTAIN:—

I have the honor to report the operations of this division on the 13th, 14th, and 15th instants, as follows:

My division reached the river at daylight on the morning of the 13th, and remained massed on the heights until half-past ten A. M., when Captain Sumner, of General Stoneman's staff, delivered me an order to cross with my division, and report with it, on the left, to General Reynolds.

The head of the division reached the field designated, at half-past eleven o'clock A. M. I, upon reporting in person to General Reynolds, was ordered to deploy my division in the field in rear of General Meade's division, as a support to the intended attack by that division. The road bounding the rear of the field was edged with high embankments, with ditches next to the road, some six feet deep. Through this embankment were two narrow wagon-ways, making it impossible to retire from the field except by the flank.

Ward's brigade on the right, and Berry's brigade on the left, were deployed in two lines, leaving Robinson's brigade, which had not yet reached the field, as a reserve.

The enemy's batteries commanded the open field, and General Reynolds ordered me to retire my command from the field, holding it in hand behind the embankments. When the movement consequent on this order was half completed, General Meade's division was being severely pressed, and he sent to me for assistance. I immediately reversed the movement of Ward's brigade, placing the Ninety-ninth Pennsylvania, Colonel Leidy, Fifty-seventh Pennsylvania, Colonel Campbell, and Fifty-fifth New York, Colonel De Trobriand, in support of Meade's batteries, ordering forward the Thirty-eighth New York, Lieutenant-colonel Birney, Fortieth New York, Lieutenant-colonel Gesner, and Fourth Maine, Colonel Walker, under General Ward, to the support of the disordered troops in front.

I returned Berry's brigade to its position on the left. The batteries attached to Meade's division having exhausted their ammunition, I ordered forward to relieve them, Randolph's and Livingston's batteries, belonging to this division, and they went immediately into action, under my chief of artillery, Captain Randolph, of the Rhode Island artillery.

Finding that Meade's and Gibbon's divisions were in full retreat, I sent forward Colonel Campbell, with the Fifty-seventh Pennsylvania volunteers, to report to General Ward, and to support my advanced regiments, and ordered the Third Maine and Fifty-fifth New York regiments in the field to the right, to support one of General Gibbon's batteries. The retreating troops poured through my ranks, and, at General Meade's request, I ordered the Ninety-ninth Pennsylvania, Colonel Leidy, on the field to the right, to try and stop his troops. It was useless, as they sullenly and resolutely marched to the rear.

The enemy now appeared in full force upon my entire front, with a brigade deployed in line and one doubled on the centre on each flank, and charged upon the four batteries under my command. General Berry, at my orders, sent me the Seventeenth Maine volunteers to support the batteries, and advanced his line to front and right, to fill the vacancy caused by sending forward a portion of Ward's brigade. General Gibbon's batteries having withdrawn, and his division not being in sight on my right, I advanced the Ninety-ninth Pennsylvania, Colonel Leidy, Third Maine, Colonel Lakeman, and Fifty-fifth New York, Colonel De Trobriand, to form the right.

The Fifth Michigan, Lieutenant-colonel Gillesley, Thirty-seventh New York, Colonel Hayman, One-hundred-and-first New York, Colonel Chester, and Seventeenth Maine, Colonel Roberts, under command of Brigadier-general Berry, met the brunt of the attack and poured a withering fire into their line. The portion of Ward's brigade on the right of the road did gallant service by its oblique fire.

General Ward, now returning with his thinned veteran regiments, was ordered by me to the right; and, reforming his lines, held an imposing attitude with his gallant command.

Robinson's brigade now arriving, I ordered immediately to the front and centre his two first regiments, the One-hundred-and-fourteenth Pennsylvania, Colonel Collis, and Sixty-third Pennsylvania, Major Danks, who poured a most effective and galling fire into the now retreating foe.

The enemy being repulsed, I formed new lines: Berry's brigade on the left, Robinson's brigade in the centre, and Ward's brigade on the right, with my two batteries on the crest of the hill, receiving also the efficient aid of the batteries of Captains Cooper and Leprieu, of General Reynolds' command. During the remainder of Saturday, the firing was constant between pickets and the advanced lines. The enemy holding the edge of the woods, the railroad embankment, rifle-pits, and ditches in our front, at three o'clock, P. M., I ordered skirmishers to advance and seize a ditch parallel with my front. They did so, gallantly capturing in the ditch some sixty prisoners. At four and a half o'clock, P. M., the enemy, uncovering ten guns on the hill opposite my left, opened a concentrated fire on Doubleday's division. My chief of artillery directed the fire of the two division batteries, and, aided by Leprieu's battery on my left, silenced the guns in twenty minutes. The enemy then opened upon our left a battery of Whitworth guns that enfiladed my command, which annoyed us greatly.

At five o'clock, P. M., General Reynolds sent to me orders to take command of the entire front. During Saturday night, Sunday and Monday, my tired regiments remained without a murmur on the field, (lying on the damp ground,) without blankets, and exposed to the most galling fire from the sharpshooters.

During Monday afternoon, an informal arrangement was made, on the suggestion of General Ewell, commanding the forces opposite, to stop the picket firing. This was done; and our commands, within one hundred yards of each other, passed Sunday night and Monday without firing a shot.

On Monday night, under orders from General Stoneman, this division was withdrawn in good order without loss of public property.

I have to mark out for the high commendation of the General-in-chief, Generals Berry, Robinson and Ward. To their reputation, established on other fields, they have added greater lustre.

My regiments all did well, and the new regiments equalled all their comrades have done before. The loss of officers is great, and shows that they were at their posts.

Randolph's and Livingston's batteries did admirably; and Captain Randolph, as chief of division artillery, was then, as always, skillful, prudent, daring, and contributed greatly to the result. Between his batteries and this division there exists the strongest attachment.

There are many instances of heroism and gallantry entitling the persons to distinction. Their names will be promptly forwarded. My staff was very efficient, and exercised a great influence on the result. Captain F. E. Bliss, commissary of subsistence, volunteered his services in the field, and was indefatigable. Lieutenant Briscoe, my engineer officer, rendered also the most efficient aid, and the maps annexed to illustrate my report are from his field notes.

Colonel Campbell, Fifty-seventh Pennsylvania volunteers, with his arm still in a sling from Fair Oaks, fell, severely wounded. I would ask that one of the new regiments be assigned to this division, and that my request for the consolidation of some of my skeleton regiments be duly considered.

I am your obedient servant,

D. B. BIRNEY,

Brigadier-general commanding Division.

CAPTAIN ALEXANDER,

Assistant Adjutant-general, Third Corps.

THE EMANCIPATION PROCLAMATION.

BY THE PRESIDENT OF THE UNITED STATES OF AMERICA:

A PROCLAMATION.

WHEREAS, on the twenty-second day of September, in the year of our Lord one thousand eight hundred and sixty-two, a proclamation was issued by the President of the United States containing among other things the following, to wit:

"That on the first day of January, in the year of our Lord one thousand eight hundred and sixty-three, all persons held as slaves within any State, or designated part of a State, the people whereof shall then be in rebellion against the United States, shall be then, thenceforth and forever free; and the Executive Government of the

United States, including the military and naval authorities thereof, will recognize and maintain the freedom of such persons, and will do no act or acts to repress such persons, or any of them, in any efforts they may make for their actual freedom.

"That the Executive will, on the first day of January aforesaid, by proclamation, designate the States and parts of States, if any, in which the people therein respectively shall then be in rebellion against the United States; and the fact that any State, or the people thereof, shall on that day be in good faith represented in the Congress of the United States by members chosen thereto, at elections wherein a majority of the qualified voters of such States shall have participated, shall, in the absence of strong countervailing testimony, be deemed conclusive evidence that such State and the people thereof are not then in rebellion against the United States."

Now, therefore, I, Abraham Lincoln, President of the United States, by virtue of the power in me vested as Commander-in-chief of the Army and Navy of the United States in time of actual armed rebellion against the authority and Government of the United States, and a fit and necessary war measure for suppressing said rebellion, do, on this first day of January, in the year of our Lord one thousand eight hundred and sixty-three, and in accordance with my purpose so to do, publicly proclaimed for the full period of one hundred days from the day of the first above-mentioned order, and designate, as the States and parts of States wherein the people thereof respectively are this day in rebellion against the United States, the following, to wit: Arkansas, Texas, Louisiana, except the parishes of St. Bernard, Plaquemines, Jefferson, St. John, St. James, Ascension, Assumption, Terre Bonne, Lafourche, St. Mary, St. Marrin, and Orleans, including the city of New Orleans; Mississippi, Alabama, Florida, Georgia, South Carolina, North Carolina, and Virginia, except the forty-eight counties designated as West Virginia, and also the counties of Berkeley, Accomac, Northampton, Elizabeth City, York, Princess Ann, and Norfolk, including the cities of Norfolk and Portsmouth, and which excepted parts are, for the present, left precisely as if this proclamation were not issued.

And by virtue of the power and for the purpose aforesaid, I do order and declare that all persons held as slaves within said designated States and parts of States are and henceforward shall be free;

and that the Executive Government of the United States, including the military and naval authorities thereof, will recognize and maintain the freedom of said persons.

And I hereby enjoin upon the people so declared to be free to abstain from all violence, unless in necessary self-defence, and I recommend to them that in all cases, when allowed, they labor faithfully for reasonable wages.

And I further declare and make known that such persons, of suitable condition, will be received into the armed service of the United States, to garrison forts, positions, stations, and other places, and to man vessels of all sorts in said service.

And upon this, sincerely believed to be an act of justice, warranted by the Constitution, upon military necessity, I invoke the considerate judgment of mankind and the gracious favor of Almighty God.

In witness whereof I have hereunto set my hand and caused the seal of the United States to be affixed.

[L. S.] Done at the city of Washington, this first day of January, in the year of our Lord one thousand eight hundred and sixty-three, and of the Independence of the United States of America the eighty-seventh.

ABRAHAM LINCOLN.

By the President:

WILLIAM H. SEWARD,
Secretary of State.

BIRNEY'S REPORT OF CHANCELLORSVILLE.

HEADQUARTERS FIRST DIVISION THIRD CORPS,
May 9, 1863.

COLONEL:—

I have the honor to report, for the information of the major-general commanding the corps, the part performed by this division in the recent operations against the enemy.

The division moved from its camp on the 29th April, at four o'clock, P. M., and by a route through the ravines reached the position assigned to it, some four miles below Fredericksburg, near the river, and bivouacked. On the 30th April my command advanced to a position immediately in rear of the Sixth Corps, and near the bridges used by it. At two o'clock, P. M., I received orders from the major-general commanding corps to march my division to the United States ford, and cross it by half-past seven o'clock, A. M., next day, taking care to move through the ravines, concealing my troops from the enemy. I reached "Hammett's" on the Warrenton turnpike, at eleven and a half o'clock, P. M., and bivouacked. The march was resumed on the first day of May, at five and a half o'clock, A. M., crossing the bridges at United States ford at seven and a half o'clock, A. M., and reaching a point near Chancellorsville at about eleven o'clock, A. M.

At one o'clock, P. M., under orders from Major-general Sickles, I sent Graham's brigade and Turnbull's battery to Dowdall's tavern to take position, sending with them Lieutenant Briscoe of my staff. Upon reaching the tavern indicated, General Graham was told by Major-general Howard that there was some mistake in the brigade and battery being sent there, as he was sufficiently strong, and they would interfere with the disposition of his own forces, which were ample.

Brigadier-general Graham reported this to me, and I immediately sent the information to Major-general Sickles, and was ordered to permit the troops to remain there for the present.

At five o'clock, P. M., the enemy attacking General Slocum's front, I took position in the rear of the Chancellor House with Ward's and

Hayman's brigades, and sent to the tavern for Graham to return. When Graham's brigade reported, a position was assigned to it in support of one of General Slocum's batteries, where it was subjected to a heavy and well-directed artillery fire. With Ward and Hayman's brigades I marched up the plank road towards Dowdall's tavern, and meeting Generals Williams and Knipe, of Slocum's command, and finding the right of their line weak, bivouacked my two brigades in its rear, and replaced two of their regiments with the Twentieth Indiana and Thirty-seventh New York volunteers, throwing pickets well to the front, and dislodging the enemy from a house in the little field in my front. At daylight of May 2d, after consultation with Major-general Howard, I occupied a line through the woods south of the plank road, and connected with his left. At this time General Graham reported with his brigade. About eight o'clock I reported to Major-general Sickles that a continuous column of infantry trains and ambulances was passing my front towards the right, and that I should give it a few shots from Clark's rifled battery. Sending a section to a good point in the little field in my front, it opened with effect, the column double-quicking past the point reached by our shots. I then ordered the remainder of the battery to the same position, and threw the column into great confusion, as the battery poured its well-directed shot into its midst.

At twelve o'clock, M., I received orders from Major-general Sickles to follow the enemy, pierce the column, and gain possession of the road over which it was passing. Colonel Berdan reported to me at the same time with his sharpshooters. The Twentieth Indiana, Colonel John Wheeler, entered the woods, ascending the hill, driving the skirmishers of the enemy before them. We quickly bridged Scott's Run with rails, and crossing the sharpshooters, I ordered Colonel Berdan to advance rapidly towards the road at the point we had reached with our artillery, which was to the left. Hayman's brigade was ordered to follow, and attack the enemy, if found between the point of entrance and the road alluded to.

The firing increasing, I sent for Graham's brigade, to keep my connections complete, and then sent for Ward's brigade as we advanced, crossing all over the small creek, which was some five feet deep, with high banks. We met with no serious opposition until reaching the "Forge," which was occupied by a company. Berdan's Sharpshooters with great skill captured this company. The enemy now opened on us with a battery placed near Welford's house, near the road that I intended to take. I sent back for Turnbull's battery, which after an exciting artillery duel drove off the enemy. The fire upon our left flank from musketry was galling, and at this point I received orders from Major-general Sickles to wait for the advance of General Whipple's division, and a brigade from the Twelfth Corps on my left. I rode to the rear, and pointed out to General Whipple the position to be taken by him on my left. On my return to the front, Brigadier-general Barlow, commanding a brigade of the Eleventh Corps, reported to me that he was on my right, and had completed the connection between it and his corps. I now sent forward the Twentieth Indiana and Fifth Michigan to support the sharpshooters, and ordered them to advance towards the road. The movement was quite successful, as a capture of some one hundred and eighty prisoners was almost immediately made by the party. At about half-past six o'clock, P. M., I received orders from Captain Alexander Moore, of Major-general Hooker's staff, to advance rapidly, which I did, taking the road, and, placing Randolph's battery, which I had ordered up in position, poured a well-directed fire on the retreating column of the enemy. In this advance Hayman's brigade led, followed by Graham and Ward's, the latter keeping open the connection to the "Forge." Sending out scouts I found the enemy in some force on three sides, and, disposing my troops to meet attack from any direction, I was preparing to bivouack, when I was informed by Lieutenant-colonel Hart, Assistant Adjutant-general, who had gallantly reached me, that our right, occupied by the Eleventh Corps, had given away in entire disorder, and Major-general Sickles ordered my immediate return.

I withdrew my command in good order, using the Twentieth Indiana and Sixty-third Pennsylvania as a rear guard, and sent an order to Brigadier-general Barlow to follow with his brigade. I returned to the field in which I had placed Clark's battery in the morning, and found Major-general Sickles with the batteries belonging to the corps, supported by some thousand cavalry under General Pleasanton, with which he had checked the advance of the enemy on the plank road. My division was formed in line of brigades in rear of the batteries.

At midnight I received an order from Major-general Sickles to make necessary dispositions to drive the enemy from the woods in our front, and retake the plank road and earthworks on it. I placed Ward's brigade in the front line, with Hayman's in the second line, one hundred yards in rear, and gave orders that all pieces were to be uncapped and not discharged until the plank road and earthworks were reached. This movement was by right of companies to the front, until the enemy's line was reached. Upon the left of the line of battle a wide road had been cut through the woods, perpendicular to the plank road, upon which I sent in, by column of companies at full distance, the Fortieth New York, Seventeenth Maine, and Sixty-third Pennsylvania. The movement was successfully executed, amidst the most terrific musketry and artillery fire. In moving through the thick undergrowth of these close woods at midnight, there was necessarily some disorder, but the object was successfully gained. Among those under my immediate eye in this movement, Colonel Thomas W. Egan was distinguished for his energy, dash, and enthusiasm. I would call the attention of the major-general commanding the corps to this officer, and recommend his promotion.

At daylight, Sunday morning, I received orders to follow Whipple's column in withdrawing from the field, and form on the next line, near the plank road. Before my division had left the field, Graham's brigade was attacked by the enemy, with infantry and artillery. It however replied to it and fell back in good order. I formed my brigades in column of regiments just beyond the crest of the hill, and, placing two batteries on the crest, opened upon the enemy, who appeared on the field from which we had just withdrawn. After this, say at six o'clock, A. M., I sent Graham's brigade, composed of the One-hundred-and-fourteenth, Fifty-seventh, Sixty-third, Sixty-eighth, One-hundred-and-fifth and One-hundred-and-forty-first Pennsylvania volunteers, called the Pennsylvania brigade, to the front, to relieve one of General Slocum's brigades, which was nearly out of ammunition. It went in gallantly, and for some two hours held the ground, driving the enemy out of some barricades that he had taken.

The troops on the right of the plank road withdrawing, the enemy flanked this brigade, but, sending troops to his rear, I led a portion of Hayman's brigade to the charge, driving him back in confusion and capturing a large number of prisoners, relieving Graham's brigade, which was then withdrawn in good order.

During this time Brigadier-general Ward, under orders from Major-general Sickles, had moved to the right of the plank road to form on the right of Carr's division, but reports that he was not able to find General Carr in the woods and was ordered by Major-general French to fall to his rear.

Graham's and Hayman's brigades continued to support the artillery at the Chancellor House, until I received orders to take position in the front of the new line, when they were withdrawn. Ward's brigade had received orders to support an intended attack by Meagher's brigade, and moved again to the left for that purpose, but the order was countermanded. Taking the final position assigned to my command, with the few tools within our reach my men at once intrenched themselves, and we remained subjected to the occasional fire of sharpshooters and artillery until Wednesday morning, when, at four o'clock, A. M., my division moved without interruption to the rear.

To Brigadier-general Graham, a new-comer in our division, fell the post of honor, and with three new regiments in his command I looked with some anxiety for the result. But braver men never drew a trigger than those in the first brigade, and General Graham has gained in this fight, by his coolness, firmness and enthusiasm, the entire confidence of myself and the division.

Of Brigadier-general Ward I need not speak more than to say that he fully sustained all my previous reports of him, in the battles of Williamsburg, Fair Oaks, Glendale, Malvern, Manassas, Chantilly, and Fredericksburg.

Colonel S. B. Hayman, Thirty-seventh New York volunteers, commanding third brigade, has been specially recommended by me for promotion for gallantry on this occasion.

Captain Clark, chief of artillery of the division, was of great service, and displayed skill and gallantry in the management of his batteries.

Colonels Tippen, Madill, Sides, Pierce, Egan, Wheeler, Lieutenant-colonels Kirkwood and Sherwood were distinguished for their gallantry.

My staff were efficient. Major H. W. Brevoort was ever by my side, and my aides-de-camp, Captain Fassitt and Lieutenants Briscoe and Clarke, showed the greatest enthusiasm and ardor in carrying my orders. Lieutenant Clarke was seriously wounded. Captain Markle, Division Provost Marshal, deserves much credit for taking the large number of prisoners captured by us safely to the Provost Marshal-general. Captain Fergus Walker, Assistant Inspector-general, acted as an aide, and was very gallant and efficient. He received on Sunday a serious wound in his leg.

The division medical department under Surgeon Lyman, Fifty-seventh Pennsylvania volunteers, was admirably conducted. The wounded were immediately taken to the division hospital at Potomac Creek, where every attention was bestowed upon them. The hospital of this division is unsurpassed by any field hospital in this army.

Lieutenant C. H. Graves, Fortieth New York, the division ordnance officer, kept us well supplied with ammunition, and preserved his train from capture during the stampede of the Eleventh Corps.

The loss of this command has been heavy, and we mourn for many good and brave comrades; but I am happy to say that the division is impatient again to meet the enemy with strengthened confidence.

I am your obedient servant,

D. B. BIRNEY,

Brigadier-general commanding Division.

LIEUTENANT-COLONEL O. H. HART,

Assistant Adjutant-general, Third Corps.

THE KEARNY MEDALS.

HEADQUARTERS FIRST DIVISION THIRD CORPS,
May 16, 1863.

[GENERAL ORDERS, NO. 48.]

The Brigadier-general commanding division congratulates it on its achievements of the 2d and 3d of May. The division pierced the centre of the enemy's column, captured over seven hundred prisoners, then returning, breaking through the enemy who had closed in its rear, executed successfully the order of the Major-general commanding the army to attack at midnight; then receiving the enemy's attack at daylight, held his hordes in check and at bay until ordered to withdraw and hold a position of honor given to it in the front of the new line.

The division has added to the reputation gained at Williamsburg, Fair Oaks, Glendale, Malvern, Manassas, Chantilly, and Fredericksburg, and can now add to those names "The Cedars" and "Chancellorsville."

With strengthened confidence in the gallant generals commanding the corps and the army, this division awaits with impatience the order to again meet the enemy of our country. Our rejoicing is mingled with regret for the slain and wounded; but the recollection of their bravery and martyrdom will be fresh with us evermore and incite us to still greater efforts.

The Brigadier-general commanding division announces the following names of meritorious and distinguished non-commissioned officers and privates, selected for their gallantry, as recipients of the "Kearny Cross," the division decoration.

Many deserving soldiers may have escaped the notice of their commanding officers, but in the selection after the next battle they will doubtless receive this honorable distinction.

This cross is in honor of our old leader, and the wearers of it will always remember his high standard of a true and brave soldier, and will never disgrace it.

GRAHAM'S BRIGADE.

RANK.	NAME.	CO.	REGIMENT.
	Anna Etheridge		5th Michigan.
	Mary Tepe		114th Pennsylvania Vols.
Private	John Brantz	A	"
"	Francis Hopkins	A	"
"	Christian Robrig	A	"
Corporal	Andrew Strotz	B	"
"	Samuel N. Cass	B	"
Private	William Werber	B	"
Sergeant	William J. Miller	C	"
Color Sergeant	Benjamin J. Bayletts	C	"
Corporal	Michael Cannon	C	"
Sergeant	George W. Gower	D	"
"	Herman Grasley	D	"
Corporal	Brian McLaughlin	D	"

RANK.	NAME.	CO.	REGIMENT.
Sergeant	Andrew J. Cunningham	E	114th Pennsylvania Vols.
"	Henry C. Muns	E	"
"	John Guinness	E	"
"	John Waterhouse	F	"
"	Isaac Fox	F	"
Private	James Maguire	F	"
"	William Fowler	F	"
Sergeant	Joshua Bates	G	"
"	John A. Burk	G	"
Private	Matthew Patton	G	"
Sergeant	H. McCarthy	K	"
Corporal	William Larky	K	"
Color Corporal	Charles Borie	K	"
Sergeant	William J. Brown	A	68th Pennsylvania Vols.
"	James P. Frazer	A	"
Private	George B. Kenney	A	"
Sergeant	Elisha Warne	B	"
"	George S. Paul	B	"
Private	John Brown	B	"
Sergeant	Hiram McAllister	C	"
"	George Smith	C	"
"	Henry Mohn	D	"
"	Henry Morgan	D	"
Private	Charles Collins	D	"
Sergeant	Charles Kime	E	"
"	Samuel Wardlaw	E	"
"	Castner Jones	F	"
Private	Edward R. Winchell	F	"
Corporal	Jeremiah Cowley	G	"
Private	William H. Hazard	G	"
"	Edward A. Nutall	G	"
Sergeant	David Allbright	H	"
Corporal	Peter J. Skeen	H	"
Private	Albert W. Burkhart	H	"
Sergeant	Thomes V. Miller	I	"
"	Lewis Meredith	I	"
Private	Henry Bowers	I	"
Sergeant	Jonathan Neil	K	"
"	Alexander H. Mitchell	A	105th Pennsylvania Vols.
"	Samuel S. Hayden	A	"
"	A. McPherson	A	"
"	John C. Kelso	B	"
"	George Heigs	B	"
"	Charles C. McCaully	B	"
Corporal	Andrew A. Harley	C	"
Private	Charles C. Weaver	C	"

RANK.	NAME.	CO.	REGIMENT.
Private	Samuel H. Mays	C	105th Pennsylvania Vols.
Sergeant	James Sylois	D	"
Corporal	Milton Craver	D	"
Sergeant	Josiah E. Geiger	E	"
Corporal	George Weddle	E	"
"	James M. Shoal	E	"
Sergeant	Robert Doty	F	"
Corporal	Henry P. McKillip	F	"
Private	Perry C. Cupler	F	"
Sergeant	George W. Harthorne	G	"
Private	William D. Kane	G	"
"	Thomas McRea	H	"
"	Robert Feverly	H	"
Sergeant	Oliver C. Redick	I	"
"	Joseph Kennier	I	"
"	James Miller	K	"
"	George S. Reed	K	"
Sergeant Major	Joseph G. Fell		141st Pennsylvania Vols.
Sergeant	Edwin M. White	A	"
Private	Benjamin A. Oliphant	A	"
"	Edwin Lee	A	"
Corporal	Josiah A. Bosworth	B	"
Private	Isaac Potter	B	"
Corporal	Charles Scott	C	"
Private	G. W. Fell	C	"
"	Seldon Worth	C	"
Sergeant	David C. Palmer	D	"
Corporal	Martin Berry	D	"
Private	Jacob W. Palmer	H	"
"	John Stockholm	H	"
"	Joseph McShurd	H	"
Sergeant	S. S. Hager	F	"
Private	A. J. Baldwin	F	"
"	O. A. Oakley	F	"
Sergeant	James H. Terwillegar	G	"
Private	Marcus C. Roencrantz	G	"
"	William O. McGreary	G	"
Corporal	Archibald Sinclair	K	"
"	John N. Dunham	I	"
Private	Alfred Allen	I	"
Corporal	James B. Ellsworth	I	"
Private	James M. Buch	E	"
Corporal	George Gibson	A	63d Pennsylvania Vols.
"	Isaac McKeng	A	"
Sergeant	David Strachan	B	"
Corporal	George F. House	B	"

RANK.	NAME.	CO.	REGIMENT.
Sergeant	Henry Kelly	C	63d Pennsylvania Vols.
Corporal	David Lesseig	C	"
Private	Samuel Hart	C	"
Sergeant	Thomas Cahoon	D	"
"	John C. Gray	D	"
"	Robert Henry	E	"
Corporal	John Heist	E	"
Private	John Cyphert	F	"
"	Stewart W. Fulton	F	"
Sergeant	William R. Nicholson	G	"
Private	A. J. Moore	G	"
Corporal	Frank Johnston	G	"
Sergeant	Peter Weaver	H	"
"	Hugh Kenney	H	"
Corporal	Henry Campbell	H	"
"	Philip Alletrand	I	"
Private	John Alletrand	I	"
"	James Gallatin	I	"
"	James Carney	K	"
Corporal	John M. Smith	K	"
"	Frank Rafter	K	"
Sergeant	Charles P. Post	A	57th Pennsylvania Vols.
Corporal	J. W. Granger	A	"
"	Sumner E. Lines	A	"
Sergeant	Ira E. McKnight	B	"
Private	James Ramsey	B	"
"	Simeon Hahn	B	"
Sergeant	Jeoria Allen	C	"
"	Michael Maloy	C	"
Private	David Mourihad	C	"
Sergeant	Walker Rice	E	"
Private	Henry Krenninger	E	"
Corporal	M. A. Irwin	F	"
"	J. K. Hamilton	F	"
Sergeant	Franklin Shaw	H	"
"	John Burnsides	H	"
Private	Amos Miller		"
Sergeant	Samuel Shields	I	"
Private	Levi Christ	I	"
"	Charles Maxum	I	"
Sergeant	H. R. Douglass	F	"
"	John C. Taylor	F	"
Private	Horace Sweet	K	"
"	Jonas Snow	K	"
"	William Murray	K	"

WARD'S BRIGADE.

RANK.	NAME.	CO.	REGIMENT.
Sergeant	William Garvie	A	38th New York Vols.
"	Henry Quinn	A	"
Corporal	George Traver	A	"
Sergeant	Robinson Hopper	B	"
Private	Hobart G. Acker	B	"
Sergeant	Fritz Miladophiky	C	"
"	Jacob Schaffer	C	"
Private	Henry Liehte	C	"
Sergeant	John Brothers	D	"
Corporal	Charles Stone	D	"
Sergeant	Girtlow Garing	E	"
"	Dennis McCarthy	E	"
Corporal	Joseph Walsh	E	"
Sergeant	C. F. Morgan	F	"
"	William Norris	F	"
"	Joseph Meyan	G	"
Private	Louis Fredolf	G	"
Sergeant	Robert Moll	H	"
Private	Jacob Geiss	H	"
"	Frederick Bromaharst	H	"
Sergeant	John Kavanagh	I	"
Corporal	John O'Connor	I	"
Private	John Meister	I	"
Sergeant	William Germond	K	"
Corporal	Hugh W. Burns	K	"
Sergeant Major	Jacob D. Bennett		40th New York Vols.
Sergeant	Thomas Walton	A	"
Corporal	Gustavus Vass	A	"
Private	Job Shermann	A	"
Sergeant	Henry K. Brown	B	"
Color Sergeant	Andrew J. Wadleigh	B	"
Sergeant	Allen Smith	C	"
"	William J. Miller	C	"
Corporal	Daniel H. Mayer	C	"
Sergeant	Washington Peel	D	"
Private	Edward Clifford	D	"
Sergeant	Edwin J. Sweet	E	"
"	Andrew Hollywood	E	"
"	Thomas Crawford	F	"
"	Anthony Collins	F	"
"	Philip M. Harden	G	"
Corporal	G. W. Chamberlain	G	"
Sergeant	Thomas Braslin	H	"
"	James Shuter	H	"

RANK.	NAME.	CO.	REGIMENT.
Private	William Gilbert	H	40th New York Vols.
Sergeant	William Moyne	I	"
Private	Isaac Garrison	I	"
"	Peter Farrill	I	"
Sergeant	William Edwards	K	"
"	John Curtin	K	"
"	William B. Parris	A	3d Maine Volunteers.
Private	J. L. Little	A	"
Sergeant	H. Johnson	B	"
Corporal	A. C. Rowe	B	"
Sergeant	L. Crawford	C	"
"	G. M. Houghton	C	"
Corporal	D. Maxey	C	"
Sergeant	H. H. Shaw	D	"
Corporal	H. Kennerson	D	"
Sergeant	G. L. Chamberlain	E	"
Corporal	C. J. Dalton	E	"
Private	H. J. Roach	E	"
Sergeant	O. M. Nason	F	"
"	J. Durgin	F	"
Private	A. Luce	F	"
Sergeant	G. E. Davis	G	"
"	H. C. Webber	G	"
Corporal	P. F. Rowe	H	"
Private	R. Cochrane	H	"
Sergeant	N. W. Jones	I	"
Private	L. W. Brown	I	"
"	Lemuel Powell	I	"
Sergeant	B. W. Smart	K	"
Corporal	A. G. Wood	K	"
"	W. G. Wilson	K	"
Private	James Gall	A	4th Maine Volunteers.
"	Horace Speed	A	"
Sergeant	Henry O. Kipley	B	"
Private	Robert Grant	B	"
Corporal	George G. Gardner	C	"
"	Warren W. Austin	C	"
Sergeant	James McLaughlin	D	"
Corporal	Henry O. Davis	D	"
Private	Henry Marshall	D	"
Corporal	William Barstron	E	"
"	Nathaniel Waters	E	"
"	F. K. Chapman	E	"
Sergeant	A. H. Rose	F	"
"	Henry Leach	F	"
"	F. O. J. S. Hill	F	"

RANK.	NAME.	CO.	REGIMENT.
Private	Bradford Blime	G	4th Maine Volunteers.
"	Daniel O. Howard	G	"
"	Horace Tellison	H	"
Corporal	George P. Wood	H	"
"	C. W. Gray	I	"
Private	John Donaghue	I	"
"	Juan Millano	I	"
Sergeant	John A. Toothacher	K	"
Private	Robert Whitehead	K	"
"	P. J. Carter	K	"
Corporal	Reuben Richardson	A	20th Indiana Volunteers.
Private	John B. Fairman	A	"
Sergeant	James B. Jones	B	"
"	Thompson Farmer	B	"
"	George W. Milliken	B	"
"	John W. Williams	C	"
Private	E. Griffith	C	"
Corporal	Franklin Barwick	D	"
"	Lemuel J. Orwing	D	"
Private	Charles W. Sentman	D	"
Corporal	John H. Hendricks	E	"
Private	Elicot Wilson	E	"
"	William C. Hatfield	E	"
Sergeant	Jesse L. Cornwell	F	"
"	George H. Reddick	F	"
Sergeant	William P. Thompson	G	"
Corporal	Francis H. Downing	G	"
"	David Taylor	G	"
Private	John Anderson	H	"
"	Michael Powers	H	"
Sergeant	William H. Robinson	I	"
Corporal	Mahlon Smith	K	"
Private	Stephen C. Wilson	I	"
Sergeant	William Horine	K	"
Corporal	James C. Stephens	K	"
Sergeant	D. S. Hunsberger	H	99th Pennsylvania Vols.
Private	Henry Landis	H	"
"	Charles H. Farnacht	H	"
Sergeant	William Thomas	B	"
Private	Frederick Klein	B	"
"	David Brolly	B	"
Sergeant	Harvey M. Munsell	C	"
"	Thomas O'Neil	C	"
Sergeant	John Wendler	D	"
Private	Hugh Kennerly	D	"
"	Joel Porter	D	"

RANK.	NAME.	CO.	REGIMENT.
Corporal	William J. Harmer	E	99th Pennsylvania Vols.
Private	Charles W. Cooper	E	"
"	John Jackson	F	"
"	Joseph Ansback	F	"
"	Robert Martin	F	"
Sergeant	John Armstrong	G	"
Private	Cornelius Winters	G	"
Sergeant	William J. Firhn	H	"
Sergeant	James T. Taylor	H	"
Corporal	Henry C. Ipshording	I	"
"	David G. Wilson	I	"
"	James Quinn	K	"
Private	Patrick Coggins	K	"
"	Philip Clause	K	"

HAYMAN'S BRIGADE.

RANK.	NAME.	CO.	REGIMENT.
Sergeant	Charles A. Van Dusen	A	3d Michigan Volunteers.
Corporal	Ransom B. Howell	A	"
"	Webster J. Kniffin	A	"
Private	John Laraway	A	"
Sergeant	William S. Coughters	B	"
Corporal	William W. Bennett	B	"
"	Silas H. Compton	B	"
Sergeant	Leonard Diedrick	C	"
"	Frank Muhlberg	C	"
Corporal	Peter Myers	C	"
Private	William Schumaker	C	"
Sergeant	Richard E. Arthur	D	"
Corporal	Lewis Pettitt	D	"
Private	William Rennick	D	"
Sergeant	Daniel E. Bordsell	E	"
Corporal	Edwin Van Went	E	"
Private	George H. Wesilogh	E	"
Sergeant	James D. Van Dusen	F	"
Corporal	Daniel G. Grotty	F	"
"	Job Brewer	F	"
Private	Mortimer Bonner	F	"
Sergeant	Charles A. Price	G	"
Corporal	Ira M. B. Crane	G	"
Private	John Broad	G	"
Sergeant	Martin Biber	H	"
Corporal	Cada White	H	"
Private	George W. Lemon	H	"
Sergeant	James F. McGinley	I	"
"	Benjamin C. Parker	I	"

RANK.	NAME.	CO.	REGIMENT.
Corporal	Charles Nelson	I	3d Michigan Volunteers.
Sergeant	Reuben Tower	K	"
Corporal	James Hannah	K	"
"	Alexander French	K	"
Private	Benjamin C. Gardener	K	"
Q. M. Sergeant	John H. Sumner		"
Corporal	August Busson	A	5th Michigan Volunteers.
"	Nicholas Henry	A	"
Private	Henry Jervine	A	"
Corporal	Herman Schmidt	B	"
"	George Newton	B	"
Private	William Rupp	B	"
"	Henry C. Brady	B	"
Sergeant	James Hazzard	C	"
"	Donald Sinkley	C	"
Corporal	Reuben Howe	C	"
Private	Luther Franklin	C	"
Sergeant	John Wickam	D	"
Color Sergeant	Otto A. Berger	D	"
Sergeant	Peter Lennon	D	"
"	Othello W. Phelps	E	"
Private	James Harkness	E	"
"	Hugh Madison	E	"
Private	William J. Moore	E	"
Sergeant	Joseph Kemp	F	"
"	James Darling	F	"
"	Francis McElroy	F	"
Corporal	Peter Kenney	G	"
"	Thomas Lipscomb	G	"
Private	John E. Lee	G	"
Sergeant	William Bowles	H	"
Private	Milton Matoon	H	"
"	Alfred B. Crane	H	"
Corporal	Patrick Waters	H	"
Sergeant	Stewart A. Boyd	I	"
Corporal	Charles Abrams	I	"
"	Charles Thayer	I	"
Private	Alva W. Schofield	I	"
Sergeant	Peter Boffinger	K	"
"	Charles J. Zwissler	K	"
Corporal	William Budde	K	"
Sergeant	Fayette M. Paine	A	17th Maine Volunteers.
"	Edward H. Crie	A	"
Corporal	Joseph F. Lake	A	"
Private	Jacob C. Brown	A	"
"	James G. Holt	B	"

RANK.	NAME.	CO.	REGIMENT.
Private	Monroe Quint	B	17th Maine Volunteers.
"	B. T. Trueworthy	B	"
"	John Lehanne	B	"
"	J. M. Hall	C	"
"	S. C. Pratt	C	"
Corporal	J. L. Fuller	C	"
Private	S. W. Burnbam	C	"
Sergeant	Stephen Graffam	D	"
Corporal	F. L. Whittemore	D	"
Private	Charles H. Hayes	D	"
"	Amos G. Winter	D	"
Sergeant	Herman Q. Mason	E	"
"	A. S. Osyar	E	"
Corporal	George F. Small	E	"
Private	Charles Greeley	E	"
Sergeant	Wellington Hobbs	F	"
Corporal	Austin Hanson	F	"
Private	Henry Day, jr	F	"
"	Charles D. Noble	F	"
Corporal	Jeremiah P. Wyman	G	"
Private	James B. Robinson	G	"
"	George A. Frederick	G	"
Private	A. L. Dunnell	G	"
Sergeant	George A. Whiddin	H	"
"	S. P. Hart	H	"
"	J. S. Lor'ng	H	"
Private	M. P. Leary	H	"
Corporal	John W. Kendrick	I	"
Private	D. A. Wentworth	I	"
Private	John H. Simpson	I	"
"	A. J. Harmon	I	"
Sergeant	Isaac O. Parker	K	"
Private	Edward G. Parker	K	"
"	F. A. Butland	K	"
"	G. J. Strout	K	"
Q. M. Sergeant	James B. Shepard		37th New York Volunteers.
Sergeant	David Meskill	Pioneers	"
"	Samuel B. Wilson	A	"
"	John O'Connell	A	"
"	John Donovan	A	"
Corporal	Laurence Cahill	A	"
Sergeant	Thomas Feehery	B	"
"	John Doherty	B	"
Corporal	Patrick Sheehan	B	"
Private	Walter Gladson	B	"
Sergeant	John Collins	C	"

RANK.	NAME.	CO.	REGIMENT.
Sergeant	Daniel J. Kelly	C	37th New York Volunteers.
"	John F. Morton	C	"
"	Peter Moran	C	"
"	Charles Foley	D	"
Corporal	Owen Gorman	D	"
"	James Cosgrove	D	"
Private	Cornelius Driscoll	D	"
Sergeant	Patrick Cooney	E	"
Corporal	James Reddy	E	"
Private	Anthony Smith	E	"
Sergeant	Michael Cuddihy	F	"
Corporal	Michael Duffy	F	"
Sergeant	Patrick Gilespie	F	"
"	Hugh Murphy	G	"
"	John Broderick	G	"
"	James McManus	G	"
Private	Patrick Stackpole	G	"
Sergeant	Harmon E. Wentworth	H	"
Corporal	Conrad Snyder	H	"
Private	John D. Lyons	H	"
"	Jacob Albrecht	H	"
Sergeant	Clark C. Foster	I	"
"	Jerome D. Andrews	I	"
"	Charles Lattin	I	"
"	Julius C. Schultz	I	"
"	John McCarthy	K	"
"	Timothy Spillam	K	"
"	Thomas Murray	K	"
Corporal	John Madden	K	"
	William Torpey		Battery E, 1st R. I. Art'y.
	John McAlees		"
	Martin Harvey		"

An official copy of this order will be given to each soldier entitled to wear the cross.

D. B. BIRNEY,

Brigadier-general Volunteers, commanding Division.

BIRNEY'S REPORT OF GETTYSBURG.

HEADQUARTERS FIRST DIVISION THIRD CORPS,
August 7, 1863.

COLONEL:—

I have the honor to submit the following report of the part taken by my command at the battle of Gettysburg.

At seven o'clock, A. M., on the 2d of July, under orders from Major-general Sickles, I relieved Geary's division, and formed a line resting its left on the Sugarloaf mountain, and the right thrown in a direct line towards the Cemetery, connecting on the right with the second division of this corps. My picket line was beyond the Emmettsburg road, with sharpshooters some three hundred yards in advance.

At twelve o'clock M., believing from the constant fire from the enemy that a movement was being made towards the left, I received permission from Major-general Sickles to send one hundred of Berdan's Sharpshooters, with the Third Maine regiment as a support, to feel the enemy's right. I sent Captain J. C. Briscoe, of my staff, with the reconnoissance, which was under Colonel Berdan's command. They advanced from the Peach Orchard, out the Millerstown road, and entered the woods in order to flank the enemy. The skirmishers of the enemy were driven in, and three columns of his forces were found marching to our left. The force sent by me was driven back by overwhelming numbers, with the loss of about sixty killed and wounded. Communicating this important information to General Sickles, I was ordered by that officer to change my front to meet the attack. I did this by advancing the left five hundred yards and swinging around the right so as to rest on the Emmettsburg road, at the Peach Orchard. He also informed me that a division from the Second and one from the Fifth Corps had been ordered to be in readiness to support me.

My line was formed with Ward on the left, resting on the mountain, De Trobriand in the centre, and Graham on my right in the Peach Orchard, with his right on the Emmettsburg road. Smith's battery of rifled guns was placed so as to command the gorge at the base of the Sugarloaf mountain; Winslow's battery on the right of Ward's brigade, and a battery from the Reserve artillery. Also Clark's and Ames' batteries to the right, in rear of the Peach Orchard, supported by Graham's brigade, and the Third Michigan from the third brigade, and Third Maine from the second brigade. Randolph's, Seely's, and Turnbull's batteries were placed near the Emmettsburg road, on the front parallel with it.

I immediately sent an aide to Major-general Sykes, asking for the division promised to support my left. I opened—say at three and a half o'clock P. M.—with Clark's and Smith's batteries, upon the columns of the enemy moving towards our left and parallel with the Emmettsburg road. At four o'clock the enemy returned the artillery fire on my entire front, and advanced his infantry *en masse*, covered by a cloud of skirmishers.

Major-general Sykes reached my left opportunely, and protected that flank. A portion of his command under General Barnes had been placed in rear of the right of De Trobriand's brigade, but during the hottest of the fight he withdrew this force, saying that his men could not see to fight in the woods, and formed them some three hundred yards farther in the rear.

As the fight was now furious, and my line reached from Sugarloaf hill to the Emmettsburg road, fully a mile in length, I was obliged to send for more reinforcements to General Sickles; and Major Tremain, A. D. C. to the commanding general, soon appeared with a brigade of the Second Corps, which behaved most handsomely, and leading them forward it soon restored the centre of my line, and we drove the enemy from that point, to fall with redoubled force on Ward's brigade.

My thin lines swayed to and fro during the fight, and my regiments were moved constantly, on the double-quick, from one part of the line to the other, to reinforce assailed points. I cannot estimate too highly the services of the regiments from Burling's brigade, second division, the Fifth, Sixth, and Seventh New Jersey volunteers, and Second New Hampshire. These regiments were sent to me during the contest, and most gallantly did they sustain the glorious reputation won by them in former battles.

Graham's brigade was subjected, at the point of the angle of the line on the Emmettsburg road, to a fearful artillery fire, enfilading his line, but this brigade, with the assistance of the Third Maine from the second brigade, and Third Michigan from the third brigade of this division, held the Peach Orchard until nearly dusk, when, finding the right was unsupported, they fell back to the next ridge.

At six o'clock I found Major-general Sickles seriously wounded, and at his request took command of the corps. After this I rode to the second division, and, finding it in some confusion, aided its officers in rallying it. The officers and men responded with great alacrity, and, changing front, again advancing, they recaptured many pieces that were in the possession of the enemy. Major-general Hancock reached me about half-past seven o'clock with a brigade of fresh troops, and, at his request, I assigned them a position. My division was relieved from the front line by the Second and Fifth Corps towards dusk.

The annexed tables of casualties show the nature of the engagement, and its terrific character. Several of my regiments lost more than fifty per cent. of their number, and almost every officer. One regiment, the One-hundred-and-forty-first Pennsylvania volunteers, Colonel Madill, lost out of two hundred men taken into the fight, one hundred and forty-nine men and officers killed and wounded. Every regiment of my command did its whole duty, and officers vied with each other in honorable emulation to repel the masses that were hurled on my small division for three hours. The batteries were well handled, and I have no reports of any guns being lost, as in retiring we hauled the disabled pieces from the field.

The first brigade, composed of Pennsylvania regiments, commanded by Brigadier-general C. K. Graham, tried with its skeleton ranks to even outdo Chancellorsville. General Graham was wounded and fell into the hands of the enemy, with Lieutenant-colonel Cavada of the One-hundred-and-fourteenth Pennsylvania, and Major Neeper of the Fifty-seventh Pennsylvania. The Fifty-seventh Pennsylvania, Colonel Sides; Sixty-third Pennsylvania, Major Danks; Sixty-eighth Pennsylvania, Colonel Tippin; One-hundred-and-fifth Pennsylvania, Colonel Craig; One-hundred-and-fourteenth Pennsylvania, Lieutenant-colonel Cavada; and One-hundred and-forty-first Pennsylvania volunteers, Colonel Madill, compose this brigade, and have made its reputation equal to any in this army. General Graham showed the same coolness, daring and endurance under the terrible fire, that distinguished him at Chancellorsville.

The second brigade, Brigadier-general Ward, held also a post of great honor and importance, and fully sustained its old reputation. The First United States Sharpshooters, Colonel Berdan, and Second United States Sharpshooters, Major Stoughton; Third Maine, Colonel Lakeman; Fourth Maine, Colonel Walker; Twentieth Indiana, Colonel Wheeler; Ninety-ninth Pennsylvania, Major Moore; One-hundred-and-twenty-fourth New York, Colonel Ellis; and Eighty-sixth New York, Lieutenant-colonel Higgins, compose this brigade.

Colonel Walker, who has so distinguished himself on the Peninsula, and at Manassas, Chantilly, Fredericksburg, and Chancellorsville, was seriously wounded; and those gallant officers, Colonels Ellis and Wheeler, "fell dead with their crowns to the foe," at the head of their regiments.

General Ward sustained me, as he always has, by his judicious arrangements and dispositions, holding the most hotly-contested point of the line for three hours.

The third brigade, Colonel De Trobriand commanding, held the centre of my line. The Fortieth New York, Colonel T. W. Egan; Third Michigan, Colonel Pierce; Fifth Michigan, Lieutenant-colonel Pulford; Seventeenth Maine volunteers, Lieutenant-colonel Merrill, and One-hundred-and-tenth Pennsylvania, Lieutenant-colonel D. M. Jones, compose this brigade Colonel De Trobriand deserves my heartiest thanks for the skillful disposition of his command, gallantly holding his advanced position until relieved by other troops. This officer is one of the longest in commission as colonel in the volunteer service; has been distinguished in nearly every engagement of the Army of the Potomac, and certainly deserves the rank of brigadier-general of volunteers to which he has been recommended.

The Fortieth New York volunteers, Colonel Egan, was sent by me under charge of Captain Briscoe, A. D. C., to strengthen General Ward's line; and, led by its gallant, dashing colonel, charged the enemy and drove him back from his advanced point, and poured the most terrific fire into his ranks. This regiment is composed of the old Fortieth, and gallant men from the Eighty-seventh, One-hundred-and first, Thirty-eighth, and Fifty-fifth New York consolidated with it, making a glorious unit.

The Seventeenth Maine volunteers, Lieutenant-colonel Merrill, was driven back from its position by an overwhelming force; but, responding to my personal appeal, again charged the enemy across the small wheat field, and retook their position. This regiment behaved most gallantly, and evinced a high state of discipline. The enthusiasm was cheering, and the assistance rendered by its charge most important.

I have already mentioned the valuable aid rendered me by the command of Colonel Burling, commanding the third brigade of the second division. This officer and his gallant old regiments never did better service at a better time.

Colonel Berdan, of the sharpshooters, and Captain Briscoe, of my staff, deserve mention for their services in leading the reconnoissance before the battle, and for the valuable information derived from it. The two regiments of sharpshooters under Colonel Berdan and Major Stoughton were of the most essential service in covering my front, and pouring a constant and galling fire into the enemy's line of skirmishers.

All of the members of my staff were efficient and ready with their services in the field.

During the 3d of July this division, under command of General Ward, was held in reserve, and during the heavy artillery fire of that day was brought up under it to support General Newton's line. The enemy was, however, repulsed without its assistance.

I am your obedient servant,

D. B. BIRNEY,

Major-general comd'g first division Third Corps.

LIEUTENANT-COLONEL O. H. HART,

Ass't Adjutant-general Third Corps.

CASUALTIES IN BIRNEY'S DIVISION, THIRD ARMY CORPS, AT THE BATTLE OF GETTYSBURG, PA.

GRAHAM'S BRIGADE.

STAFF.

Brigadier-general Graham wounded and a prisoner.
Lieutenant Charles H. Graves, A. A. A. G., wounded.
Lieutenant Willard Bullard, A. D. C., wounded.

REGIMENTS.	KILLED.		WOUNDED.		MISSING.		Aggregate.
	Commis'd officers.	Enlisted men.	Commis'd officers.	Enlisted men.	Commis'd officers.	Enlisted men.	
Brigade Staff			3				3
57th Pennsylvania volunteers	2	9	9	37	3	55	115
63d " "		1	3	26		4	34
68th " "		4	9	117		19	149
105th " "	1	7	13	101		9	131
114th " "		8	1	85		57	151
141st " "		25	6	97	3	21	152
Total	3	54	44	463	6	165	735

WARD'S BRIGADE.

REGIMENTS.	KILLED.		WOUNDED.		MISSING.		Aggregate.
	Commis'd officers.	Enlisted men.	Commis'd officers.	Enlisted men.	Commis'd officers.	Enlisted men.	
Headquarters Second Brigade			1				1
3d Maine volunteers	1	17	2	60		32	112
4th " "	3	11	2	54	4	68	142
20th Indiana volunteers	2	28	9	101		11	151
99th Pennsylvania volunteers	1	17	5	79		9	111
86th New York volunteers	1	9	3	46	1	4	64
124th " "	4	24	3	54		4	89
1st United States Sharpshooters	2	5	3	33		6	49
2d " "	0	5	4	23		12	44
Total	14	116	32	450	5	146	763

DE TROBRIAND'S BRIGADE.

REGIMENTS.	KILLED.		WOUNDED.		MISSING.		Aggregate.
	Commis'd officers.	Enlisted men.	Commis'd officers.	Enlisted men.	Commis'd officers.	Enlisted men.	
Headquarters Third Brigade			1				1
40th New York volunteers	1	28	6	114		5	154
17th Maine volunteers	1	17	7	105		2	132
110th Pennsylvania volunteers		8	6	39			53
5th Michigan volunteers	2	17	8	74		4	105
3d " "		7	2	29		7	45
Total	4	77	30	361		18	490

RECAPITULATION.

BRIGADES.	KILLED.		WOUNDED.		MISSING.		Aggregate.
	Commis'd officers.	Enlisted men.	Commis'd officers.	Enlisted men.	Commis'd officers.	Enlisted men.	
First Brigade	3	54	44	463	6	165	735
Second "	14	116	32	450	5	146	763
Third "	4	77	30	361		18	490
Total	21	247	106	1274	11	329	1988

CAPT. J. C. BRISCOE'S REPORT OF GETTYSBURG.

HEADQUARTERS FIRST DIVISION THIRD CORPS,
SULPHUR SPRINGS, VA., *August* 4, 1863.

CAPTAIN:—

I have the honor to report the following as what came under my observation, of the part taken by this division in the late battle of Gettysburg.

The division marched from Emmettsburg, Maryland, July 1, 1863, and bivouacked one and a half miles south of Gettysburg and a quarter of a mile east of the Emmettsburg road. On the following morning De Trobriand's brigade, which had been left behind at Emmettsburg, came up and we went into position, the left resting on the Taneytown road, north of the Sugarloaf mountain, the right swung round so that it was parallel with the Emmettsburg road and connected with the Second Corps. About ten, A. M., the major-general commanding directed me to take out one hundred and fifty sharpshooters under Colonel Berdan and feel the enemy, who were supposed to be in the woods west of and parallel to the Emmettsburg road. The sharpshooters drove in the enemy's pickets twice, and Colonel Berdan reported him in force with infantry and artillery.

At noon I received orders to take one hundred sharpshooters, with the Third Maine as a support, and feel the enemy's right. Advancing from the Peach Orchard, out the Millerstown road, we entered the woods so as to, if possible, flank the enemy, found him in line of battle ready for us, drove in his skirmishers, and after receiving a few volleys retired with a loss of about sixty killed and wounded. During this affair, from the roof of a blacksmith's shop on the Millerstown road I saw the enemy's artillery and infantry in rear of the woods, evidently preparing for a demonstration on our left. Returning to headquarters I found that General Birney, in anticipation of the attack, was about changing his line, by advancing the left five hundred yards and swinging round the right so as to rest on the Emmettsburg road at the Peach Orchard.

Our new position then was, Ward's brigade with Smith's battery on the extreme left, his line on a rocky ridge running east and west with his left resting on the Sugarloaf. On the right of this brigade Colonel De Trobriand was placed, in the woods, with Winslow's battery in the wheat field between the two brigades. General Graham's command was deployed in the open fields, with his right resting on the Emmettsburg road at the Peach Orchard, where also the Third Maine was placed as an outpost; Clark's battery took position at this point, and a battery from the reserve came up on his left.

It was now four, P. M., and the new order of battle had scarce been established, some of the batteries just going into position, when the enemy opened his artillery with good effect and his advancing columns bore down on us with a yell in the usual style. Previous to this I represented to General Birney, and by his order to General Sickles, that we wanted another regiment to occupy the Sugarloaf; General Sickles said he had no more troops and would send to General Meade.

The division was deployed in a single line of regiments, covering the left flank of the army, and occupying the space between the Peach Orchard and the Sugarloaf.

General Ward sent for reinforcements, and General Birney directed me to take him two of De Trobriand's regiments. I started with the Fortieth New York and another regiment, the name of which I have been unable to ascertain, which lagged behind when we got under fire, and I saw nothing more of it. Not finding General Ward immediately to report the Fortieth to him, I placed it on his left and rear. The enemy had now occupied the Sugarloaf and was endeavoring to flank Ward. I suggested a charge to Colonel Egan, which he made in the most gallant style, driving the enemy back and up the mountain. The Pennsylvania Reserves came up about this time, and taking position on a ridge north of the Sugarloaf kept up a very rapid musketry fire at long range. General Ward now informed me that he could not hold his position much longer without more reinforcements. Captain Cooney, his assistant adjutant-general, said in ten minutes it would be too late. I reported the fact to General Birney, who directed me to take a regiment from Colonel De Trobriand; but on going to his front I found he had enough to do to take care of himself. Two regiments, under Colonel Burling, from the New Jersey brigade of the second division, having

51

reported, were placed by General Birney in front of Winslow's battery, filling the gap between Ward and De Trobriand.

The enemy still continuing to press us, it became necessary to withdraw Winslow's battery, which was done in good order, the regiments of the New Jersey brigade and the Seventeenth Maine covering the withdrawal in a determined manner, under a severe musketry fire from the woods in front. While this was going on, General Barnes' division had gotten up and were massed in rear of De Trobriand. I represented to General Barnes more than once that we were hard pressed in front.

Seeing the batteries on our right and the infantry falling back, Captains Birney, Randolph, and myself, tried to rally them, and with Colonel Tippen's assistance succeeded to some extent.

It was now six and a-half, P. M., when I learned General Sickles was wounded, and, looking for General Birney, saw him leading a brigade from the Second Corps, which advanced in good order and checked the onset of the enemy. From this time I directed my efforts towards getting our men together.

By ten, P. M., the division was bivouacked by General Birney's order in the open field, east of the Taneytown road and about two hundred yards in rear of the position assigned us in the morning. General Birney, having assumed command of the corps, next morning placed the first division in rear of and supporting the right of the Fifth Corps. At one, P. M., the enemy opened with artillery along his whole line, directing his fire mainly on the Cemetery Hill; under cover of which fire his infantry advanced in two lines and endeavored to force the position. General Birney directed me to report the first division to General Newton, commanding the front line. General Newton distributed the regiments from right to left along the front line, and they remained until the following day, when the command was again concentrated in rear of the Second Corps, and was kept in reserve during the day and night.

On the morning of the 5th of July, General Birney directed me to take one hundred of Berdan's Sharpshooters and find what the enemy was doing. We advanced across the Emmettsburg road and entered the enemy's works without opposition, discovered his column in retreat on the Fairfield road and the hospitals on Willoughby's creek, containing thousands of his wounded, abandoned. I reported the matter to headquarters, and received orders to remain where we were and report at intervals whatever transpired.

By one, P. M., the rear of the enemy's column had passed, and half an hour later the Sixth Corps came up and took possession of the road over which the enemy had just retreated.

I have the honor to be

Your obedient servant,

J. C. BRISCOE,

Captain and A. D. C.

CAPTAIN F. BIRNEY,

Assistant Adjutant-general.

BIRNEY'S REPORT OF MINE RUN.

HEADQUARTERS BIRNEY'S DIVISION, THIRD CORPS,
CAMP BRANDY STATION, *December* 4, 1863.

COLONEL:—

I have the honor to submit the following report of the operations of the division during the recent movements from November 26th to the 3d instant.

I broke camp on the morning of 26th ultimo, and at eight and a half o'clock, A. M., followed Carr's division, keeping close up to it during the day, reaching the pontoon bridge at dark, crossing and bivouacking in the field half a mile from the river.

It was found impracticable to ascend the bluffs opposite Jacob's Mill with even an empty ambulance, and, under orders from the corps commander, the battery attached to the division (Bucklyn's) and all the trains, ambulances, ammunition, etc., were ordered to Germania ford. After laboring all night over almost impassable roads, Bucklyn's battery reached the division about daylight with jaded, unfed horses, and being the only battery that had succeeded in surmounting the difficulties presented by the road between Germania and Jacob's ford, was transferred to Prince's, the leading division.

At seven o'clock, A. M., 27th November, the march was resumed, my division bringing up the rear of the corps following Carr's division.

The head of the column encountering the enemy near the Raccoon ford road, I was ordered by Major-general French to form a second line in rear of the centre of the first line, composed of the divisions of Generals Prince and Carr, and to grant support to either when necessary during the expected battle.

I marched my division parallel to Carr, through a thick wood, some two hundred paces to rear, moving by the flank, and Carr soon becoming hotly engaged, formed in line of battle. I deployed the third brigade (Egan) in his rear as my first line, massing the second brigade (Ward) in the rear of its right, and the first brigade (Collis) in rear of its left. Before the formation was completed, say within twenty minutes, General Carr informed me that the right of his line was hardly pressed and ammunition nearly expended. I immediately ordered the second brigade, General Ward, to move up, and relieve Carr's right connecting with Prince's left. He did so, however, without pressing the enemy.

General Carr now reporting his centre hard pressed, I moved forward the third brigade, (Egan,) relieving his entire line excepting one regiment of Kieffer's brigade, which had enjoyed favorable cover. Finding that Smith's brigade of Carr's division did not connect on the left, and that the enemy was endeavoring to turn it, I moved the third brigade to the left, and ordered up my first brigade (Collis) to the centre. The musketry fire was incessant, and the enemy made constant efforts to break through my line. They were driven back, and the ridge was firmly held by us, but Prince's division not advancing equally with us, enabled the enemy to plant a battery on the right that completely enfiladed my line.

At dusk I advanced, my line of skirmishers holding the battle-field. During the night the enemy retired, leaving their dead, wounded, and hospitals.

At four o'clock, A. M., 28th November, under orders from major general commanding the corps, I withdrew the division a mile to the rear, massing it near the widow Morris' house. My picket line remained. My ordnance officer collected on the battle-field such small arms as he was permitted by the short time allowed him through the rapid movements of the corps, and destroyed a large number for which he had no transportation.

At eight o'clock, A. M., same day, I followed Carr's division toward Robertson's tavern. I soon received orders to pass it, and found it in line of battle. On reaching the left of the Sixth Corps I massed my division; thence I marched to a point near Muddy Run, in rear of the left of the First Corps, and again massed. Under orders from Major-general French I bridged Muddy Run, and pushing forward a strong reconnoissance to the heights of Mine Run, driving away a small party of the enemy posted there, I advanced my division and bivouacked on the heights, connecting on the right with the First Corps, my line forming almost a right angle with the line of that corps, occupying the position indicated by Major Duane, Chief Engineer.

During the 29th, my division was held in readiness for the expected assault.

Before daylight on the 30th, Prince's and Carr's divisions were withdrawn to the support of the movement by General Warren, and I received orders from General French to be prepared to assault the enemy in my front, crossing Mine Run. Detaching the Third Michigan, One-hundred and-twenty-fourth New York, First and Second United States Sharpshooters, all under command of Colonel B. R. Pierce, Third Michigan, I relieved my entire picket line, and deploying them as an advanced line of skirmishers, connected with the First Corps on the right and General Warren on the left, and driving the enemy's pickets from the bank of Mine Run, made crossings of rails and logs, and two bridges for artillery, so that the run would be no obstacle to a rapid advance in line of battle. I deployed the second brigade (Ward) as the second skirmish line, in open order, with four companies from each regiment as supports, with orders to follow the advance line at two hundred paces. The first and third brigades were formed in line of battle, excepting the regiments detached for the support of the batteries. At eight o'clock, A. M., the batteries opening on the right and centre, Colonel Pierce gallantly pushed forward the advanced line, driving the first line of the enemy out of the advanced rifle pits, capturing a few prisoners. Finding that the expected attack on the left was not made by General Warren, I had despatched an aide (Lieutenant Moore) to Colonel Pierce, ordering him not to advance any further, when Major-general French ordered me to retire my demonstration and resume the position and formation of the 29th, the day before.

At six and a half o'clock, P. M., on the first of December, my command followed Carr's division, bringing up the rear of the corps in the withdrawal by Culpepper ford. The movement was a little delayed by the bad condition of the woods road, forcing the batteries to double teams to reach the plank road. On reaching the plank road the movements of this division were greatly embarrassed by the cutting of the column by the ambulances, trains, and a column of a division of the Sixth Corps and the Second Corps. I reached this side of the Rapidan by Culpepper ford, at five and a half, A. M., 2d instant, and bivouacked. The roads were so occupied by trains and troops that my division did not reach my former camp near Brandy Station, until five o'clock, A. M., 3d instant.

Captain E. L. Ford, division ordnance officer, whose efficiency in bringing up the ammunition train, supplying the division, taking from the battle-field the arms and destroying others, deserves especial commendation.

The third brigade (Egan) was the most hotly engaged, and acquitted itself most gallantly. Colonel Egan, for the first time in command of the brigade, exhibited much skill in handling the troops.

The division is now in camp, in good condition and spirits, and I have the pleasure to report that the straggling, considering that the marches were for two nights, was confined to a few.

I regret to say that the command has experienced a serious loss in the death of Lieutenant-colonel Trepp, commanding First United States Sharpshooters, killed in the skirmish and advance at Mine Run.

I am, Colonel,

Your obedient servant,

D. B. BIRNEY,

Major-general Volunteers, commanding Division.

LIEUTENANT-COLONEL O. H. HART,

Assistant Adjutant-general, Third Army Corps.

PICKET DUTY.

HEADQUARTERS TENTH ARMY CORPS,
IN THE FIELD, NEAR HATCHER'S, VA., *July* 27, 1864.

[GENERAL ORDERS, No. 19.]

The system of picketing for this corps will be that of Butterfield, with the following modifications:

The picket guard is divided into four reliefs. On marching on the first relief goes to the outposts, consisting of the groups of three and the outer sentinels. The second to the supports. The third and fourth to the grand guard. At the end of six hours the second relief moves from the supports to the outposts, the first relief going to the supports. At the end of twelve hours the third and fourth reliefs go forward from the grand guard, the outposts first falling back on the supports. Each relief has thus twelve consecutive hours on the grand guard. The outer sentinels are to be relieved every two hours, and the groups every six hours. In extremely inclement weather division commanders may authorize sentinels and groups to be relieved more frequently. Twelve and three quarters men per sentinel's post gives the proper detail, with extra men for fatigue purposes, supernumeraries, etc. As a general rule there should be in each relief one corporal for every three sentinels' posts, one sergeant for every six posts, one subaltern for every ten posts, and a captain or field officer commanding. For example: twenty posts gives, say two hundred and fifty-five privates, twenty-eight corporals, twelve sergeants, eight lieutenants, and four captains.

Division commanders are responsible for the manner in which picket duty is performed on their division picket line, and that the prescribed system of picketing and the regulations on the subject are followed.

The pickets of each division will be regularly mounted as a grand guard, under the direction of the division commander. In permanent camps the guard may be continued for three days.

The picket line of the corps, when once established, will not be changed or modified, unless such change shall be sanctioned at these headquarters, or by orders from the corps officer of the day to the division officer of the day.

On the march the pickets will be thrown out immediately on arriving in camp, by the commander of each division, (about one-tenth of his force,) making their lines connected from right to left and their camps secure. The corps officer of the day will also see that this connection is duly made, and that all the exposed points of the camp are securely guarded.

No officer or soldier on picket will be allowed to return to camp during his tour, or to leave his post, unless so ordered by his commander then on duty, or from sickness.

A medical officer will accompany each division picket.

The pickets will not be permitted to converse with citizens, save on duty, or with the pickets of the enemy.

Small fires may be permitted by division commanders, at the groups, never at the sentinel's post. When fires are permitted they must be made so as to be concealed from the observation of the enemy.

The guard at the "reserve" and "supports" will habitually turn out at the approach of officers entitled to that honor. Sentinels will stand at "attention," at "ordered arms," when officers on duty pass their posts.

The picket reserve and support will be under arms at daylight. The groups always under arms.

The pickets of each division, after they have been relieved, will all be assembled and marched in a body to division headquarters. They will not be permitted to straggle back to their camps.

No discharging of arms whatever, except in action, will be permitted without authority from these headquarters.

Refugees, contrabands, and deserters, presenting themselves at the picket line, will be sent under guard to the provost marshal at these headquarters. They will not be examined, except when, in the opinion of the division commanders, it may be essential to the safety of his command.

Citizens will not be allowed to pass inside the lines with the intention of returning, except by orders from department headquarters, signed by the major-general commanding, the chief of staff, assistant adjutant-general, or provost marshal-general. They will be detained on the picket line until such orders can be communicated. When provided with proper authority they will be sent under guard to these headquarters.

When the corps is detached, passes from the corps commander, signed by himself, or by his order by his chief of staff, assistant adjutant-general, or provost marshal, will be recognized.

Officers or soldiers, belonging to infantry or cavalry detachments, on duty beyond the picket lines of the corps, will, when on duty, be permitted to pass the pickets on an order from the commanding officer of their detachment, or his immediate superiors. These passes must be dated, and the entry and exit by the main and direct roads.

Organized bodies of troops recognized as friends will be subjected to no other detention than that prescribed in army regulations.

Corps officers of the day will be taken from commanding officers of regiments. When officers are detailed as corps officer of the day, who are not present for duty, the detail will immediately be returned to these headquarters.

The corps officer of the day will report to the general commanding the corps, at nine o'clock, A. M.

The corps officer of the day will visit the division officers of the day, on the picket line, at least once during his tour, to see that the orders are properly executed and that the line is connected throughout, and shall make such further inspections as may be practicable.

The division officers of the day will visit their picket lines at least once during the day and once after twelve o'clock at night. They should notify the corps officer of the day of the location of their headquarters.

Each division officer of the day will be furnished with one mounted orderly from division headquarters. The corps officer of the day will be furnished with two mounted orderlies from corps headquarters.

When the corps officer of the day marches off, he will submit to the assistant adjutant-general of the corps a report of his tour, enumerating all irregularities which he has observed, specifying the division in which they occurred. Division officer of the day will make like reports to division commanders, noting all irregularities and unusual circumstances that have occurred during their tour.

These reports will be transmitted by commanders to these headquarters, on the day of their date.

The occurrence of any unusual circumstances on the picket line should be instantly submitted to the division officer of the day, and by him to the commanding officer of the division, and to the corps officer of the day, at these headquarters, and by the division commander to the assistant adjutant-general at these headquarters.

These orders are published to secure uniformity.

By command of Major-general D. B. Birney:

EDWARD W. SMITH,
Assistant Adjutant-general.

ACTION OF COUNCILS.

THURSDAY, *October* 20, 1864.

Councils met:—The following message was received from the Mayor:—

OFFICE OF THE MAYOR OF THE CITY OF PHILADELPHIA,
October 20, 1864.

TO THE PRESIDENT AND MEMBERS OF THE
COMMON COUNCIL OF THE CITY OF PHILADELPHIA:

GENTLEMEN:—

Major-general David Bell Birney, United States volunteers, died on the night of Tuesday last, at his residence in this city. Four weeks ago your chamber adopted a joint resolution of welcome to General Birney, tendering to him the Hall of Independence that he might receive the merited congratulations of his fellow-citizens.

The conspicuous and successful military career of General Birney since the beginning of the rebellion has reflected honor upon the city of his adoption, and it is proper that Philadelphia should evince a grateful appreciation of his eminent self-devotion and patriotism, and should manifest a sense of the public loss in the decease of this able soldier and honored citizen.

Respectfully,

ALEXANDER HENRY,
Mayor of Philadelphia.

Mr. Isaac Sulger thereupon (on leave)

Read in his place and presented to the chair the following resolutions in honor of the late Major-general David Bell Birney:

Whereas, It has pleased Almighty God to remove by death from our midst Major-general David B. Birney, at a time when our citizens were seeking an opportunity to do honor to his worth and bravery; when his many deeds of valor had commended him to our highest consideration and warmest sympathy; when with Hancock and Meade and Grant, and a long list of others, he had gained for himself undying honors, and ranked himself a brave, bold, and courageous officer; when, after slow advances, flank movements, dashing charges and severe battles, the "Army of the Potomac," under fearless and able generals, had driven the Confederates within the rebel capital, and when Richmond was almost within the grasp of the Union forces. And

Whereas, It is due to the memory of the deceased, that our citizens should honor him with a public burial; therefore,

Resolved, By the Select and Common Councils of the City of Philadelphia, That the use of Independence Hall be tendered to the family of the late Major-general David B. Birney, for the purposes of a public funeral.

Resolved, That we deeply deplore the loss of a brave general, a courageous soldier, a distinguished civilian. His many deeds of valor, his many sacrifices, his bold and fearless example will be held in grateful esteem by us his fellow-citizens. And while we regret his departure from amongst us, at a time when his courage, his efficient services, his best energies, together with those of his honored associates of the "Army of the Potomac," were about to be crowned with success, and victory was about to be proclaimed in the occupation and possession of the rebel capital, we humbly submit to the decree of Heaven in this sore and afflictive dispensation.

Resolved, That we tender to the family of the deceased our heartfelt sympathy and condolence, and hereby testify our sincere appreciation of his worth and merit, his valor and courage, his many sacrifices and services in defence of our firesides and homes, our flag and our country.

Resolved, That a committee of five members from each branch of Councils be appointed, together with the Presidents of each chamber and the Mayor of the city, to make arrangements for a public funeral of the deceased from Independence Hall, if agreeable to the wishes of his family. And that a copy of these resolutions be engrossed and presented to his consort in grateful appreciation of the distinguished courage, bravery, and devotion that marked her husband's promotion from the lieutenant-colonel to a major-general of volunteers in the United States army.

Passed unanimously.

The President appointed Messrs. Sulger, Everman, Gratz, Loughlin, and Wolbert the committee on the part of Common Council.

The Select Council passed the following after his burial:—

RESOLUTIONS OF RESPECT TO THE MEMORY OF GENERAL BIRNEY.

Major-general David Bell Birney is no more. This distinguished officer, after a severe illness, induced by a protracted service in the field, was compelled to return to his family for a short period of repose, but he had too long devoted himself to his country's service to be within the reach of human aid, and he now, at the early age of thirty-nine, rests in a soldier's grave, honored by the gratitude and affection of the nation. It would not be fitting that his life should be permitted to glide unnoticed to its close, and the Councils of the city of his adoption desire to make such acknowledgment of his services as shall, in some degree, express the public sense entertained of his worth and the profound regret felt for his death; therefore,

Be it resolved, By the Select and Common Councils of the City of Philadelphia, That the authorities of the city have been greatly pained by the decease of Major-general David Bell Birney, United States volunteers. The citizens of Philadelphia generally have felt a just pride in the appreciation of the public services of one of her soldiers by the general government, as manifested in the regular advancement of the deceased from the rank of a lieutenant-colonel to the command of one of the army corps of the national forces; and it is a subject of regret that his early death forbids those public evidences of gratitude which would most surely have crowned his riper years. To the youth of the city, the life, devotion, and patriotism of General Birney form a bright example, while his successes in the field secure to his name a glowing page in the history of the country.

Resolved, That the Councils of the city offer the sympathy of the citizens of Philadelphia to the family of the late Major-general Birney, and direct that the minutes of these proceedings be sent to them.

Approved 28th of October, A. D. 1864.

GENERAL BIRNEY'S COMMAND.

The following regiments and batteries served under General Birney as a division commander:—

First Maine Heavy Artillery.
Sixth " Battery, Dow's.
Third " Infantry.
Fourth " "
Seventeenth Maine Infantry.
First Massachusetts Heavy Artillery.
First " Battery. Sleeper's.
Eleventh " Infantry.
First Rhode Island Battery. Randolph's.
First New York Infantry.
Thirty-seventh New York Infantry.
Thirty-eighth " "
Fortieth " "
Fifty-fifth " "
Seventy-first " "
Seventy-third " "
Eighty-sixth " "
Eighty-seventh " "
Ninety-third " "
One-hundred-and-first New York Infantry.

One-hundred-and-twentieth New York Infantry.
One-hundred-and-twenty-fourth " "
Sixth New York Battery. Bramhall's.
Third New Jersey Infantry.
Fifth " "
Sixth " "
Seventh " "
Eighth " "
Eleventh " "
First New Jersey Battery. Clark's.
Fifty-seventh Pennsylvania Infantry.
Sixty-third " "
Sixty-eighth " "
Eighty-fourth " "
Ninety-ninth " "
One-hundred-and-fifth Pennsylvania Infantry.
One-hundred-and-tenth " "
One-hundred-and-fourteenth " "
One-hundred-and-forty-first " "
Third Michigan Infantry.
Fifth " "
Twentieth Indiana Infantry.
First United States Sharpshooters.
Second " "
Second " Artillery, Battery G.
Third " " E.
Third " " K.
Ames' Battery.
Seeley's "
Turnbull's Battery.
Winslow's "
Bucklyn's "

STAFF OFFICERS.

The following-named officers served at different times on the staff of General Birney. The list is necessarily imperfect; for, besides the impossibility of obtaining the names of all, it has been difficult to trace the subsequent career of those who are known to have served in this connection.

*FITZHUGH BIRNEY, Major and A. A. G.
HENRY W. BREVOORT, Major and A. A. G.
J. C. BRISCOE, Major and A. D. C. Afterwards Colonel One-hundred-and-ninety-ninth Pennsylvania volunteers, and Brevet Brigadier-general U. S. V.
G. C. BRADLEY, Lieutenant-colonel and Chief Q. M. Afterwards Colonel and Q. M.
*A. J. H. BUZZEL, Third New Hampshire volunteers, Medical Inspector.
F. E. BLISS, Captain and C. S.
PAUL BRODIE, Lieutenant and Signal Officer.
W. W. BRAMAN, Ninety-third New York volunteers, Captain and Provost Marshal.
F. F. CAVADA, One-hundred-and-fourteenth Pennsylvania volunteers, Lieutenant-colonel and Chief of Staff.
BENJ. S. CALEF, Second U. S. Sharpshooters, Lieutenant and A. D. C.
FRANK CLARK, One-hundred-and-fourteenth Pennsylvania volunteers, Lieutenant and A. D. C.
LEVI B. DUFF, One-hundred-and-fifth Pennsylvania volunteers, Major and A. A. I. G. Afterwards Colonel.
*J. H. DANDY, One-hundredth New York volunteers, Captain and A. C. S. Afterwards Major One-hundredth New York volunteers.
THOS. J. DIEHL, Volunteer A. D. C., with rank of Captain.
JOS. DAVIS, Fortieth New York volunteers, Lieutenant and A. A. D. C.
ORPHEUS EVARTS, Twentieth Indiana volunteers, Medical Director.

---

* Deceased.

J. BARCLAY FASSITT, Twenty-third Pennsylvania volunteers, Captain and A. D. C.

E. L. FORD, Ninety-ninth Pennsylvania volunteers, Captain and A. D. C.

LOUIS FITZGERALD, Fortieth New York volunteers, Captain and A. D. C.

CHARLES H. GRAVES, Captain and A. A. G. Now Major and A. A. G. on staff of Major-general Terry.

JOHN HANCOCK, Major and A. A. G. Afterwards Lieutenant-colonel and A. A. G.

Surgeon HILDRETH, Third Maine volunteers, Medical Director.

G. C. HUNKINS, Fourth Maine volunteers, Medical Director.

J. C. HENSHAW, Major and Judge Advocate.

W. V. HUTCHINGS, Captain and A. Q. M. Afterwards Acting Chief Q. M. of Twenty-fifth Army Corps.

G. O. HOWARD, Fortieth Massachusetts volunteers, Captain and Ordnance Officer. Afterwards Ordnance Officer Twenty-fifth Army Corps.

G. W. JOHNS, Captain and A. Q. M. Afterwards Major and Q. M.

R. H. JACKSON, Lieutenant-colonel and A. I. G. Afterwards Brigadier-general U. S. V. and Brevet Major general.

E. F. KOEHLER, One-hundred-and-fourteenth Pennsylvania volunteers, Captain and Judge Advocate.

*J. W. LYMAN, Fifty-seventh Pennsylvania volunteers, Medical Director. Afterwards Lieutenant-colonel Two-hundred-and-third Pennsylvania volunteers.

S. P. LEE, Third Maine volunteers, Lieutenant and A. D. C. Afterwards Major Third Maine volunteers, and Veteran Reserve Corps.

—— LAMBERT, Third New Jersey volunteers, Lieutenant of Guard.

JAMES M. LINNARD, Twenty-third Pennsylvania volunteers, Captain and A. D. C. Afterwards Captain and A. A. G.

—— LLOYD, Third New Jersey volunteers, Captain and A. A. I. G.

*F. MCGILVERY, First Maine Artillery, Lieutenant-colonel and Chief of Artillery.

C. MACMICHAEL, Ninth U. S. Infantry, Captain and A. D. C.

W. E. MORFORD, Captain and A. Q. M. Afterwards Lieutenant-colonel and Chief Q. M. Third Corps.

---

* Deceased.

J. RIDGEWAY MOORE, One-hundredth-and-sixteenth Pennsylvania volunteers, Lieutenant and A. D. C.

G. W. MINDIL, Twenty-third Pennsylvania volunteers, Captain and A. A. A. G. Afterwards Colonel Twenty-seventh New Jersey volunteers, and Brevet Brigadier-general U. S. V.

CASSIUS C. MARKLE, One-hundred-and-fifth Pennsylvania volunteers, Captain and Provost Marshal.

DR. MCCRUER, Medical Director.

DONALD MCINTYRE, Captain and C. S.

CHARLES NOBLE, JR., One-hundred-and-nineteenth Pennsylvania volunteers, Captain and A. D. C.

W. H. OWENS, Captain and A. Q. M. Afterwards Colonel and Q. M.

C. H. PHILLIPS, Fourth Massachusetts Cavalry, Lieutenant and Chief of Ambulances.

H. W. PHILLIPS, Fourth Massachusetts Cavalry, Lieutenant and Assistant Provost Marshal.

—— PHILLIPS, One-hundred-and-first New York volunteers, Lieutenant and A. D. C.

G. H. PANCOAST, Medical Director.

J. R. PANCOAST, One-hundred-and-tenth Pennsylvania volunteers, Lieutenant and Chief of Ambulances.

C. M. ROBINS, Captain and C. S. Afterwards Acting Chief C. S. Twenty-fifth Army Corps.

J. F. RANDLETT, Third New Hampshire volunteers, Major and Provost Marshal. Afterwards Lieutenant-colonel.

—— ROGERS, Fourth Maine volunteers, Lieutenant of Guard.

ED. W. SMITH, Lieutenant-colonel and A. A. G., Brevet Colonel.

R. J. SMITH, Medical Director.

A. H. STEVENS, Fourth Massachusetts Cavalry, Major and Provost Marshal. Afterwards Provost Marshal of Twenty-fifth Corps.

J. E. SWEET, Twentieth Indiana volunteers, Captain and A. D. C.

WILLIAM P. SHREVE, Second U. S. Sharpshooters, Lieutenant and C. M. Afterwards Commissary of Musters, Twenty-fifth Corps.

LEWIS A. STIMSON, Volunteer Aide, with rank of Lieutenant. Afterwards with Major-General A. H. Terry.

H. J. STRAIT, Fortieth New York volunteers, Captain, Judge Advocate.

J. H. TALMAN, Captain and A. Q. M. Afterwards Major and Q. M.

JOSEPH F. TOBIAS, Volunteer Aide, with rank of Major.

John Willian, Eighth New Jersey volunteers, Captain and A. A. I. G. Afterwards Colonel Twelfth New Jersey volunteers, and Brevet Brigadier-general U. S. V.

D. C. Winebrenner, Ninety-ninth Pennsylvania volunteers, Captain and Assistant Provost Marshal.

Fergus Walker, Thirty-eighth New York volunteers, Captain and A. A. I. G.

A. C. Warberg, (Royal Swedish Army,) Lieutenant-colonel and A. D. C. Afterwards A. I. G. Twenty-fifth Army Corps.

THE END.

www.ingramcontent.com/pod-product-compliance
Lightning Source LLC
LaVergne TN
LVHW020555110826
845149LV00002B/281

* 9 7 8 1 4 1 8 1 8 8 3 5 1 *